Managing Migration

Nation states must today contend with large numbers of non-citizens living within their borders. This phenomenon has largely been understood in terms of the decline of the nation state or of increasing globalisation, but in *Managing Migration* Lydia Morris argues that it throws up more complex questions. In the context of the European Union the terms of debate about immigration, legislation governing entry, and the practice of regulation reveal a set of competing concerns, including:

- anxiety about the political affiliation of migrants;
- continuing employer demand for labour;
- the desire to protect national resources;
- human rights obligations alongside restrictions on entry.

The outcome of the ensuing tensions is presented in terms of increasingly complex systems of civic stratification. The heart of the book considers the operation of such systems in three contrasting countries: Germany, Italy and Great Britain. Morris then moves on to examine the way in which abstract notions of rights map on to lived experience when filtered through other forms of difference such as race and gender, and to an elaboration of the theoretical implications of her work.

This book will be essential reading for students and researchers working in the areas of migration and the study of the European Union.

Lydia Morris is Professor of Sociology at the University of Essex.

Managing Migration
Civic stratification and migrants' rights

Lydia Morris

London and New York

First published 2002
by Routledge
11 New Fetter Lane, London EC4P 4EE

Simultaneously published in the USA and Canada
by Routledge
29 West 35th Street, New York, NY 10001

Routledge is an imprint of the Taylor & Francis Group

© 2002 Lydia Morris

Typeset in Bembo by
BOOK NOW Ltd
Printed and bound in Malta by
Gutenberg Press Ltd.

All rights reserved. No part of this book may be reprinted or reproduced or utilized in any form or by any electronic, mechanical, or other means, now known or hereafter invented, including photocopying and recording, or in any information storage or retrieval system, without permission in writing from the publishers.

British Library Cataloguing in Publication Data
A catalogue record for this book is available from the British Library

Library of Congress Cataloging in Publication Data
Morris, Lydia, 1949–
    Managing migration : civic stratification and migrants rights / Lydia Morris.
    p. cm.
    Includes bibliographical references and index.
    1. European Union countries–Emigration and immigration–Government policy.
  2. Immigrants–Government policy–European Union countries. 3. Immigrants–Civil rights–European Union countries. 4. Social stratification–European Union countries. I. Title.

JV7590 .M62 2002
325.4–dc21   2002069953

ISBN 0-415-16706-X (hbk)
ISBN 0-415-16707-8 (pbk)

Contents

Acknowledgements		vii
Abbreviations		ix
	Introduction	1
1	A cluster of contradictions: the politics of migration in the European Union	10
2	Rights and controls in the management of migration: the case of Germany	28
3	The ambiguous terrain of rights: Italy's emergent immigration regime	53
4	The shifting contours of rights: Britain's asylum and immigration regime	80
5	Stratified rights and the management of migration: national distinctiveness in Europe	103
6	Gender, race and the embodiment of rights	122
7	Managing contradiction: civic stratification and migrants' rights	143
	Notes	159
	Bibliography	166
	Index	175

Acknowledgements

This book was made possible by the support of a large number of people and institutions. The first chance to apply my framework for the understanding of migrants' rights came unexpectedly, with the offer of a Fellowship at the Hanse Wissenschaftskolleg. There I spent six months at the start of 1998, and three months at the end of 2000. I am deeply indebted to my co-Fellow, Martin Kronauer, and to my host Walter Siebel, with whom I discussed many aspects of this work and who also supported me in many other ways. The Italian research was made possible by a small grant from the Nuffield Foundation, and relief of teaching for one term, funded by the Research Promotion Fund at Essex. I am extremely grateful to Enzo Mingione, Enrico Pugliese and Fabio Quassoli for their intellectual and practical support, and their companionship in the course of the five months I spent in Italy (four months in 1999 and one in 2001). I also thank Nicoletta and Marcello Carmi, and Elena Spinelli for their friendship. The research in Britain was made possible by sabbatical leave from the University of Essex and I am grateful for the advice and the contacts supplied by Steve Peers in the Law Department there. My greatest debt is, of course, owed to the people I interviewed, who gave freely of their time and expertise with extraordinary patience and generosity. Against the 168 interviews conducted, I met with only two refusals – both of them in Britain. The views expressed in these interviews are those of the individuals concerned, and not of the institutions for which they work.

With the exception of Chapter 6, the chapters of this book have already appeared in the form of journal articles and I have kept to the titles of those original articles, details of which are given below. Most of the articles have been extended and updated, and sometimes substantially reworked for the current volume so that the book is not a collection of free-standing essays but an unfolding and integrated argument about the comparative analysis of migrants' rights. I would like here to record my thanks to the journals which originally published the articles, and especially to their various anonymous referees:

'Globalisation, migration and the nation state: the path to a post-national Europe?', *British Journal of Sociology*, 48 (1997): 192–209.
'A cluster of contradictions: the politics of migration in the EU', *Sociology*, 31 (1997): 241–59.

The above two articles together form the basis of the Introduction and Chapter 1.

'Rights and controls in the management of migration: the case of Germany', *Sociological Review*, 48 (2000): 224–40.
'The ambiguous terrain of rights and controls: Italy's emergent immigration regime', *International Journal of Urban and Regional Research*, 25 (2001): 497–516.
'The shifting contours of rights: Britain's asylum and immigration regime', *Journal of Ethnic and Migration Studies*, 28 (2002): 409–25.
'Stratified rights and the management of migration: national distinctiveness in Europe', *European Societies*, 4 (2001): 387–411. <http://www.tandf.co.uk>.
'Managing contradiction: civic stratification and migrants' rights', *International Migration Review*, 36 (2002).

These five articles appear in amended form as, respectively, Chapters 2, 3, 4, 5 and 7.

A majority of the interviews on which this work is based were conducted in English. However, I am grateful to Martin Kronauer for translating in three of the German interviews. In Italy more than half of the interviews (40) were conducted in English. For the remainder I am grateful for the translating skills of Roberto Pesci, Gloria Lowenthal, Michela Sorgoni, and in two cases Ana Germani.

Lydia Morris
University of Essex

Abbreviations

BBA	Beauftragte der Bundesregierung für Ausländerfragen
CDU	Christlich-Demokratische Union (Christian Democratic Union)
CGIL	Confederazione Generale Italiana del Lavoro (General Italian Confederation of Labour)
CIR	Consiglio Italiano per i Refugiati (Italian Refugee Council)
CISL	Confederazione Italiana Sindicati Lavorotori (Italian Confederation of Workers' Trade Unions)
CPT	centri di permanenca temporanea (temporary holding centres)
CSU	Christlich-Soziale Union (Christian Social Union)
EC	European Community
ECHR	European Convention on Human Rights
ECJ	European Court of Justice
ECRE	European Council on Refugees and Exiles
ECtHR	European Court of Human Rights
EEA	European Economic Area
ELR	exceptional leave to remain
ERCOMER	European Research Centre on Migrations and Ethnic Relations
EU	European Union
FCFA	Federal Commissioner for Foreigners' Affairs
FEANTSA	Fédération Européenne d'Associations Nationales Travaillant avec les Sans-Abri (European Federation of National Organisations Working with the Homeless)
FES	Federal Employment Service
FL	Foreigners' Law
FMLSA	Federal Ministry of Labour and Social Affairs
FPWP	foreigner present without permission
GC	Geneva Convention
HRA	Human Rights Act
IAA	Immigration and Asylum Act
ILO	International Labour Organization
ILR	indefinite leave to remain
IND	Immigration and Nationality Directorate

JCWI	Joint Council for the Welfare of Immigrants
JR	judicial review
JSA	job seeker's allowance
NAA	National Assistance Act
NACAB	National Association of Citizens Advice Bureaux
NASS	National Asylum Support System
NGO	non-governmental organisation
NHS	National Health Service
NI	national insurance
SEA	Single European Act
SPD	Sozialdemokratische Partei Deutschlands (Social Democratic Party)
TCN	third country national
TP	temporary protection
UIL	Unione Italiana del Lavoro (Italian Federation of Trade Unions)
UN	United Nations
UNHCR	United Nations High Commission for Refugees
ZDWF	Zentrale Dokumentationsstelle der Freien Wohlfahrtspflege für Flüchtlinge

Introduction

Post-war developments in Europe have shown a number of contradictory trends, with increasing national closure alongside the emergence of trans-national and multi-national forces. It is the latter tendency which has dominated academic debate, with emphasis commonly placed upon trans-national flows of 'global' capital,[1] the development of global communications and the compression of time and space (Giddens, 1990; Smith, 1995). Also featured are the large population flows which have led to a growth in numbers of permanent foreign residents in host societies, together with an expanding recognition and enforcement of the rights of individuals over and above those rooted in membership of a particular nation state (Brubaker, 1989; Freeman, 1986; Soysal, 1994). Hence the view that 'formerly independent states and nations are being bound by a complex web of interstate organisations and regulations into a truly international community' (Smith, 1995:1). Taken together, it has been argued that these phenomena constitute a challenge to central features of the modern nation state, representing what Smith (1995:96) terms an external crisis of autonomy and an internal crisis of legitimacy.

Whilst these developments raise questions of interest to sociologists, they are not readily addressed by the traditions of a discipline which is inherently nationalist in orientation. Despite its broader theoretical scope, the empirical thrust of sociology has until recently been focused on the internal analysis or cross-national comparison of 'societies' which are taken to be contained within the boundaries of the nation state − what Beck (2000) has termed a 'methodological nationalism'. There has, however, been a recent change in this focus. For example, one of the most frequently cited sociological works on citizenship (Marshall, 1950) has been criticised (Anthias and Yuval-Davis, 1992) for its failure to question the constitution of the 'community of reference', that is, the nation state. Indeed, for Giddens (1990), assumptions about the bounded nature of 'society' and its alignment with the nation state epitomise a phase in modernity which we are now transcending.

Globalisation

It is argued that we are moving into a new phase of modernity in which 'We have to acount for the extreme dynamism and globalising scope of modern institutions and explain the nature of their discontinuities from traditional cultures' (Giddens, 1990:16). Furthermore, society is held to be undergoing a 'stretching process' whereby different social contexts and regions become networked across the globe, albeit with no unified direction of change and displaying some inevitable tensions. A number of writers have addressed these issues by reaching for a new and deceptively simple concept, 'globalisation', which for Beck (2000) signals a break with the categories of the nation state, and the development of a world society without a world government. As a result, it is argued, the nation state must share the global arena with international organisations and trans-national social and political movements.

This issue is addressed by Sassen (1998:6), also writing under the broad heading of 'globalisation', but with specific reference to population flows. She identifies a process of '*de facto* trans-nationalisation of immigration issues', citing as evidence the expansion of international agreements and conventions dealing with migrants' rights, and the increasing use of human rights' instruments to contest the authority of the state. There is a tendency in some of this literature for any trans-national force to be termed global, and much of Sassen's interest is in fact focused on the European Union (EU) as a key example of the gradual ceding of national control over immigration in the drive for a single market (Sassen, 1998:10). A more overtly global theme is addressed by Meyer *et al.* (1997), who emphasise the force of 'world culture' in shaping the form and actions of nation states which are viewed not as independent rational actors but as culturally embedded occupants of a role. It is argued that they show strong consensus for principles such as citizenship, development, justice and human rights, for which they claim universal applicability and which have come to form the basis of a constraining institutional framework. States are thus depicted less as autonomous agents who are collective authors of their own history and more as enactors of 'conventionalised scripts'.

However, Meyer *et al.* also note that the principles of world culture may not mesh with practical experience, so that the 'broad and diffuse goals' of nation states lead to a 'decoupling' of purpose and structure, intention and result (pp. 154-5). In other words, one likely outcome is a clash of national interests with global culture, or at the least an eclectic mix of conflicting principles. In fact, adherents of the globalisation thesis make no commitment to a linear, developmental perspective (see Giddens, 1990:64), whether cultural, economic or social, though its implicit presence is hard to escape.[2] The explicit emphasis, however, lies with the many ambiguities and contradictions built in, and the globalisation thesis thus becomes hard to fault. Giddens (1990), for example, notes the 'dialectical' nature of globalisation, and the 'trade-off' whereby concerted action increases national influence within the global state system but diminishes sovereignty.

The crisis of the nation state?

Embedded in these global concerns is a set of much more specific interests, some of which focus on national closure. Hall (1991), for example, has identified a related cultural crisis whereby – in response to the erosion of the nation state – national economies and national cultures adopt a defensive and regressive exclusionism, most apparent in policies and attitudes concerned with immigration. Despite the supposed transcendence of the nation state, and the growth in institutions for the trans-national assertion of rights, we have seen pockets of racial violence, selective tightening of immigration controls and the demonisation of asylum seekers. Thus Smith (1995:15) writes, 'Fears of immigrant waves have fuelled resentments and spurred renewed interest in cultural identity, national solidarity and defence of national interests.'

The European nation has, at least in principle, grown up around an 'ideal' of cultural homogeneity, established and reinforced through state control over the transmission of literate culture (Gellner, 1983), as well as entry to the territory and the acquisition of citizenship. Thus the nation represents territorialised cultural belonging while the state formalises and controls legal membership, though the extent of correspondence between the two has increasingly come into question. Hence the continuing debate on the concept of multi-culturalism, which has focused on cultural rights for minority groups and on the problem of social cohesion given a culturally diverse citizenry (Taylor, 1994; Kymlicka, 1995). This focus on culture contains an implicit critique of overly legalistic approaches to citizenship, but in doing so leaves aside the issue of how far citizenship creates further inequalities by virtue of the designation of non-members.

The quest for cultural recognition should not divert attention from the question of access to rights more generally. As Smith observes (1995:99): 'Modern nations are simultaneously and necessarily civic and ethnic. In relation to the national state, the individual is a citizen with civic rights and duties, and receives the benefits of modernity through the medium of an impersonal, and impartial, bureaucracy.' How then are we to assess the sociological impact of international migration, multi-ethnic societies, multi-state bureaucracies and trans-national institutions asserting the rights of migrants? If the nation state is no longer a sovereign power, is there some new institutional basis on which to build the relations of civic society?

Some writers have addressed this issue through the idea of an emergent 'post-national' society, a concept which arguably makes a lesser claim than globalisation and focuses in part on the demands that non-citizens might legitimately make upon national states. The idea of a global system is still present, however, and sociological neglect of global processes and trans-national networks again draws critical comment (Soysal, 1994:164). A key component of the post-national argument places emphasis on a 'discourse of universal personhood', which is deemed to have transformed the position of non-citizens in such a way that national citizenship has now been superseded by the rights of long-term residence. However, an alternative view (Brubaker, 1992:23) emphasises the continuing material and symbolic significance of citizenship – not least in conferring full political rights which have so far been denied to long-term resident non-citizens, and in being the only ultimately secure basis for residence.

4 Introduction

The foundation for much sociological thinking about citizenship has been the work of T. H. Marshall and his account of the evolutionary development of civil, political and social rights as the basis for 'membership' in modern society. His concern was thus with citizenship from the inside, with reference to the rights and obligations that accompany the status, though some have seen the growing interest in universal human rights as a potential fourth phase which can be grafted on to Marshall's model (e.g. Parry, 1991; Bottomore, 1992). However, Marshall himself does not address the question of the rights of non-citizens, and a number of thinkers (Alexander, 1988; Turner, 1988) warn against any assumed evolutionary unfolding of rights. Indeed, as Brubaker has made clear (1992), citizenship is also an exclusionary device and despite speculation about the possible transformation of the nation state, 'societies' still operate as national territories. The most fascinating aspect of migration is, therefore, its impact on the substance of and criteria for membership, the rights that attach to inclusion and the mechanisms that lead to exclusion. These questions become more complex for the nation states of Europe which are negotiating their responses in the context of multi-national collaboration within the European Union.

Many of the member states of the EU have inherited permanent populations of foreign residents as a result both of their colonial past and of various guest-worker systems (Castles and Kosack, 1985). Despite the stops on immigration into Europe that have been in place since the early 1970s there has been continuing entry through family reunification and a dramatic increase in the numbers of asylum seekers – both affected by international conventions on human rights, as well as by the constitutional commitments of some states. Labour migration has also continued, though on both more selective and more clandestine bases, with the result that in 1990 there were roughly 14.25 million foreign nationals resident in the member states of the European Community (EC) (Salt *et al.*, 1994), of whom about two-thirds were 'third country nationals', i.e. nationals of states outside the European Economic Area (EEA). Of particular concern to the member states wishing to exert control over their borders, however, is the unknown extent of unofficial migration – sometimes dealt with by regularisation – and the lucrative smuggling trade bringing in migrants from further and further afield. There is a continuing struggle between those seeking entry and the capacity of the nation state to secure and police its borders.

Theorising contradiction

The available theoretical approaches seem increasingly inadequate to address the position of these third country nationals (TCNs), rendering only partial or poorly substantiated accounts, and ill-equipped to address the multiple logics at work. Indeed, the sociology of migration reflects a series of chronological shifts in the phenomenon itself. A political economy approach to migration offered a persuasive interpretation of post-war recruitment of both colonial labour and temporary 'guestworkers' by a number of European countries – a means of supplying cheap labour for the jobs rejected by nationals at a time of full employment. Within this framework, nation states were implicated in the structuring of a reserve army of labour to meet the needs of capital (Castles and Kosack, 1985) and to fill the jobs rejected by the national population.

This neat coincidence of economic demand and political supply was soon to unravel with internal tensions and rising unemployment. As capital itself became more mobile, defying national control, and as temporary migrants started to look permanent, political concern became more narrowly focused on securing the resources of the welfare state and the closure of national boundaries. In this setting, the short-term interests of employers seeking cheap labour are not so easily accommodated by the long-term interests of state welfare systems (see Freeman, 1986). A focus on the political economy of labour recruitment thus gave way to concern with national protectionism and closure, though a new phase may now be emerging in the face of skill shortages.

Against the logic of national or regional exclusions came another distinctive post-war development: the emergence of rights located outside national belonging in the form of trans-national human rights. These rights lie at the heart of speculation about an emergent 'post-national membership' (Soysal, 1994) or a 'global society' (Giddens, 1990), and certainly the development of trans-national rights cuts across any other dynamic through which we might seek an understanding of current policies with regard to migration. It is through the assertion of rights to asylum and family reunification that migration has continued and grown, in the face of explicit attempts in the 1970s to bring it to an end. Whilst there is considerable evidence of recalcitrance on the part of many European states, any full-blown denial of established human rights is (so far) inconceivable.

Mediating these accounts of labour demand, welfare protectionism and trans-national rights is a 'race relations' perspective, which sees post-war labour supply, subsequent national closure and even human rights restrictions as part of a process of 'racialisation' of particular populations. It has been argued by some that this account is tailored to a distinctively British history of migration (Miles, 1990; Layton-Henry, 1992), while others (Sivanandan, 1991) have identified a 'pan-European racism' in aspects of EU migration policy. In this broader context, however, there has also been a growing emphasis on the cultural construction of 'difference' (Rattansi, 1994) which accommodates a wider variety of excluded groups (see Solomos, 1995), and it has even become possible to refer to a 'typology of racisms' (Miles, 1993:42). There is a related literature variously addressing issues of migration, racism, citizenship and so on, but sometimes conflating analytically distinct concepts and categories (e.g. Cross, 1991). This is unsurprising, since attempts to establish a European immigration and asylum regime alongside existing national policies reveal both complementary and competing dynamics, which as a result are rarely amenable to easy theorising.

Despite a predominant discourse of closure, migration into Europe continues in a number of forms: the professional élite of technical and administrative experts, the families of the post-war labour reserve, growing numbers of asylum seekers granted either refugee status or, more commonly, humanitarian leave to remain, the revival of a 'guestworker' system through a variety of bilateral agreements and, not least, the persistence of undocumented workers. The result is an elaborate hierarchy of statuses with varying attendant rights, not easily captured by any single political dynamic. The logic of the market is weighed against welfare protectionism; welfare and labour market regulation against demands for labour; and national resource concerns against trans-national obligations. The outcome may be presented in terms of an increasingly complex system of civic stratification (see Lockwood, 1996), only hinted at in the conventional distinction between citizens, denizens and aliens (Hammar, 1990). This nascent structure of inequality built upon the differing rights conceded by the state raises a further contradiction: discriminatory exclusion and partial inclusion set alongside assertions of equal treatment. How then do we deal sociologically with these cross-cutting pressures, and what is their impact in terms of the emerging structure of migrants' rights?

A sociology of migrants' rights

Sociological interest in the issue of rights is relatively recent (see Therborn, 1995: 85), and in fact Turner (1993) has argued that sociology as a discipline has no obvious foundation for a contemporary theory of rights, and that a sociology of citizenship has served in its place. As we have seen, one response to the question of how to think sociologically about rights has been to move beyond nationally bounded citizenship and to invoke the universal. Turner's own solution, for example, is largely aspirational in seeking an ontological grounding for universal rights lodged in human frailty, while Soysal (1994) argues that a discourse of 'universal personhood' underlies the emergence of post-national societies which increasingly incorporate fundamental rights for non-citizens. However, alongside the quest for ethical certainty (Turner) and the somewhat uncritical acceptance of trans-national universality (Soysal), we also find reminders of the enduring power of the nation state (Smith, 1995; Joppke, 1999), and accounts of rights – especially human rights – as politically negotiated (Waters, 1996).

A more traditionally sociological approach to the issue of rights is found in an emphasis on boundary drawing, as in Brubaker's (1992:23) analysis of citizenship as 'both an instrument and an object of social closure', and his application of this argument to the expansion of positions of partial membership as a response to trans-national migration (1989). This phenomenon is largely to be understood in terms of the defence of national resources with respect to welfare and labour market systems (see Freeman, 1986) not yet superseded by any fully fledged alternative (Morris, 1997b). Even universal human rights, as for example embodied in the European Convention on Human Rights (ECHR), contain their own hierarchy of absolute, limited and qualified rights which is largely defined in terms of national interests. So when it comes to the practice of rights, rather than ascendancy of the universal over the particular, the global over the local, or the post-national over the national, we more often find a negotiated pragmatism.

It is in documenting and analysing the outcome that the idea of a system of stratified rights, or civic stratification (Lockwood, 1996; Morris, 1997b), has been most useful: a system which in practice can serve as both a statement of rights and as an apparatus of surveillance and control. I take this concept from the work of David Lockwood, who describes what he terms four types of civic stratification – civic exclusion, civic gain and deficit and civic expansion, which are in fact two sets of paired oppositions. Civic gain and deficit refer to the enhanced or impaired implementation of rights by virtue of largely informal processes. Civic exclusion refers to the formal denial of rights, while civic expansion may refer either to the expanding claims of particular groups or to the expanding terrain of rights more generally. Human rights are given as one example. Bechhofer (1996) has already argued that civic exclusion and expansion sit uneasily together, and here I suggest a slight amendment, pairing exclusion with inclusion to denote formal access to rights, and introducing a third opposition, civic expansion and contraction, to refer to the shifting character of a regime of rights or of a particular area within its ambit.

Cultural rights may be seen as one currently contested area, but key works in the debate about multi-culturalism have principally addressed the problem of equality among citizens, through the drive for cultural recognition of minorities (Taylor, 1994; Kymlicka, 1995). The framework I have proposed here calls attention to the creation of further inequalities through a variety of exclusions and attendant statuses of partial membership. This phenomenon is not readily incorporated into existing theories of citienship *per se*, but invites analysis of the granting and withholding of rights as a possible basis for the management of migration. The questions raised by the application of this framework to the area of migration and migrants' rights concern the classificatory system – that is, the structure of legal statuses – which governs eligibility for particular rights; the sorting of migrants into these different positions by processes of inclusion and exclusion; the actual realisation of rights formally associated with these different locations; and the shifting character of the whole regime both with respect to the delivery of rights and to the broader practice of governmentality.[3]

Some of these issues will engage questions of human rights, some will relate to rights conferred by Community law, while others lie entirely within the scope of domestic policy-making. In the chapter to follow I attempt to assess quite how post-national Europe really is, and how far the concept of globalisation offers any help in unravelling the complexity of empirical evidence. In the body of the book I move on to examine the various dimensions of civic stratification in a comparative analysis of asylum and immigration regimes in three European countries, thus offering an analysis of the management of contradiction and a framework for the sociology of migrants' rights.

Chapter outline

Chapter 1 outlines the European objective of a frontier-free market and an associated concern with immigration control. Alongside developments to secure the free movement of labour, there has simultaneously been a heightened interest in the policing of external borders. This chapter examines the tensions and contradictions entailed, focusing specifically on the positions of TCNs and their location in the emergent system of civic stratification. The issue is taken up in more detail with respect to three contrasting national regimes which are considered respectively in Chapters 2–4. The countries studied – Germany, Italy and Britain – have been chosen with a view to national distinctiveness in Europe. Indeed, each stands in a different position in relation to a harmonised European Union – Germany shows notional commitment but acts as a constraining system of reference; Italy is still shaping its legal regime, swayed by EU priorities but with its own distinctive dilemmas; and Britain remains cautious, having negotiated selective involvement.

Germany represents a guestworker regime in which migrant workers have gradually accrued secure residence, and attendant family rights, while remaining predominantly non-citizens; Italy represents a country only recently established as a receiver rather than a sender of migrants, whose legal regime of rights is still unfolding; and Britain represents an ex-colonial regime in which many early migrants arrived with full citizenship. All three countries have also been affected, though to differing degrees, by the expanding numbers of people seeking asylum. In some specific respects the position of TCNs will be shaped by Community Law, through the limits on free movement, the rights of family members of EEA migrants and the functioning of various association agreements, for example. However, these rights and constraints operate in the context of national regimes for the granting, withholding and delivery of rights.

The three-country study which forms the core of this book is therefore built around the possible legal statuses occupied by TCNs (including asylum seekers), and their associated rights in relation to the central issues of residence, social support and employment. The outcome is analysed in terms of an emergent system of stratified rights through which it is possible to identify migrant careers in terms of the potential for movement through the system, both individually and cross-generationally. Such movement may involve the accumulation of rights and security or the reverse dynamic. In the chapters to follow the focus of the analysis is the structuring of rights in each national regime, the identification of points at which the objective of control and the assertion of rights cohere or conflict, and the intended and unintended consequences of different aspects of the management of migration.

The material for these three case studies has been collected through semi-structured interviews with key actors in the field of immigration, notably lawyers, NGOs and support organisations, and local and state officials, supplemented by documentary sources. A total of 168 interviews were conducted and transcribed personally by the author, focusing on the legal position of TCNs and their access to rights both in theory and in practice.[4] The individual studies do not constitute an exhaustive account of each system, but rather are designed to capture their key characteristics and the tensions most commonly identified by practitioners in the field of immigration and asylum.

Each regime is thus depicted in its active implementation rather than through a static account of its legal features.

An attempt is therefore made in analysis to detail the distinguishing features of each national regime, and this material is placed in more systematic comparative context in Chapter 5, which draws up a typology based on the three national systems. With different labour market and welfare regimes, different immigration histories and different formal and informal structures for dealing with migrant populations these three cases serve to highlight some of the difficulties confronting any attempt at a harmonised asylum and immigration regime for Europe. The chapter therefore includes some comment on the nature of this endeavour, and the progress so far achieved.

Chapter 6 moves from a consideration of the structuring of rights to the question of their embodiment with respect to differences of gender and race. I examine the way in which abstract regimes of rights translate into lived experience when filtered through differences which are to some degree written on the body. In the case of gender, access to rights is shaped to a significant extent by women's association with the private domain, whether as carers or as objects of sexual gratification. In the example of race, access to rights is shaped by the classification of migrants with respect to visible difference, ethnicity and/or nationality. The chapter considers how these dynamics of difference interact with the formally constructed framework of rights represented by different modes of civic stratification. Chapter 7 then reflects on the analysis of migrants' rights more generally, returning to some of the problems posed in this introduction and arguing for a more nuanced approach than generalised assertions of globalisation or post-national membership have so far permitted.

1 A cluster of contradictions

The politics of migration in the European Union

The European Union has been cited by some as a paradigm case in the unfolding of a post-national or even global dynamic. Giddens (1995), for example, has argued that the EU stands as both a response to and an expression of globalisation, whereby member states relinquish some aspects of sovereignty with a view to promoting national interests – an expression of the dialectical nature of globalisation. Soysal (1994) also sees Europe as a key reference point for post-national membership, describing the EU as 'the most comprehensive legal enactment of a trans-national status for migrants' (p. 147). She is referring here to free movement and the attendant rights conferred on nationals of all member states (and additionally those of the EEA), though not yet extended to TCNs resident in one of the member states.[1] In fact, in tandem with efforts to establish a single market, we find that much of the collaborative effort with respect to migration has focused on control and that this, as much as the expansion of migrants' rights more generally, has been at the heart of post-national developments. It is in this context that a harmonised European immigration regime is seen as a necessary part of moves towards a free market (see Sassen, 1998).

Multi-state collaboration

The creation of a law-making body which stands above the member states, whose laws have direct effect and override any inconsistencies with domestic law, is perhaps the strongest manifestation of a post-national (rather than global) dynamic. Yet the process of establishing a single market met with resistance at various stages from the member states, and there have been a number of significant moments in negotiating a balance. Concern about sovereignty with respect to migration was initially reflected in the 'three pillar' structure of the treaty on European Union (the Maastricht Treaty), which placed Justice and Home Affairs outside Commission competence so that action in the field of migration was negotiated in inter-governmental fora on the basis of unanimity. Such caution may seem surprising, given broad agreement on the need for harmonisation of admission policies, a common approach to illegal migration, a policy on labour migration and a common position on third country nationals.[2] However, implicit in this programme of work was the acknowledgement that a frontier-free zone carries with it a series of implications for immigration, as in practice the external boundaries of Europe become the boundaries for each individual member state.

The Amsterdam Treaty (1997) marks a fundamental change in previous arrangements by moving immigration and asylum from the third pillar of intergovernmental negotiation to the first pillar of community competence, under a new Title IV of the EC Treaty (as amended by the Amsterdam Treaty). The move was opposed by Denmark, who opted out completely, and by Britain and Ireland, who negotiated a selective opt-in and also secured exclusion from the requirement to abolish controls at internal borders. The remaining thirteen member states are committed to the latter development, as expressed in the incorporation of the Schengen Acquis into the Amsterdam Treaty (Statewatch, 1997). Yet in so far as 'free movement' has been established, it operates alongside a continuing emphasis on external control in European policy and debate, and the familiar formula of combating illegal migration while ensuring integration for those legally present is repeated in the related Council Action Plan (European Union Council, 12028/1/98 Rev 1).

Though the Amsterdam Treaty explicitly embraces the European Convention on Human Rights (Article F(2)), there has been something of a shift in terminology, with the result that the domain of Justice and Home Affairs under the Maastricht Treaty has now become an area of 'Freedom *Security* and Justice'. Indeed, the associated programme of measures to be adopted within five years (that is, by May 2004) includes a set of control-related issues, which have been among the first to reach agreement (Immigration Law Practitioners' Association, 2001). Areas of continuing debate are minimum standards of reception, qualification and procedures for refugees; conditions of entry and residence for TCNs (including family unification); and the conditions for their residence or employment in other member states. There is as yet no commitment to extending full rights of free movement to this group (beyond permitting three months visa-free travel), though the issue is addressed in a proposed directive from the Commission (European Commission, 2001b). Overall, Peers (2000: 105) describes the treaty as a missed opportunity for securing the position of resident TCNs which 'damages the internal market, infringes the basic principles of equality, and contributes to indirect racism'. These issues are explored below, in the context of the broader question of quite how post-national Europe really is.

A frontier-free market

The principle objective of the European Union has been the realisation of a Common Market, envisaged in the Treaty of Rome (1957) and given urgency by the Single European Act (SEA) (1986) with its commitment to establish an internal market for goods, capital, services and persons. The act immediately raised two questions which proved contentious: what categories of person were to be granted free movement (and with it the right to work and reside); and, in the absence of internal frontiers between member states, where should ultimate authority over entry to the national community lie?

The first of these questions was answered restrictively when the European Court of Justice (ECJ) interpreted 'persons' as meaning 'workers of the Member States', third country nationals being dealt with in secondary legislation. The related question of authority was addressed by a General Declaration appended to the SEA to the effect that nothing in its provisions 'shall affect the right of the Member States to take such measures as they consider necessary for the purpose of controlling immigration from third countries' (Handoll, 1994:11.41). This right was also confirmed in a much documented decision by the ECJ in 1987 which upheld a challenge to the Commission's proposal for prior communication on migration issues, brought by Germany, France, The Netherlands, Denmark and the UK (Hoogenboom, 1992; Handoll, 1994). This judgement has been largely superseded by the Amsterdam Treaty, and in fact the failed Communication of 1985 has resurfaced in updated form as part of the current drive for harmonisation (*Migration News Sheet*, August, 2001). However, while the Amsterdam Treaty has changed the legal framework for dealing with immigration and asylum, there is nothing to suggest that control will not continue to be at a premium.

The right for citizens of member states to work and reside in other member states has now been established, and extended to EEA countries, with accompanying relaxation of national control. Free movement between the relatively affluent countries of Europe is viewed as necessary for the establishment of a single market, but ease of entry and stay for TCNs has been much less acceptable. The fear has been that generous policies or lax control on the part of one member state could rebound on the whole Community, and hence the logic of the single market has been restricted from the outset. This issue derives its significance from the fact that there are at least 10 million legally resident TCNs in the EU (Salt *et al.*, 1994), and an unknown number who are undocumented.[3] In March of 2001, the Commission proposed a directive on resident TCNs that would grant free movement after five years, but in terms which are hedged with caution (see p. 15 below).

The diverse origins of TCNs in Europe reflect the colonial ties of the member states, the sources of their guestworkers and the range of refugee-producing regimes throughout the world. Thus steps towards the realisation of a frontier-free Europe immediately set up a series of tensions such that a high level of mutual trust was required between Member States with regard to their immigration policies and practices.[4] In fact, border controls between certain countries have sometimes been reintroduced for this reason, as for example between Italy and Germany. At a practical level problems stem from the impossibility of exercising complete and effective control over entry to the EU. More significantly, the problem of control differs according both to the physical nature of the border and to its socio-economic significance, the southern and eastern borders being clearly the most vulnerable to clandestine entry. Among the reasons for concern have been the national character of labour markets and their associated welfare systems, and the significant differences which exist in this respect between member states.

To date, European workers have been the principle focus of the drive for free movement, with entry and residence for non-workers initially conditional upon proof of adequate resources. Treatment of third country nationals has been very much more restrictive, granting only three months visa-free travel in another member state: 'Member countries do not want them to demand work in their countries because until now they did not have any say in the way the entrance policies of the other Member countries have worked' (House of Lords, 1992, Commission evidence: 9). The Commission has consistently argued against this restriction, and the white paper on social policy (European Commission, 1994a), for example, made a case for extending the freedom to work and reside to legally resident non-EEA nationals. As labour supply supersedes unemployment as a pressing problem there may be growing support for this view. We have noted there is now a Commission proposal on this issue – from which Britain and Denmark have opted out.[5]

The logic of welfare?

The key sociological question concerns the sources of resistance to extending free movement, or conceding ease of entry, and for some writers this is predominantly an issue of national resources. Thus Freeman (1986:51) has argued that the welfare state is necessarily bounded; that 'national welfare states cannot co-exist with the free movement of labour'; and that in establishing a principle of distributive justice dependent on membership of a limited community, the welfare state necessarily departs from market principles. Of course this constraint can be overridden by other principles, as, for example, when a strong argument for 'membership' is made,[6] raising other questions about the criteria for inclusion and exclusion. Broadly speaking, however, welfare provision has developed hand in hand with the nation state and has traditionally required the exclusion of less affluent peoples. As Freeman argues, this has been the central concern in control over entry to the national territory, a concern the 'single market' has slowly had to address.

Welfare provisions serve at least two purposes: to provide for needy categories of the population, and to guide, indirectly, the dynamics of the labour market. Thus the setting of assistance benefit is likely to affect the minimum acceptable wage, while the conditions for receipt of such benefit are always set with an eye to work enforcement. Take, for example, the increased emphasis in the UK on proof of job search and tests of availability. Here the policy preference is to force the unemployed into low-paid work rather than allow employers to recruit migrant labour from outside the welfare community, though this strategy can rebound on other member states as the unemployed or low paid seek opportunities elsewhere. There was, for example, resistance in Germany to an influx of migrant workers (many of them British) undercutting local labour (*Guardian*, 2 October 1995; 21 March 1996), while in France, British sub-contractors have been prosecuted for flouting French and European labour laws (*Guardian*, 3 December 1996). Trans-national migration thus threatens the national capacity to regulate both the labour market and the welfare system. Though the Posted Workers Directive[7] now requires observation of the host state's employment rules – a requirement which arguably conflicts with the market principle underpinning the philosophy of European integration (see O'Leary, 1995) – informal practices are an obvious means of evasion.

The welfare state/labour market package as it stands is still, to a considerable degree, a bounded national relationship and access to social provisions remains a contentious area. So, for example, entry for residence as divorced from employment requires that EU citizens and their dependants should carry medical insurance and have sufficient resources not to be a charge on the state (Council Directives 90/364/EEC, 90/365/EEC, 93/96/EEC). The exercise of 'free movement'[8] has therefore excluded a certain category of people who may well hold EU citizenship. This was made clear in a European Commission white paper on social policy (1994a:35) which states, with reference to the rights of EU citizens to move and reside freely: 'In reality, certain persons without resources are hindered from exercising this right, in particular unemployed people without benefits, those who live on social benefits and certain disabled people, and gypsies, who encounter practical and administrative difficulties in residing in the Member State of their choice.'

These constraints could gradually be eroded at the level of the single market and a recent decision by the ECJ ruled – in the case of a student – that EU citizens can rely on the prohibition of discrimination on the grounds of nationality in claiming access to non-contributory benefits (*Migration News Sheet*, October 2001). However, the problem is by no means new and a likely response is either the tightening of eligibility rules for benefit, or heightened requirements for proof of sufficient resources. In 1996, in an attempt to prevent benefit claims from EU nationals in the course of seeking employment, the British social security system introduced a 'habitual residence test'(Allbeson, 1996), designed to prevent what was termed 'benefit tourism' (*Guardian*, 14 February 1996). This was despite an earlier ruling by the ECJ (Case C – 292/89 Antonissen (1991) ECR 1-745; see Handoll, 1994:110-11) granting a 'reasonable' period of jobsearch, though even EU citizens have been requested to leave if they become long-term dependent, a practice which has itself been recently called into question.[9]

While the detailed operations of the single market slowly unfold under Community Law, the position of TCNs has been governed principally by domestic law, which commonly denies welfare rights until full residence has been achieved. In fact, it is argued by some that labour migrants are net contributors to the welfare state (e.g. Carens, 1988) because of the limited circumstances under which they can make a claim. The early stages of residence are commonly tied to employment, or at least are conditional on not being a charge on the state, while clandestine migrants in particular are likely to pay in more than they can ever take out as claimants or service users. Indeed, the Commission's proposed directive on long-term resident TCNs would grant free movement but impose exclusions from social support: 'to ensure that the person concerned does not constitute a burden on the member state where they exercise the right of residence' (*Migration News Sheet*, April 2001). Continuing concern over welfare resources is also apparent in debate about the appropriate system of support for asylum seekers (see chapters to follow), while a claim for social assistance by the family dependent of a TCN can in many cases mean non-renewal of their residence permit (Joint Council for the Welfare of Immigrants, 1993). Thus, in Baubock's terms: 'The more substance the internal rights of citizenship acquire, the more important it seems to police the frontiers of the state' (1991:3), or at least to limit access to those rights.

Trans-national rights

Nevertheless, despite national resistance, and with little overt adjustment of the ideal, the nation as a territorial unit of cultural and civic membership has been challenged by shifting populations and differing dimensions and degrees of inclusion. In fact, the continuing migrant flows into Europe have been echoed, over the same period, by the emergence of trans-national conventions for asserting the rights of migrants which many feel in themselves pose a challenge to national autonomy. These conventions are not part of the legal framework of the European Union, but are rather international commitments which have been entered into by individual member states (see Peers, 2000: 103). The most widely known derive from the human rights machinery developed in the aftermath of World War II, though there are many other less celebrated organisations and conventions asserting the rights of resident foreigners (see Soysal, 1994).

An impressive array of international instruments laying down standards for the protection of migrants has emerged from such organisations – for example, from the United Nations (UN), the International Convention on the Protection of the Rights of all Migrant Workers and their Families (1990); from the International Labour Organization (ILO), the Convention on Migrant Workers (1975); and from the Council of Europe, the European Convention on the Legal Status of Migrant Workers (1977). The impact of such instruments is not always as powerful as might appear, since they depend on ratification by individual states, which is not always forthcoming and is more easily secured among sending than receiving countries. The UN convention, for example, is not yet in force and has certainly not been signed by any of the EU member states. Indeed, concern has been expressed over the often small numbers of states which sign and ratify international conventions designed to protect minority groups (Cator and Niessen, 1994).

Insofar as such conventions represent a challenge to national autonomy, this largely takes the form of moral pressure, as individual nation states are free to opt in or out of such agreements. Even where there is full endorsement, the efficacy of international conventions is often in doubt (Cator and Niessen, 1994). The rights conferred may be conditional, they are commonly limited to co-signatories, and implementation can easily fall short of entitlement. Such tensions raise the question of how far trans-national rights do in fact erode national sovereignty. Certainly individual rights may be established in supra-national fora, but their immediate guarantor is the nation state, which Meyer *et al.* (1997:157) see as strengthening the role of the state as society's primary manager. While a claim to rights will sometimes derive from trans-national instruments, the mechanism for delivery will inevitably operate at national level.

The case of EU citizenship serves as one rather particular example of this arrangement. In November 1993, as a result of the Maastricht Treaty, 93 per cent of residents of Europe gained EU citizenship in addition to their national citizenship. Guild (1994), however, has argued that from a legal perspective the status is meaningless since it is attached to an administrative machinery with no clear territory. EU citizenship is a derived status, dependent upon citizenship of one of the member states of the EU, and loss of the principal citizenship will also mean loss of the derived status. Citizenship of the EU cannot be conferred independently of citizenship of a member state and thus 'does not break the association between citizenship and nationality but renews it in a slightly different way' (Martiniello, 1994:35). Its acquisition and deprivation lie outside EU control and in the hands of nation states.

Human rights

Despite the limitations of some international conventions, a good deal of contemporary migration is accounted for by human rights commitments on asylum and family reunification, which undermine attempts at national closure, though not without resistance often linked to concern about resources. This tension is apparent in a number of areas. The 1993 Commission Resolution on harmonisation of national policies on family reunification was described as a balance between 'favourable admissions policies resulting from international Conventions and national laws . . . and the need to control migration flows' (Handoll, 1994:11.98) and attempts at harmonisation since the Amsterdam Treaty have not yet reached a satisfactory conclusion (see Chapter 5). Although the European Convention on Human Rights, to which all EU member states are signatories, asserts the universal right to respect for private and family life, and thus provides a basis for claims by third country nationals, the right is normally conditional. In practice, the conditions which attach to family reunification – notably the provision of adequate maintenance and accommodation – are quite restrictive, given the position of most non-EU migrants in the host society. In contrast, for EU citizens and EEA nationals who are exercising their right to free movement, the right to family life is much less problematic.

Asylum seekers are the other major source of continued migration into the EU, alongside the suspicion that many are in fact disguised 'economic' migrants. One legislative response has been to impose penalties on the carriers responsible for passengers lacking adequate documentation, in effect impeding the flight of many asylum seekers. The impact of this legislation is compounded by visa policy for the EU since: 'the list for which visa restrictions [were] proposed contains all those [countries] from which asylum seekers [had] fled to Europe over the last five years' (British Refugee Council, House of Lords, 1989, Evidence:162). Asylum seekers are likely to have difficulty in obtaining a visa before travel, and thus to fall foul of the carriers' liability law. This is an arrangement argued by Fernhout (1993) to contravene Article 31 of the Refugee Convention, which forbids criminal sanctions for illegal border crossings by refugees, and described by Cruz (1994) as 'the gradual elimination of the possibility of flight to industrialised countries for those fleeing persecution'.

Reservations over carrier sanctions have been expressed by the United Nations High Commission for Refugees: 'If States consider recourse to carrier sanctions unavoidable they should, at a minimum, implement them in a manner which is consistent with refugee protection principles, and which does not hinder access to status determination procedures' (cited in Cruz, 1994:17). In practice, the response to increased applications has been an attempt to block access. Finally, the Dublin Convention (1990), now incorporated into the Amsterdam Treaty, is based on the principle that asylum applications are to be dealt with by one country on behalf of the EU as a whole. The fear is that states will adjust their procedures on restrictive lines, in order to avoid becoming a magnet for asylum seekers, who will have only one chance of applying to an EU member state. Each of these responses has been the focus of considerable criticism,[10] and so far, as in the case of family unification, harmonisation efforts have not reached any clear conclusions (see Chapter 5).

Irregular employment

However, while human rights may undermine national closure by virtue of transnational commitments, demand for foreign workers can undermine closure from within, and here regulation of labour, political concerns and economic imperatives have been out of step. One of the reasons clandestine migration continues to the extent that it does is the availability of employment of some kind, offering a standard of living far superior to that available in the countries of origin. The availability of labour for inferior pay and carrying reduced (if any) social protections is clearly attractive and can be seen as the logic of the market reasserting itself. Thus, the Director-General of Italy's Confindustria could meaningfully state: 'We need immigrant labour. There is no competition between Italians and immigrants on the labour market' (European Commission, 1993). In part this is because, particularly in southern countries, labour migrants fuel a parallel economy in jobs which bypass regulations, typically in small-scale firms though, as we see in Chapter 3, Italy has attempted to combat this tendency through the use of regularisations and immigration quotas. Throughout the EU, however, there are concentrations of migrants in insecure or seasonal work in construction and agriculture, in small-scale workshops, and also in large-scale industries such as textiles and diamonds. Some, but not all, of this work is undertaken within the law through an arrangement which in effect resurrected the 'guestworker' system, allowing recruitment of temporary labour through bilateral agreements with non-EU countries (see Groenendijk and Hampsink, 1995), but limiting potential demands on the welfare state.

Principal means of bypassing labour regulations have been by sub-contracting to firms illegally employing TCN workers, sometimes recruited from outside the EEA, or by the use of employment agencies which recruit in one member state and hire out the labour in another, below standard rates and without social security (European Commission, 1993). Penalties for employers of clandestine labour are common across the EU, one argument being that they, rather than the individual migrants, hold ultimate responsibility. However, when such penalties were introduced in Britain, they provoked much debate about their potentially negative effect on visible minority workers who are seeking employment legally and may well have full citizenship (*Guardian*, 7 April 1995; see also Chapter 4). Though they remain a part of British law these sanctions are only rarely used, and there are reasons to doubt their efficacy elsewhere, as the following chapters will show. Thus the continuing flow of clandestine migrants – often at the risk of their lives – is at least as compelling an illustration of a post-national or global dynamics as institutions for the elaboration of migrants' rights.

Exporting immigration: a hierarchy of power

In fact, a focus on migration in Europe reveals a number of limitations to what are popularly perceived to represent post-national or global trends. The balance between national sovereignty and trans-national interests raises complex questions, but reveals a tension foreseen and incorporated by many exponents of the globalisation thesis. Less easily accommodated is the hierarchy of national influence by means of which the nation states of Europe extend their power in defence of sovereign control and European exclusivity. While Giddens (1990: 67) notes that 'loss of autonomy on the part of some states or groups of states has often gone along with an increase in that of others', there is no self-evident reason for portraying this in terms of 'globalisation'. Nor is the notion of post-national society particularly helpful here.

The member states of Europe have developed various techniques to facilitate the 'export' of both migration and border control. The most overt of these is 'readmission' – as for example in Germany's agreements with Bulgaria, Romania and Poland, and Italy's with the Mediterranean countries and Albania – which involves an agreement by the sending countries to take back clandestine migrants, usually in exchange for some form of aid. The adoption of the safe third country rule has, in some senses, a similar effect in that refugees can be passed back to the first safe country of transit. So, for example, when Germany abolished its unqualified right to asylum in 1993, those wishing to enter the country after passage through the states of central and eastern Europe would not have their cases considered directly, but would be referred back to an earlier destination. This practice is also apparent in the Dublin Convention, in operation since 1997, whereby the decision of one EU member state – the state of arrival – may act as the decision for all.[11]

The countries on the eastern border of Europe have been dubbed the 'buffer zone' (Bunyan and Webber, 1995; Wallace *et al.*, 1995), and have increasingly been used to absorb the westward flow from the former Communist bloc and beyond. In effect immigration controls have been externalised by pushing responsibility on to countries eager to meet the conditions for entry into the EU. Tight control of external borders is a prominent concern, and increasingly the transit countries have been adopting a range of procedures based on visa, work permit and asylum models from the West in order to regulate immigration. The Czech Republic and Poland, for example, have readmission agreements with their eastern neighbours (Wallace *et al.*, 1994), while themselves supplying guestworkers to the West. Migrants from such countries who pass through the 'buffer' countries into the EU may be referred back across their borders, and so corresponding arrangements are required with the countries further east (O'Keefe, 1992). The projected eastward expansion of EU membership will not therefore challenge this configuration.

The other means by which the member states of the EU exert control over 'sending' countries is through Association and Co-operation agreements. These arrangements are conducted under the terms of EU conventions, but are negotiated separately by each member state involved. There are agreements with, *inter alia*, east European countries, ex-Soviet republics, Turkey and North Africa (Guild, 1992; Peers, 1996). They differ in detail, but usually offer controlled access to a particular member state, though not to the wider EU labour market, and are sometimes subject to time limits. There are formal assurances against discrimination but the very nature of the arrangement makes true equal treatment extremely unlikely. Furthermore, such arrangements usually involve an agreement on the part of the sending countries to discourage the irregular migration of their nationals and to receive back clandestine migrants. International migration may be a manifestation of 'globalisation', but the form it takes is very strongly influenced by the power of the receiving states. Though the growing need for skilled workers is currently forcing a change in the approach to labour migration, most emergent policies promise to be highly selective.

Civic stratification

This brief review of the central issues involved in migration in the EU thus reveals a series of conflicting principles: the frontier-free market against the bounded welfare state; employers' interests against state regulation; and national controls against trans-national rights. The attendant policies and practices inevitably reflect some of these tensions and one result has been the proliferation of statuses involving what has been termed 'partial membership' (Brubaker, 1989), with different bases of entry having different rights attached. These degrees of membership thus constitute a system of civic stratification – a concept briefly outlined in the introduction – whereby the rights and protections afforded by the state to different 'entry' categories constitute a system of stratified rights closely associated with monitoring and control.

Hammar (1990) has captured the key differences in his distinction between citizens, denizens and aliens, but a much more complex pattern is emerging. The fullest membership status is national citizenship, which in legal terms is indistinguishable from naturalised citizenship, although there is a residual question of cultural belonging. Some naturalised citizens will hold dual citizenship with their country of origin and there has been a growing acceptance of this as a possibility.[12] While the rules of national citizenship vary among member states, it is this status which confers entitlement to EU citizenship, and its principal substantive right, to work and reside across the Union. Thus in any single member state there may be long-term residents who are citizens of other member states and who are exercising this right.

In addition there are legal residents who have neither national citizenship nor EU citizenship, and they may be divided into nationals of EEA states, who have the same right to work and reside across Europe as EU citizens, and other third country nationals, who do not. The proposal to extend conditional free movement to those with five years' residence would introduce yet another distinction. Each of these groups may also have with them family members who were allowed entry by virtue of their familial link but whose rights are contingent upon the relationship. In most cases an independent right to remain is acquired only after a probationary period. Among other legally resident foreigners are the workers who enter under the terms of one or other of the Association or Co-operation agreements with third countries, often for a specified period (Guild, 1994). Recognised refugees are usually granted unlimited residence, while other asylum seekers may receive humanitarian leave for a specified period. There are also asylum seekers whose cases are pending and, finally, migrants present in an unlawful status, having either crossed borders undetected or exceeded their permitted period of stay.

Several commentators have argued that in terms of rights it is permanent legal residence rather than citizenship which is the crucial status (Baubock, 1991; Soysal, 1994), but this oversimplifies the case. In fact the positions listed above more or less represent a continuum in terms of their associated rights. Full political rights, notably that of voting in national elections, attach only to citizenship status, as does the unqualified right of residence. Other categories of resident are accepted subject to varying conditions concerning national resources, public order, security, health etc. Re-entry after a period away can sometimes present difficulties, and in the context of the EU the right to free movement between member states is a significant divide. Once granted a non-revocable right to remain, migrants will usually have full social rights; hence the argument that citizenship is being devalued by the rights attaching to residence. However, the denial of full political rights, and the generally conditional residence of any non-citizen suggests otherwise.[13]

Furthermore, we have seen that rights of non-EU citizens with respect to family reunification are limited by virtue of the conditions of entry, notably that the applicant should be in a position to provide reasonable accommodation and maintenance (see Joint Council for the Welfare of Immigrants, 1993). Access to the labour market for migrant family 'dependants' is varied, and may be phased, while the same is true of labour market rights under the various Association and Co-operation agreements between the EU and third countries. Here, full access to the labour market and social rights may be granted only after a specified period of time, or may be strictly limited by a temporary permit. Full refugee status carries with it social rights, family reunification rights and access to the national, but not the EU, labour market. Those granted humanitarian leave to remain have social rights but family reunification rights are delayed or denied. Asylum seekers whose status is pending are much more precariously placed – they generally have reduced social rights and are sometimes, it can be argued, denied their civil rights, if held in detention until their case has been considered.

The position of clandestine migrants raises the difficult questions of whether their illegal status should mean the denial of all rights, whether receiving states carry some responsibility for their presence and their treatment, or whether they stand completely outside any relationship with the state and therefore any protection. They are, of course, the most vulnerable category of migrants for this reason and international conventions for protecting the rights of migrant workers have ignored or specifically excluded undocumented workers, though they can lay claim to some basic human rights. The 1990 UN Convention on the protection of the rights of all migrant workers and their families (see Bosniak, 1991) is unusual in asserting a number of rights for undocumented workers, albeit much more restrictive than for other statuses, but fear of discovery will be a strong inhibitor. Strengthening the rights of this group could limit abuse and improve the state's effective regulation of the national labour market, but, significantly, the Convention has to date been signed by countries which are predominantly senders rather than receivers of migrant flows. There is an inevitable fear that increased rights will encourage clandestine migration, though so too could tighter controls, given continuing employer demand (House of Lords, 1992, Evidence:79; Sciortino, 1991; Handoll, 1994), as labour market policy is slowly coming to recognise.

Work on the gendered nature of these statuses has begun only relatively recently (see Hune, 1991; Kofman et al., 2000). Thus Anthias and Yuval-Davis (1992:96) have noted: 'Although there are about six million women migrants in Europe most of the literature on migration and race has failed to address their specific position.' Certainly gender differences do further complicate the picture sketched above, though work on gender and citizenship (Pateman, 1988) offers one approach to understanding the position of women, as we see in Chapter 6. It is argued that citizenship is implicitly a gendered status of the public sphere, with women's position often limited by their association with the private. In the case of migrant women this rebounds on their independent claim to public rights, their ambiguous position as domestic workers and homeworkers and even their potential for recognition as refugees (Phizaclea, 1996; Crawley, 1997).

As domestic workers women have often been concealed in private households, sometimes under abusive conditions, with no 'public' status of any kind, and there is evidence of a link with the largely illegal and undocumented sex industry. Women also make up the majority of entrants under family unification arrangements, while the mail-order bride syndrome is a further source of female migration. Spouses arriving from outside the EU suffer reduced rights – at least temporarily – and face considerable difficulties, including the threat of deportation on an early breakdown of marriage. Migrant women thus commonly find themselves in a position of legal dependency, with their public right to remain tied to a private status and under the control of a male employer, partner or pimp.

A cluster of contradictions

These growing positions of partial membership seem at odds with the ostensibly unifying concept of EU citizenship and the objective of a single market. They certainly raise questions over too simplistic a presentation of the EU as the paradigm post-national community. Deriving as it does from citizenship of a member state, EU citizenship excludes many legally resident migrants, and cannot (as yet) be granted independently. One means of access to EU citizenship would be naturalisation,[14] but there is an anomaly even here. We have already noted the incremental attempts to establish a harmonised approach to immigration across the EU, which is seen as a condition for the abolition of internal frontiers. Excluded from debate, however, are the very varied criteria and procedures for defining and granting national citizenship, the only means of access to EU citizenship, and it is widely agreed there should be no attempt to bring them into uniformity (House of Lords, 1992, Evidence:38; European Commission, 1994b:35). We should note the sharp contrasts between naturalisation rates for different EU countries, reflecting, in part, differing degrees of openness and different rules on dual citizenship.[15]

There are other senses in which the general principles espoused by the EU seem to conflict with specific aspects of policy. For example, the SEA, whose preamble embraces the principles of freedom, equality and social justice, prohibits discrimination on the grounds of nationality but has been interpreted as referring to member states' nationals only (Niessen, 1992). While there is continuing commitment to the 'integration' of third country nationals, since this is applicable only at the level of member states there is no provision to encompass equal treatment at Community level. There is thus no requirement to grant freedom of movement and settlement rights, and as far as these issues are concerned nationality has been the basis for discrimination, inviting charges of 'racism'.

At the Tampere European Council meeting in October 1999, it was concluded, with respect to long-term resident TCNs that 'a more vigorous integration policy should aim at granting them rights and obligations comparable to those of EU citizens'. However, the Commission's proposed directive on the status of long-term resident TCNs (European Commission, 2001b) falls short of this objective. So, for example, the proposed extension of free movement is not accompanied by full social rights, and the terms of family unification are not equivalent to those of EU citizens. Furthermore, the conditions of initial entry into a member state may anyway be indirectly discriminatory, through the impact of visa regulations, or the requirement not to be a charge on the state. Even within the host country a commitment to equal treatment does not challenge the tenuous bases of entry under some of the Association and Co-operation arrangements, their often limited access to the national labour market and the denial of family reunification rights to temporary workers (see Guild, 1992). Nor does it address the problem of the rights of undocumented migrants (see Bosniak, 1991).

A number of statuses have thus been constructed which explicitly limit rights and effectively preclude claims to equal treatment, except as very narrowly construed. Furthermore, the priority being placed on control can jeopardise existing rights in a variety of ways and, in doing so, challenge some of the fundamental principles espoused by the member states. Human rights are one example, with asylum being increasingly treated as an immigration rather than a humanitarian issue. Another example lies in the intensification of internal controls (Owers, 1994) which involve both random and systematic checks by a variety of enforcement agencies. The land borders of the 'frontier-free' Europe are policed by mobile units authorised to check the documents of any person within a range of 20 km of the border.

Such measures – as with the spread of responsibility to agencies (private and public) whose primary concern is not immigration enforcement, for example, hospitals, social security offices, housing departments, employers, and so on[16] – are anyway contradictory. Internal controls are more than ever being used to compensate for the inadequacy of external controls and as a substitute for internal frontiers, but with attendant fears that freedom of movement is bought at the cost of an erosion of civil liberties. In particular, internal checks make it difficult for some groups to realise their formal entitlements, whether they be undocumented migrants in fear of discovery, or legally resident 'visible minorities', whose contact with public authorities will always expose them to excessive scrutiny in the exercise of their rights.

Immigration controls and 'racism'

These issues eventually run up against the fact that the equal treatment of third country nationals espoused in aspects of EU policy is undermined by the exclusive approach to entry and the negative image of migrants with which it is associated. The conditions of entry are exempt from commitments to equal treatment; yet it has been argued that an endorsement of non-discrimination cannot be viewed independently of the laws on immigration. Thus 'any apparent determination to keep out more of their kind sends out a very disquieting message' (Commission for Racial Equality, House of Lords, 1992, Evidence: 53). In recent years the discussion of 'integration' has been increasingly paired with expressions of concern about racism and xenophobia, which must eventually confront the question of whether the policy of strengthening external controls and national policies on immigration are themselves in contradiction with such a commitment. We have at least the appearance within the EU of immigration regulations which discriminate at the point of entry, alongside explicit limitations on free movement and settlement, together with commitments to remove discrimination from the internal operations of the member states.

Balibar (1991) has argued that racism is written into the EU through the creation of categories of foreigners with unequal rights. This is, of course, a reference to the restrictions on free movement for third country nationals which are central to much of the debate about equal treatment (e.g. Hoogenboom, 1992). However, many would wish to retain a distinction between individual prejudice and rules or procedures which have discriminatory consequences (e.g. Allen and Macey, 1994), while political intent in the framing of such procedures is yet another issue. Others (Brah, 1994) also emphasise the distinction between race and ethnicity, to which we could add cultural difference, while Solomos criticises 'simplistic and monolithic accounts of racism'(1995:48), identifying a plurality of categories and contested notions (cf. Miles, 1993:42). In this context the notion of 'race' becomes so fluid in its meaning and application as to be of little help in detailed analysis and increasingly we find the concept displaced by a focus on the 'cultural construction of difference' (e.g. Rattansi, 1994).

It is useful to recognise that (gender, disability and sexuality aside) anti-discrimination law may cover race, colour, ethnic origin, nationality and language,[17] and may incorporate both direct and indirect discrimination. From this perspective, it is quite clear that the immigration policies and restrictions on free movement embraced by the member states of the EU are discriminatory in different ways: directly by nationality and indirectly through their disproportionate (but not exclusive) impact on non-white populations and non-European cultures. The precise political dynamic which underlies this outcome is more difficult to establish, especially in comparative context, and for this reason a number of writers have attempted to broaden the terms of debate. Miles (1994: 193), for example, argues for analysis in terms of citizenship, democracy and equality rather than race, while Baubock (1991:27) asserts that the concept of citizenship has become overcharged by association with nations or cultural and ethnic communities. But arguably 'race' and discrimination need to be made more explicit in these debates, for example, in documenting the extent to which civic stratification and degrees of membership variously correspond to 'racial', ethnic and cultural hierarchies, albeit socially constructed (see Chapter 6). However, when 'racism' seems to act as a shorthand for such a range of discriminatory practices, there is a strong case for disaggregation.

In Britain, for example, more than half of the immigrant and emigrant employed population are not visible minorities (Immigration Law Practitioners' Association, House of Lords, 1994, Evidence:3), but the categories black, poor, third world, migrant, and third country national operate to some extent interchangeably. Although there are some quite strong tendencies, the lack of clear correspondence raises difficult analytical questions. As noted earlier, free movement has not been entirely confined to nationals of member states, but has also been extended to the largely white and affluent EEA countries. This discriminates against other legally resident, foreign populations in the EU – and the latest Commission proposal would continue to do so – but including as it does Poles and Ukrainians, along with Turks and Moroccans, is this discrimination helpfully termed racist? Similarly, migrant workers whose terms of employment bypass labour regulations have variously included British, East European, Turkish and North African workers, albeit ranked by wage and skill (*Guardian*, 21 March 1996). A blanket charge of 'racism' thus pre-empts a number of other analytical questions.

One of the reasons we now need a more refined framework for analysis is the growing diversity in migrants' countries of origin, and increasing comparative sensitivity as we move towards a more integrated and harmonised European picture. In fact, attempts at harmonisation – which have not to date advanced very far – immediately highlight the range of national distinctiveness. This applies both to the source of different countries' migrant populations and also the varied domestic approaches to their incorporation and/or exclusion. Thus one approach to understanding the position of 'minority' populations across different member states is through the construction and operation of the rights regimes which operate in different national settings, and their impact on migrants according to their origins and forms of entry. How far do these legal structures offer an opportunity for 'full membership', and how far do they confine migrant groups to a long-term marginal status? The answer to this question is quite complex, as the following chapters will show, because of the very varied – often conflicting – factors which are brought to bear in shaping a national regime of rights. We should also note that the boundaries of legal entitlement are shifting boundaries, and a regime of rights can expand or contract over time. Indeed, the expanding membership of the EU could at some point in the future turn the demonised gypsy beggars into co-citizens of Europe, while the once honourable status of refugee has been tainted by the notion of the bogus asylum seeker.

Competing constraints

Political concerns have very recently shown some signs of a shift, as countries have become more attuned to forecasts of ageing populations and have begun to experience a shortage of workers in key areas, notably those with IT skills, but including health service workers, teachers and other service workers and, in Italy, manufacturing workers. In October 2000 a Communication from the European Commission (COM (2000) 757) recognised the necessity for a legal framework on the admission of needed workers and espoused a more positive approach to immigration policy. There have also been shifts in orientation at national level. So, for example, we have seen the introduction of a 'green card' providing a five-year stay for IT workers in Germany, a simplification of Britain's work permit procedures and the use of quotas for migrant labourers in Italy. Increasingly the talk is of developing legal routes of entry as a way of combating clandestine immigration, but to date this approach has been quite selective with respect to needed skills, though the situation in the countries of the south is somewhat more open to relatively unskilled labour, a need which is beginning to be recognised in Britain (*Guardian*, 3 October 2001).

However, there are longer-established anxieties surrounding discussions of migration relating to cultural difference (e.g. House of Lords, 1992, Evidence: 12; 1989, Evidence:75) and political affiliation (e.g. House of Lords, 1992, Evidence:61), with the two often linked, as in the case of growing concern about an Islamic presence. Overt restrictions on movement and entry, however, are formulated not in terms of race or culture but in terms of citizenship. Discriminatory effects are thus inevitably indirect. Furthermore, as we have noted, the criteria for citizenship vary across the EU, with different bases of inclusion affecting different national, ethnic and 'racial' groups (Smith and Blanc, 1995; see also Chapter 6). Personal resources offer a further basis for restriction (as for example in family reunification), but entry may still be granted to a wide diversity of migrants where human rights commitments override other constraints. Conversely, visa regulations, carrier sanctions, resource constraints and the informal operations of border control will disproportionately affect poor, non-white populations.

Similarly, internal policing will tend to focus suspicion on the 'visibly different' minorities and have the effect of eroding their legitimate rights, affecting both employment opportunities and access to services. Britain claims among the most advanced anti-discrimination legislation in the EU, particularly with respect to indirect discrimination (House of Lords, 1992, Evidence:103–11). Yet the requirement for employers to police the legality of their workers – common elsewhere in Europe and known to discriminate against legally present minorities – was introduced in Britain by the 1996 Asylum and Immigration Act. Exclusions from social security have also been argued to produce 'racial discrimination' in the handling of all applications (Social Security Advisory Committee, 1996). Furthermore, the habitual residence test directed against 'benefit tourism' from other EU countries (Allbeson, 1996) rebounded disproportionately on black and minority British citizens with ties outside the UK.

It can then be argued that resource constraints inevitably have an indirect effect on visible minorities, even possibly by design, but there are counter-examples. In practice, the operation of the habitual residence test affected British citizens of whatever ethnic group who had worked abroad, including those exercising their right to free movement in Europe, though an ECJ ruling on this issue (Case C-90/97) prompted an amendment of the rules. In Germany the acceptance of 'ethnic Germans' (*Aussiedler*) as citizens with all the attendant rights appears as a clear example of racially defined 'belonging' overriding other resource issues. There has been growing political opposition to this arrangement (*Migrant News Sheet*, April 1996), partly in the face of perceived cultural difference. Since 1989 there has been a reversal of previous policies to encourage their entry, a tightening of the language requirement and a change in popular positive perceptions of this group (see Groenendijk, 1995).

Taken together then, the terms of debate, legislation governing entry and the practice of regulation reveal a combination of competing concerns: anxiety about both cultural and political affiliation; a clash between ostensible equal treatment and the overriding desire to protect welfare resources; and human rights commitments alongside restrictions on entry. Against a more open policy on immigration stand concern about the national management of welfare and the labour market and reservations about the 'cultural' or political character of migrant populations; while encouraging entry there is continuing demand for labour at both extremes of the class spectrum and a commitment to international human rights, which can be restricted but rarely completely denied.

This situation seems to point to the source of the difficulties experienced in arriving at an adequate theoretical framework for the analysis of migration, rights and membership. There are multiple social and political forces operating, sometimes in harmony but more often in conflict. The central policy issues are the continuing need for enhanced controls, the social integration of migrants and harmonised immigration procedures. Yet arguably the EU and its member states are on the brink of a crisis with respect to their driving principles, insofar as key social institutions are being shaped by conflicting or contradictory forces. My argument here has been that one outcome is a system of stratified rights, or 'civic stratification', which serves as a central device in the management of migration. In the next three chapters we will consider the operation and implications of such a system in three contrasting immigration and asylum regimes – Germany, Italy and Britain – identifying the key features and implications of each before considering these differences in the light of attempts at EU 'harmonisation' and their further implications for a sociology of migrants' rights.

2 Rights and controls in the management of migration

The case of Germany

The heritage of Germany's guestworker history has played a central role in shaping its immigration law and the associated system of migrants' rights. Despite the well-known intention to recruit foreign labour on a temporary basis to drive post-war economic expansion (see Castles and Kosack, 1985) it soon became apparent that the guests had come to stay. The reasons behind this transition are interesting, and have been cited as a classic example of the expansion of migrants' rights by virtue of universalistic claims to 'personhood', as opposed to nationally bounded rights based on citizenship (Soysal, 1994). However, the impulse to consolidate the position of the guestworker population did not derive directly from trans-national commitments, but from both the nature of employer demand and the recognition of a moral responsibility on the part of national politicians (see Joppke, 1999:64). More specifically, the rights of guestworkers to establish residence and seek family unification were upheld through a series of rulings by the Constitutional Court in the course of the 1970s and 1980s. Guiraudon has therefore argued (1998:280) that the extension of rights to aliens was enacted domestically, on the basis of constitutional commitments (dating from 1949) which pre-dated the emergence of a post-war human rights discourse.

Nevertheless, the result has been that an initial policy of temporary recruitment gave way to the gradual unfolding of a regime of migrants' rights which led to the (relatively) secure long-term stay of guestworkers and members of their families. One factor in the elaboration of this system, however, has been the traditionally restrictive approach to citizenship, which as a result required the development of some alternative form of incorporation for permanent foreign residents. We have already noted that there are two salient dimensions to citizenship, namely, the civic and the ethnic, the former being concerned with rights and the latter with identity or 'belonging' (see Smith, 1995:99). The linkage between these two dimensions is closest in countries like Germany, which operate a blood-based (*jus sanguinis*) system of citizenship (Brubaker, 1992) whereby citizenship derives from ancestry. In May 1999, however, Germany took a significant step away from reliance on blood-based belonging, revising its Nationality Law to introduce an element of territory (*jus soli*) in the designation of citizenship (*Migration News Sheet*, May 1999). As we shall see, the immediate impact of this law has been rather limited, but its potential for the future remains quite powerful.

The other characteristic feature of Germany's immigration and asylum regime – again rooted in the Constitution – is a guarantee of the right to seek asylum and traditionally very high numbers of applicants, which passed the 100,000 mark for the first time in 1980 (Joppke, 1999:87). While there has been a gradual consolidation of guestworker rights, there has also been a narrowing of access to asylum, achieved in part by a deterrent approach, in part by a change to the Constitution, and in part by the use of various lesser protections from which security of stay is more difficult to achieve. The overall picture is of a system based largely on the accumulation of rights by passage through a hierarchy of statuses according to a set of specified conditions, and with an associated element of selection. This process of filtering and selection has been based on the principle of self-maintenance, built around phased access to the labour market and policed to a significant extent through the welfare system. A similar hierarchical system operates for asylum seekers, some of whom have achieved secure residence despite being denied full refugee status. However, while ease of access to citizenship could eventually end the partial incorporation of Germany's non-citizen guestworker population, a subsequent generation of temporary workers has been denied this possibility and the transition to secure residence for asylum seekers has been made increasingly difficult.

This chapter offers Germany as a case study in the management of migration through a formal hierarchical system for the granting and withholding of rights, and examines the central role of social, employment and residence rights in the selection, surveillance and control of the original guestworker population and its descendants. In this context the potential impact of the revised Nationality Law (1999) is considered, alongside the emergence of a variety of legal statuses for dealing with temporary work and asylum seekers. We find Germany poised to move from a selective but cumulative approach to the granting of rights towards a bifurcated system which permits integration for some while all but denying this possibility to others – a process which current proposals for change could further consolidate. These latest proposals, embodied in the Foreigners' Law of 2002, would facilitate the entry of highly skilled workers, improve the status of asylum seekers granted subsidiary protection and broaden the definition of this category. At the same time, however, the temporary nature of such protection would be more firmly asserted and the position of those refused protection but unable to leave would be dealt with more rigorously. The law was passed in March 2002 (by one vote) for implementation in 2003. It awaits the signature of Germany's President and may yet be subject to a constitutional challenge (*Migration News Sheet*, April, 2002).

It was suggested in the previous chapter that the development of positions of partial membership may be seen as an administrative attempt to accommodate a set of contradictory tendencies which confronts all the member states of the European Union. Resource concerns and the management of the national labour market militate against immigration, while labour demand and human rights guarantees nevertheless offer a basis for entry. In practice, there are conflicting dynamics in operation, requiring some administrative system for the management of their contradictions. One result has been that, with the notable exception of political rights, some of the rights of citizenship have been extended to resident non-citizens and in this context Soysal (1994) heralds the era of 'post-national membership'. Different categories of residence, however, mean that key rights can still be withheld from certain groups, while definitions of citizenship and criteria of access are themselves open to change. It remains to study the operation and effects of this nascent system of civic stratification (Lockwood, 1996; Morris, 1997a) in national context. In Germany we find the case of a highly bureaucratised and stratified system of rights slowly confronting the need to address a new shortage of skilled labour, and to offer protection while limiting long-term stay.

The particularity of the German case

German law, more than most, shows the continuing significance of citizenship as an instrument and object of social closure: both a marker of membership and a scarce good to which access is sought and restricted (Brubaker, 1992). As we have seen, this aspect of citizenship has been the basis for a critique of the work of T. H. Marshall (1950) and his developmental account of civic, political and social rights. A number of writers (Barbalet, 1988; Bottomore, 1992; Turner, 1993; Kymlicka, 1995) have noted the inadequacy of this framework in the case of 'multi-cultural' or 'poly-ethnic' societies. While both Bottomore (1992) and Turner (1993) have argued that a human rights perspective offers an expanded (and potentially universal) framework for the sociology of rights, this argument overlooks the significance of degrees of partial inclusion, which are a particular characteristic of the German system. In fact, it will be argued here that state control over the granting and withholding of rights has been a key component in the management of migration in Germany, where we find a highly elaborated and formalised system of civic stratification.

The German case to date is of special interest, involving as it does a bureaucratic attempt to resolve contradictory pressures through a particularly complex system of classification and regulation. Its most overt effect has been a hierarchy of statuses which simultaneously represents both a structure of opportunity for some migrants (cf. Baubock, 1991) and a set of insuperable barriers for others. The elaboration of differentiated statuses seems now to have reached its limit and the new law, if implemented, would somewhat simplify the legal structure, though much of its basic rationale would remain intact. Among the reasons for the complexity of the German system to date have been the well-documented descent-based system of citizenship, the restrictive conditions for naturalisation and the limitations on holding dual citizenship[1] (Baubock and Cinar, 1994; Brubaker, 1992). Under its revised Nationality Law (1999) Germany still retains the ideal of a sole citizenship, but accepts dual citizenship for a transitional period, with those born in Germany of settled foreign parents[2] having to choose their sole citizenship at the age of 23. Naturalisation rules have also been eased[3], with a reduction in the residence requirement from fifteen years to eight, and to three years for the foreign spouse of a German citizen. This may enhance both eligibility for and take-up of citizenship, which would correspondingly facilitate family unification for many. For non-citizens family unification remains conditional on housing and maintenance, while there are hierarchical rules governing labour migration and the classification of asylum seekers has become ever more elaborate.

Germany currently shows one of the highest proportions of non-citizen residents in Europe, at 8.8 per cent of the total population, amongst whom naturalisation is extremely low. Of the two million Turks legally present only 2.54 per cent (254,000) have so far naturalised (Beauftragte der Bundesregierung für Ausländerfragen (BBA), 2000:13) while the bulk of naturalisation to date is explained by the continuing acceptance of ethnic Germans (people of German descent) who are granted immediate citizenship (Federal Commissioner for Foreigners' Affairs (FCFA), 1997:11). The recent creation of a single market in Europe introduced a new layer of rights in all member states, but the absence of citizenship for a majority of Turks has produced a particularly complex picture in Germany. Some of the original guestworker population (e.g. Italians) became privileged EU citizens, while the Association agreements between the EU and Turkey (Guild, 1992) have in turn favoured Turkish workers over other TCNs. However, these broad distinctions are augmented by a system of residence permits with associated rights and constraints such that the original guestworkers and their family members may currently under the 1990 Foreigners' Law occupy one of five different positions in terms of their legal rights, not to mention the many Turks and ex-Yugoslavs present in a variety of statuses of protection.

The recent incorporation of an element of *jus soli* into the *jus sanguinis* law and more generous rules of naturalisation could, over time, considerably simplify this picture. Conversely, Germany operates a system of bilateral agreements for the recruitment of strictly time-limited labour under yet another status, while a further layering is discernible among asylum seekers, attracted to Germany in very large numbers throughout the 1980s and 1990s.[4] Germany is unusual in offering a constitutional guarantee to asylum seekers,[5] but in 1993 became part of a trend among European countries to restrict access by denying asylum to those who have travelled through a safe third country. This is now grounds for the refusal of recognition under the Constitution, but such a case can still be recognised under the terms of the Geneva Convention (paragraph 51(1) of the Aliens Act; ZDWF, 1996), or may increasingly be offered some lesser form of protection. There has also been an expansion in the numbers of persons formally required to leave but whose continuing presence is 'tolerated', though this status is now set to be replaced.

This system of differentiated statuses has served as an administrative system for the management of migration in the context of a political rhetoric of denial, though labour demand is beginning to provoke a shift in such rhetoric (Munz,

2001). Material presented below outlines the existing structure of the German system, noting the possibility of movement up or down the hierarchy of statuses and highlighting the centrality of employment rights and social rights in this process. The granting or withholding of these rights has functioned as part of a system of selection, surveillance, deterrence and control with implications for both individual prospects of advancement and societal prospects of cohesion. The changes introduced by the 1999 Nationality Law may signal the final stage of integration for the original guestworkers, but alongside this potential consolidation of their position we find a continuing use of alternative statuses whose functioning highlights a set of complex interactions between rights and controls. The pending 2002 law to rationalise the system[6] would subsume the current five possible residence statuses under two statuses of temporary residence and settlement, but sub-divisions by purpose of stay would continue, as would a variety of statuses of protection. The overall picture of a hierarchy of statuses and a graduated system of rights would remain largely intact, and though there would be improvements for some groups, the system's bifurcated nature, and the division between those who can and those who cannot progress to security, is likely to become more marked.

The 1990 Foreigners' Law

The German Foreigners' Law (Deutches Ausländerrecht, 1997), adopted in its present form in 1990, governs the present situation and as a national law it imposes a degree of legal uniformity across the Länder. It revised and rationalised a prior legal framework for dealing with migration which dated back to 1965 and was based on the assertion of sovereign powers rather than of migrants' rights. Though there is still some room for discretion in its interpretation and application, the 1990 law marked a change in orientation by detailing the rights and conditions associated with a highly differentiated system of statuses for non-EEA nationals. EEA nationals are handled separately under European law and granted the right to work and reside in any member state.[7]

Insofar as regional variation in the operation of the law still exists, it may be seen in the restrictive tendency of southern Länder governed by the Christian Democratic Union (CDU) or Christian Social Union (CSU) and the more liberal tendencies of the northern Länder governed by the Social Democratic Party (SPD). Most of the forty-eight interviews for this research were conducted in Hamburg, which at that time (1998/2000) had a Social Democratic majority and strong Green Party influence, and was therefore located towards the more liberal end of the spectrum. Nevertheless, the interview material, supplemented by official documentation and informants elsewhere (notably Bremen and Berlin), serves as a guide to the structure and logic of the law, and also as a window shedding some light on the scope for discretion.

> There are two key aspects to the current Foreigners' Law. One is to stabilise the situation of non-EU nationals who are already legally present, and to offer them the chance of integration. The other, putting it bluntly, is to

keep the rest out – and that includes those who may be here illegally, or in a legal but temporary status.

(Spokesperson, Foreigners' Office, Hamburg)

This law has unified practice, which is in some ways a good thing. Minority rights groups were complaining that the law was too flexibile and that officials had too much leeway. They wanted a clearer statement of rights. There is a philosophy of integration built into this law, and clear conditions for achieving a secure status. It shows an acceptance of the fact of migration to date, but there is a wish now to bring it to a halt.

(Adviser, Foreigners' Commission, Hamburg)

A crisis in the recruitment of highly skilled and specialist labour prompted a review of the latter position in July 2000 (Munz, 2001), but the complex motivations operating with respect to migration will continue to be reflected in the way the system for dealing with non-EEA nationals is structured. The law essentially operates through distinctions between different groups of migrants, each of which represent one or other of the contradictory pressures identified above. There is the need to integrate established guestworkers and their families; the need to balance labour supply and demand; and a continuing (though somewhat diminished) commitment to asylum seekers. Each of these objectives must be accommodated, but in the context of a generally restrictive migratory regime, strictly limited welfare and highly differentiated employment rights.

Table 2.1 details the origins and numbers of those occupying each of the different residence statuses, outlined in the pages to follow. This distribution does not, however, represent a static picture – there is movement off the chart

Table 2.1 Non-EEA foreigners' statuses

Origin	Total	Residence permit		Right of abode	Fixed purpose	Human. leave	Asylum seeker	Toler- ation
		limited	unlimited					
Turkey	2,053,564	744,540	619,115	475,954	6,804	21,116	40,234	14,866
Ex-Yug.[1]	737,204	118,053	161,088	99,668	3,668	24,984	93,323	145,563
Bosnia–Hertz.	167,690	41,838	25,262	21,767	2,831	6,304	4,625	46,471
Poland	291,673	88,388	68,161	7,386	46,319	8,752	1,415	1,330
Croatia	213,954	46,915	77,734	68,244	6,848	747	421	2,885
Iran	116,446	24,318	45,142	12,350	2,064	8,422	11,242	1,513
Romania	87,504	20,393	14,680	580	11,623	2,361	3,229	1,157
Vietnam	85,362	22,111	27,124	1,408	1,357	3,670	3,566	13,966
Morocco	81,450	32,143	23,830	9,772	5,208	224	445	366
Afghanistan	71,955	8,530	13,574	254	298	17,988	11,204	12,894
Sri Lanka	55,085	15,481	11,850	2,661	289	5,055	7,901	3,517
Hungary	53,152	10,982	13,688	4,162	15,643	363	120	82
Lebanon	54,063	13,341	7,956	370	519	14,799	3,334	6,081
Tunisia	24,260	8,755	7,163	3,100	1,182	138	340	105
Total	**7,343,591**	**1,757,746**	**2,027,128**	**824,099**	**231,231**	**173,718**	**264,269**	**302,037**

Source: Beauftragte der Bundesregierung für Ausländerfragen, 2000 (data for December 1999).

Note
[1] Migrants registered with Yugoslav citizenship on the date of reference.

from the right of abode into full citizenship status, there is movement between statuses, and there is also movement off the chart through deportation, denial of permission, voluntary departure or the slide into undocumented status. It is these movements which are the most interesting and revealing aspects of the rationale for managing migration and which provide the key to both the political intent and its social structural effects. We therefore need to consider the rights which attach to the different statuses, the conditions for the granting or withholding of each status and the criteria for transition between statuses. This is the background against which to assess the impact of the revised Nationality Law (1999) and any pending changes in the approach to immigration.

The probationary status

Befristete Aufenthaltserlaubnis/Foreigners' Law (FL) para. 13

Time-limited residence was the status occupied by the original guestworker population, most of whom have now established a more secure residence or, more rarely, citizenship. While time-limited status may still be granted to a small number of specialist workers, as for example with the newly established 'green card' system (see p. 38), it has become the key transitional status for arrivals under family unification rules. German citizens have an immediate and absolute right to family unification, and for workers from EEA countries this is conditional only on adequate accommodation. For TCNs the situation is more complex. First-generation migrants (who declare their marriage at the point of entry) must meet stringent maintenance and accommodation requirements. Those who were born in Germany, or arrived as minors, must in addition have eight years of residence in the country, shortened to five if there is a child involved (*FL* paras 17 and 18). Self-reliance is a common requirement in European countries which attempt to honour the right to family life, but only in the context of protecting welfare resources (Joint Council for the Welfare of Immigrants, 1993), and this is one area in which there is scope for regional variation:

> The rules for limited residence say a welfare claim *could* affect an extension of your stay. You have the right to support but you might have problems with renewing your permission. You will not be directly expelled or deported, and may be given some months to find work, but if your permission is not renewed you cannot remain in the country.
>
> (Immigration lawyer 1, Bremen)

> There is a lot of discretion for the Foreigners' Office, and a lot depends on the circumstances; what are their future prospects, how integrated are they, what is their family situation and so on . . . but while it is true that foreigners in Germany have a right to social support, for those with a limited permit access is in practice controlled by the Foreigners' Office through decisions about residence.
>
> (Social Work Office, Hamburg)

Given these constraints the right to work could clearly be crucial and is at present granted independently of the residence permit, although the two permissions are closely associated and set to be merged under the 2002 legislation. There are two types of permit, governed by national regulations: first, a limited permit which is highly restrictive, granted only with labour office approval, for a specified job with a specified company, applying a strict preferential hierarchy;[8] and, second, an unlimited permit that grants full access to the German labour market (Federal Employment Service, 1995). The foreign spouse of a German citizen or an EEA worker has immediate access to a full work permit, but the spouses of other foreign residents must wait. There has been a recent improvement here (as of December 2000) and arriving spouses qualify for the full permit after two years (rather than four). Furthermore, spouses whose partners have unlimited residence may apply for the restricted permit on arrival, while those whose partners have limited residence qualify only after one year's wait. This still means that for two years the employment prospects of all joining spouses are, to say the least, rather slim, yet meeting the housing and maintenance conditions of residence is extremely difficult:

> The major problem people bring to us concerns residence permits and the right to stay. If a man with unlimited residence brings his wife but loses his job while she has only limited permission then she will have to go back. Or even if they cannot find adequate housing, and that is a big problem in Hamburg. You have to look not just at one law but how all the paragraphs of the different laws work together.
> (Turkish minority rights adviser, Hamburg)

> We see this all the time (non-renewal of a permit), when someone is unemployed, for example. The original migrant will be allowed to stay if they themselves had an unlimited permit, but a spouse with limited stay will probably not.
> (Immigration lawyer 2, Bremen)

One change under the new law would grant the family member, on arrival, the same work entitlement as the relative they are joining. However, a foreign spouse is granted independent residence only after four years of marriage.[9] In the case of divorce after this point, unless the 'dependent' spouse has already achieved secure status, then she/he receives a limited permit and is required to demonstrate an ability to maintain and house her/himself. Divorce before this time could mean a loss of the right to remain, except where return to the country of origin would cause proven 'special hardship', as in cultures which do not readily accept divorce and would stigmatise or otherwise punish the woman. In such cases a special ruling grants independent residence after two years (*Migration News Sheet*, May 2000).

A contentious aspect of the 2002 law is a reduction in the maximum age for family unification for children from 16 to 12 (but an increase for children accompanying their parents on entry from 16 to 18). Once established, such children are granted residence according to the status of the parents, but at 18 could still face obstacles in achieving security:

> Beyond 18 if they are not in education they should have their own income, unless their family can take full responsibility for maintenance[10] – and that can be a problem. If they get social benefits this restricts their chances of unlimited residence, the right of abode and also citizenship. So in practice they could move down from their parents' position of unlimited residence to find they have only a limited permit. That leaves them very vulnerable – but in the view of the system they should work.
> (Immigration lawyer 1, Bremen)

Wilpert (1999) has noted the vulnerability of second-generation migrants to unemployment and informal work, and this can rebound on future rights, affecting for example the achievement of full security (as outlined below), or the prospects of bringing a marriage partner from their home country. Of course the possibility of citizenship at birth removes such pressure, but only for children born in Germany, and of parents who have already undergone this selection process to achieve a minimum eight years of legal residence. The time-limited status also retains its significance in cases of early divorce when the spouse has not established independent security of residence and for family members of non-citizens. The 2002 law would further expand its use in cases of humanitarian protection, but on terms which are not yet clear (see below, p. 44).

The prospect of security

Unbefristete Aufenthaltserlaubnis/FL para. 24; Aufenthaltsberechtigung/FL para. 27

One of the advances made by the 1990 Foreigners' Law was in granting progression to a more secure status as a right if people met a set of specified conditions. The move from a limited to an unlimited permit can be made after five years in the former status if the applicant also holds a full work permit. The full permit is currently granted after a wait which varies from two to six years and of course the applicant must survive the intervening period without significant reliance on welfare. The accommodation and maintenance conditions must be met at the point of application and the applicant must also have a rudimentary knowledge of the German language. After achieving unlimited residence a welfare claim is unlikely to be damaging, although official note would be taken:

> The highest law regarding the transfer of information is to give any information to the Foreigners' Office which has implications for residence status. If someone continues to claim welfare for an extended period we would always report it to the Foreigners' Office, though the length of the period is

at the discretion of the officer here [Social Office]. If someone has an unlimited permit we still pass the information, because suppose they wanted to apply for the next status [right of abode], this could be relevant.

(Social Office, Hamburg)

International conventions offer only limited guarantees of social rights, but while officials were unable to identify any circumstances under which someone might routinely lose an unlimited permission,[11] receipt of welfare benefit could disqualify them from the right of abode. However:

People won't necessarily know or understand the detail of these laws, but they will know there is something about welfare support. The thing is that it has been written into the law and this will be emitted to the person as a general insecurity. The law is sitting there as a threat and they feel they must have work to be safe.

(Adviser, Foreigners' Commission, Hamburg)

This could translate into a deficit whereby people are inhibited from claiming rights to which they are formally entitled. Self-maintenance is one condition for the next incremental step, the right of abode (*Aufenthaltsberechtigung*), which as a right rather than a permission offers a more robust basis for secure residence.[12] The transition requires eight years with a residence permit (five years limited and three years unlimited, or eight years in a humanitarian status). It also requires some measure of 'integration', in the form of a five-year record with a pension fund:

In the past this used to be a language test, but in the 1990 law this was changed to having paid five years into a German pension fund. There had been some feeling that too few Turkish people were taking up *berechtigung*, and that the language requirement might have been too difficult.

(Immigration lawyer 1, Bremen)

This is a potential source of discrimination against women, who often do not have insured employment since they typically work in part-time low-skilled jobs. There is a discretionary mechanism for granting *berechtigung* where the partner fulfils the conditions, but officials are said to be reluctant to exercise authority by taking a positive decision. So once again access to employment and related rights provides a pivotal point in the accumulation of security.

The 2002 law should simplify the system, replacing unlimited residence and the right of abode with a sole settlement status (*Niederlassungserlaubnis*), and highly skilled workers perhaps having the possibility of settlement on entry. Nevertheless, outside citizenship there is no ultimately secure status and there are a number of specific circumstances under which loss of status is a real possibility. One of the changes introduced by the 1990 Foreigners' Law was a clearer specification of the conditions for expulsion, which become more stringent the weaker one's residence status:

The law here contains a *may*, a *normally*, and a *must* [FL paras 45–7]. Someone *may* be deported, for example, for receipt of welfare, endangering public order, using drugs; will *normally* be deported for one or more criminal acts warranting two years imprisonment, producing, importing or distributing drugs, or violent demonstration; and *must* be deported for more severe criminal acts or drug-related offences.

(Lawyer, Foreigners' Commission, Hamburg)[13]

In fact there have been some recent examples of expulsion for repeated offences which would fall in the middle category (e.g. *Migration News Sheet*, September 1997) and it remains to be seen how a new settlement status would operate. Citizenship at present removes a residual element of uncertainty and, without it, non-EEA nationals must surmount some difficult obstacles to secure their status. They must guarantee their own maintenance (avoiding criminal activity), but after a period of limited access to the labour market. The full right to work is thus earned only after a period of restricted rights, rather than being granted as an immediate means to self-reliance. Social rights are more widely conferred, but the link with residence has meant that they may in practice be curtailed by the non-renewal of a residence permit. While duration of stay and the ability to be self-maintaining, together with minimal language proficiency, allow some to earn their way to security, the weaker one's initial status the harder this will be.

The huge potential significance of the 1999 Nationality Law – if a large majority of the eligible population opted for German citizenship – is that the graduated steps towards right of abode, along with their staggered access to social and employment rights, would all but fade away. Automatic rights would also follow for incoming spouses, though we should note that at the age of 23 the acceptance of dual citizenship lapses and the individual must choose between German citizenship and that of their parents. While the 1999 citizenship laws may represent the final stage of the long struggle for security by the guestworker population, and the 2002 law improves the employment rights of some family members, a later population of migrants has been experiencing a different set of constraints. For them, as we shall see, the problem has been access to a residence status of any kind, a necessary condition for embarking on the route to security.

Entry for employment

Despite the stop on active recruitment of guestworkers in 1973, migration for employment continues in a number of forms and there is a discernible hierarchy here. Transfers within multi-national corporations are relatively straightforward and workers can, if they wish, graduate to full security of residence in the terms set out above. There are some skill shortages which permit the recruitment of non-EEA workers, a recent example being the introduction of 'green cards' for IT workers who are admitted for a specified period of time up to (at present) a maximum of five years. This looks rather like a replication of the guestworker logic, and may meet the same end, though there are signs of a more fundamental rethink of immigration in relation to skill shortages (*Migration News Sheet*, August 2001). The 2002 law, for example, proposes the possibility of permanence for highly specialist workers with needed skills. It represents a shift in concern from limiting the entry and restricting the rights of low-skilled labour to encouraging the entry and enhancing the rights of the highly skilled. At present, however, the most overt restrictions operate through the status of *bewilligung* (*FL* para 28), which prohibits transition and from which it is impossible to move to a more secure position – except through marriage to a German. While the chance to earn secure residence as of right was developed as a means of accommodating the original guestworker population, one other objective of the 1990 law was to deny this possibility to certain categories of migrant. A common application of *bewilligung* is for students, in which case the permit is renewable until studies are completed. More contentious has been its use to revive the guestworker pattern but with stricter enforcement of the rotation of workers. Though *bewilligung* would be abolished under the new legislation, some system for the regulation of temporary workers is likely to be incorporated into the temporary residence status.

At present, there is a range of employment possibilities, some linked to training and others to international collaboration (Federal Employment Service (FES), 1995:16), but numerically most significant has been the recruitment of seasonal workers in agriculture and the holiday trade and the use of contract labour in construction. Seasonal workers are limited to three months, and contract labourers to eighteen months (FES, 1995) and both types of labour represent attempts to contain a particular form of undocumented migration.

> Before the 1990 law, but after the stop on recruitment, there was no means of regulating labour migration and there was a lot of illegal work, particularly in harvesting and construction. This was always the case, and still is, because once people have established connections they will make their own way.
> (Adviser, Workers' Welfare Organisation, Hamburg)

The *bewilligung* status thus offers minimal opportunities as a means of regulating a previously existing but unregulated process, setting in train a number of responses. There have, for example, been attempts to displace seasonal labour by requiring the registered unemployed to take on the work. Some years ago, the Federal Ministry of Employment announced a 10 per cent reduction in seasonal recruitment as part of a policy to direct the unemployed into these jobs with the threat of loss of benefit for refusal (*Migration News Sheet*, February 1998). Contract labour has also been contentious, in relation to both German and EU labour supply.

Contract labour is largely used in the construction industry, with the worker's presence in Germany limited to eighteen months, and with immediate return or renewal prohibited. The contract of employment is made in the country of origin and the right of residence is linked to a specified job for a specified company. Even a change of site with the same employer requires a new permit, which is negotiated by the employing company, not by the workers themselves. Health and social insurance are in the country of origin and so once the job is over, or the permit expires – whichever is the earlier – the worker has no right to social support and, technically speaking, no reason or right to remain. Centralised registers keep details of named workers for whom permits are issued as a means to enforce rotation, and there is also an established system of raiding building sites to check the legality of workers.

Formally this use of non-EU labour is to be run down:

> There have been some difficulties because the German government made agreements for a quota of workers from these different countries and at the peak there were about 200,000 a year, but around the middle of 1997 the European Commission concluded that this collides with the law for a European single market, and requested a gradual reduction.
> (Foreigners' Office, Hamburg Labour Office)

Increasingly the sources of cheap labour in construction will be from other EU countries (*Guardian*, 21 March 1996), especially with the entry of eastern countries into the EU, but the issue of undocumented labour is likely to remain:

> You have to see the reality of a big construction site to imagine the possibilities – 500 people from 200 firms from seven different countries. You have to remember the notion of a firm operating on a construction site is a very loose one. Certain trades don't need much machinery to set up a firm – just a computer and paper, and after the job many of these contractors collapse; officially they go broke. This makes them very hard to control.
> (Workers' Council Representative, Construction, Hamburg)

While the restricted permits for contract and seasonal workers are the legal means through which to impose rotation and control numbers, they present only part of the picture. Movement through the hierarchy of formal statuses may be denied, but transition to an undocumented status built on the contacts and experience accumulated during the stay are an inevitable by-product of the arrangement.

We should note that, despite the rigorous control which typifies the German system, informal work (encompassing workers with and without a permit of residence) is a matter of some concern (see Wilpert, 1999). Such work takes a variety of forms, the most common being domestic work, construction and ethnic 'fast food'. Although it is anticipated that part of the problem will eventually disappear with the entry of eastern countries into the EU, such sources by no means fully account for the phenomenon. In addition to those working on visa-free travel (e.g. from Poland), there may be people with tourist visas or unlawfully present, and those TCNs who are present in a regular capacity but denied a full work permit – at present some foreign spouses of non-Germans and asylum seekers (Wilpert, 1999).

Asylum seekers

Aufenthaltsgestattung/FL para. 55

In the treatment of asylum seekers the principal area of tension – by no means confined to Germany – lies in honouring human rights commitments while restricting migration and limiting claims on welfare resources. On gaining entry to Germany and making a claim for asylum the asylum seekers are granted a temporary status of *Gestattung* (Asylum Law, 1993, para. 55). This confines them to a specific district and imposes a waiting period of one year before a restricted work permit can be requested (*Migration News Sheet*, July 1997). Asylum seekers are provided with social support, but since 1993 this has been set at a rate roughly 20 per cent below the standard minimum welfare provision. Employment was banned for asylum seekers arriving after May 1997 (*Migration News Sheet*, July 1997), but at the end of 2000 the ban was lifted and replaced with the current one-year waiting period. The employment options, however, are limited to jobs for whom no German or EEA workers are available, and a six-week search period is required to establish this:

> In some places, Berlin for example, the new rule changes nothing because there is so much unemployment. The only positive difference is that the six week search is only for the first period. Gestattung is renewed every six months and in the past each time you had also to renew the work permit, so you had to have a new search every time. Now it is only if you want to change your job, but to get a job under this system is very difficult.
>
> (Adviser to Pro Asyl, Berlin)

For at least the first three months asylum seekers are placed in a reception centre with provisions made in kind, reflecting the dual objectives of support and control.

> The point of these centres was to have better control, at least in the first few months, to speed up decisions on weak cases and make deportations easier at the point of failure, so there would be less chance of people disappearing. The provision in kind during this early period is meant as a deterrent to anyone who might see an asylum claim as a quick route to some income. The point is to make things as unpleasant as possible.
>
> (Social worker, asylum reception centre, Hamburg)

These centres tend to be situated in marginal locations which both impose practical difficulties and convey a symbolic message about the place of asylum seekers in society. For example, in Hamburg the reception centre is housed in accommodation floating on rafts on the River Elbe, where the floors move beneath your feet. Another example in nearby Oldenburg is a disused hospital for the mentally ill, located in its own grounds and surrounded by empty marsh land. Conditions in the eastern Länder are more intimidating, with the implicit threat of racial harassment and violence.

Provision in reception centres is in kind, but thereafter the form of provision varies. Hamburg is unusual in providing financial support paid directly to asylum seekers through the social office. A system of vouchers to be exchanged for food and sometimes clothes is much more common (typically in the northern Länder), or alternatively food packages (more common in the southern Länder). Adults are permitted DM80 (£26) spending money per month.

> Most places use vouchers, though there are differences in the detail of the system. Some don't give change, although normally you can get up to 10 per cent in change from vouchers, but this can be difficult to calculate when you are buying. Some places only allow shopping on two designated periods in the week. . . . Food packages are a bigger problem[14] because you can't decide what you need and find yourself with too much of one thing but lacking something else.
>
> (Adviser to Pro Asyl, Berlin)

Housing at this stage in the process could be in large or small hostels or, more rarely, in small shared apartments. There is no possibility of opting out of dispersal, or even the housing element of support, by seeking hospitality from relatives and friends, though it is argued by migrant support groups that the administration of the system is itself quite costly. However, a mass system of dispersal and support offers greater potential for control and deterrence:

> In the case of vouchers you lose 2 or 3 per cent to the company administering the system. With food packages the value inside the package is much less – you pay the packers, the trucks to carry the packages and so on, all from the aid for the refugees. Compared to an individualised system of support it can cost up to DM3000 a month to treat a family badly – we have a lot of money for this in Germany.
>
> (Adviser to Pro Asyl, Berlin)

Confinement to a particular district also has financial implications in terms of access to advice, and has been the focus of active protest (Statewatch, 2001b). Permission must be requested before leaving the district, and even this can involve a journey to the main town of the area before a further journey to consult a lawyer can be made – all of which eats into the DM80 cash allowance. The only means of evading dispersal has been to make a local application for humanitarian leave, usually in the form of protection against deportation (a *duldung*, see p. 47). The decision is made locally and the local area remains responsible for the individual concerned – one example of the considerable variety in forms and degrees of recognition. Although the status of *duldung* is to be abolished, it is likely to be replaced with some form of certification.

Degrees of recognition for asylum seekers

Refugee status/Basic Law article 16a; Geneva Convention recognition/FL para. 51; Protection from deportation/FL para. 53

As well as the residence statuses already discussed, there are distinctive routes for asylum seekers in terms of types of recognition and their associated rights. Again the interplay of rights and controls is central. The recognition rate for asylum seekers in 1999 was about 12 per cent (Beauftragte der Bundesregierung für Ausländerfragen, 2000:table 8) and most secure are those granted protection under the German Constitution, which means an unlimited residence permit. Those recognised under the Geneva Convention (paragraph 51 of the Foreigners' Law; ZDWF, 1996), usually if they have passed through a third safe country but cannot be returned (the so-called small asylum), are granted the lesser humanitarian protection of *befugnis*. Neither recognition applies in cases of non-state agents of persecution or gender-based persecution, but the 2002 law should extend the use of 'small asylum' to such cases – strongly contested by the CDU opposition. Both recognitions already carry full employment rights and social rights, as well as rights of family unification; for those with full recognition this latter should be unconditional, though the practice is in fact varied (for discussion see Heinhold, 2000:165). The new law should consolidate family rights and grant both categories of asylum a residence permit to be reviewed after three years, but with the possibility of settlement thereafter. There is, at present, the opportunity of progressing to a right of abode for those who are self-maintaining, unless there is a reason to revoke their protection. In fact a request for family unification can trigger this, and represents another possible instance of deficit:

> This reopens the case with the Bundesampt to see if the problems still exist. People from Iraq, for example, should never apply for family unification because their recognition could be withdrawn. This means they will never have a chance to bring their family unless the family make their own individual application for asylum.
>
> (Adviser, Red Cross, Hamburg)

A change in the home country can itself be the reason for a review of cases, and those with a *befugnis* are most vulnerable as this status is issued for exceptional purposes. The 2002 law would replace *befugnis* with temporary residence, and reviews are likely to be more rigorous – a trend which has already begun:

> Yes the recognition can be taken back. This won't be a problem for those who are integrated, but there are many losers – those who cannot establish roots here, or are workless and still live on welfare. This is a big problem.
>
> (Adviser, Red Cross, Hamburg)

44   *Rights and controls – Germany*

> Now they seem to be reviewing the situation in the home countries, and starting to withdraw the refugees' status. The asylum law is quite clear about this possibility. It is not a problem for those who have graduated to the right of abode; they can remain unproblematically in that status if they are prepared to request their original national passport. The problem is for those who only have a residence permit – even if it is unlimited. Unlimited permission is still a permission and it can always be cancelled.
>
> (Immigration lawyer 3, Hamburg)

At present the right of abode (*berechtigung*) offers the possibility of a secure stay, and settlement may operate in the same way, though to date employment has been central in determining future prospects:

> One of the things we have to be careful about when advising refugees is to make them think through their long-term aims. If they wish to remain in Germany they have to move from *befugnis* or *unbefristet* to *berechtigung*, otherwise they are vulnerable to losing their status. To do this they must get a job – but there are very large numbers of recognised refugees in Hamburg living on welfare and they do not qualify for the more secure status.
>
> (Social Work Office, Hamburg)

Constraints of this kind are of growing significance as aside from Geneva Convention refugees the *befugnis* category contains a number of other subdivisions which normally grant full employment rights only after six years' residence and carry no right to family unification. The changes proposed would subsume *befugnis* into the category of temporary residence, but it remains to be seen how employment and the progression to secure residence would be handled, as the intention is to assert the temporary nature of protection.

The treatment of Bosnian civil war refugees[15] offers one model. They have been by far the largest group in the *befugnis* category (see Table 2.1), and have received distinctive treatment in a number of ways:

> Many Bosnians were given *befugnis* at the start, and they were allowed to work without restriction. There were a lot of people and it was felt they shouldn't be on social support. But it was also the case that the work would be no use to them in getting a better status because it was made clear from the start their stay was temporary.
>
> (Adviser, Red Cross, Hamburg)

When war conditions no longer prevailed, Bosnian refugees were offered only a status of toleration (*duldung*), from which transition to more secure residence was prohibited. They were also excluded from 'old cases' rulings:

> Periodically the Conference of Ministers for Home Affairs for all the Länder can decide to give a *befugnis* to all asylum seekers who arrived before a

certain date, for example, for families before July 1990, and for single people before January 1987 – if they have been in Germany since that time, earn their own money, have adequate accommodation and are integrated. Bosnians were excluded from this offer because they were always meant to be temporary.

(Social worker for asylum seekers, Hamburg)

However, a 'hard cases' ruling in November 2000 granted *befugnis* to a number of traumatised Bosnians, and those aged over 65 with no family in Bosnia who have been present in the coutry since before 1995 with only a tolerated status (see p. 47).

The other common circumstance under which *befugnis* has been granted is when people are in flight from a situation in which their lives or freedom are in danger, but which does not qualify them for asylum. Aside from recognition under the Constitution and under the Geneva Convention, there are a variety of other circumstances which at present could result in either a *duldung* or *befugnis*. An applicant for asylum whose case is rejected may still qualify for protection from deportation under para. 53 of the Foreigners' Law, which incorporates aspects of protection under the ECHR (for discussion see Heinhold, 2000: 82). Those qualifying for such protection are granted temporary suspension of deportation (*duldung*), but if the impediment to deportation continues then strictly speaking a *befugnis* should be granted (Heinhold, 2000: 84). In practice many remain for the longer term with a *duldung*, though even the superior status of *befugnis* is far from secure.

The pending 2002 law would abolish the *duldung* status and instead grant temporary residence to those who qualify for protection, extending the criteria to include gender-based persecution and non-state agents of persecution (Statewatch, 2001a). The interesting question will be the scope for transition to a more secure status, an issue in the past for many of those granted *befugnis* under para. 53(6). Again the situation has turned upon employment:

> Since the beginning of this year (1998) they have started to apply paragraph 7 to these people – which says that you should only have a residence permit (*Aufenthaltsgenehmigung*), which includes *befugnis*, if you are financially independent. This wouldn't apply to those with Geneva Convention recognition,[16] but they started to check all the paragraph 53 people.
> (Adviser, Red Cross, Hamburg)

> If they are not working and not trying to find work they will get a *duldung*. The first step is their social support is cut by 20 per cent. When it comes to renewal of their *befugnis* they may be given some time to find a job, but if they are dependent on social support the *befugnis* won't be renewed.
> (Social workers, refugee housing complex, Hamburg)

> It really seems that they regret allowing the possibility of secure residence

from *befugnis*. It is a residual status but suddenly they didn't know what to do with war refugees and others who don't strictly qualify for asylum so they placed them under this status. Now their social support is being reduced and you have the feeling the authorities wish they would go.

(Adviser, Hamburg Foreigners' Commission)

The 2002 changes would improve the position of this group with respect to social rights, but the rules on self-maintenance and transitions to security under the status of temporary residence would be very important. Under current arrangements there are certain barriers in the way of an improved status for some of the *befugnis* group, notably the stringency with which the requirement to be self-maintaining is interpreted. Those with recognition under the Geneva Convention receive children's benefit (*Kinder Geld*) while the other categories of *befugnis* do not. This can be a problem when they wish to apply for an unlimited permit:

> To be self-maintaining in low-paid work and with a large family without this benefit is very difficult. But the decision for an unlimited permit rests on the level of income they have at that moment, not what they will have in the future – because an upgrading would qualify them for the benefit. In Hamburg this is very strict. They only count what is there. They don't look forward. This is the internal instruction.
>
> (Adviser, Red Cross, Hamburg)

With housing the interactions are even more complex:

> Asylum seekers granted *befugnis* are mostly still in the centres. They should not be there and should qualify for social housing but a few years ago there was a decision here for some that *befugnis* should only be extended for 11 months. There is a big housing shortage in Hamburg and one qualification is to hold at a minimum a 12-month residence permit. So anyone with a permission for 11 months, however many times it is renewed, cannot qualify. This is a misuse of the Foreigners' Law to regulate the accommodation situation.
>
> (Social Office, Hamburg)

Again this could have implications for transition to unlimited residence as adequate housing is one of the conditions.

It is not yet clear what the prospects for security would be under the 2002 law. With *befugnis* we have a status from which this transition is possible but the requirement to be self-maintaining, restricted employment rights (for up to six years) and the manipulation of certain key social provisions can act in concert to make such progression extremely difficult. Again a number of different aspects of the law are in interaction, with interpretive decisions also playing a central role, so that the granting and withholding of rights affects not only present circumstances but, more crucially, shapes future prospects. The granting of social support in the absence of employment opportunities can be a short-term boon but a long-term liability if the conditions of stay require self-maintenance.

Duldung

FL paras 55–6

Duldung refers to a situation of tolerated presence, rather than a full legal status. It is a problematic status which the new proposals seek to abolish:

> The [2002] law is actually avoiding the term *duldung*, but it arises anew in the term *bescheinigung* [certificate]. This status will in future be mainly applied to people that cannot be deported for factual reasons [no passport, no ways of transport, not accepted by the home country, illness, etc.].
> (Asylum adviser, Red Cross, Berlin)

Civil war refugees granted temporary protection have increasingly fallen into the *duldung* category, as have many protected under para. 53, though the new law could grant them temporary residence. However, the failure to achieve recognition has not meant the end of the stay for many rejected asylum seekers, and those who cannot be deported for practical reasons (rather than a risk to life or freedom) have been granted a toleration (*duldung*). The administration of this system is itself felt to have a deterrent quality:

> A *duldung* can be for different periods of time up to a year, and can even be for just one day. There is always the possibility of renewal but this is unpredictable. They have to go to the Foreigners' Office for renewal; it is very cold with an atmosphere like a prison and a lot of steel doors. One person goes in and comes out with a new *duldung*, and another goes in and doesn't come out at all – they go to the prison and then to the airport. It's like Russian roulette and many can't stand it, they just break down or they come to us and say 'Help me to go home.'
> (Adviser, asylum support organisation, Hamburg)

The possession of a *duldung* is crucial for claims to social support and accommodation, which are offered on the same terms as for asylum seekers. In June 1997, the period during which asylum seekers and tolerated foreigners are held to this lower rate of support was extended from one year to three (*Migration News Sheet*, July 1997), and the 2002 law would confine anyone deliberately extending their stay to the lower rate indefinitely. However, the link between this status and effective access to support has provided a means of control by virtue of the incentive to remain within the legal system. This became apparent in a debate during the first half of 1998 about completely removing benefit rights from the tolerated group (see *Frankfurter Rundschau*, 20 May 1998):

> At the Bundestag Committee at the end of April [1998] it was interesting to find that all these people from city government institutions were against this law. They said we do not need it and the people in our Social Offices cannot work it. Even some of the conservative part of the CDU asked questions which showed they were very hesitant about whether it could work. Of course the welfare and church organisations would oppose it, but the others we thought would be very friendly to this law as it could save them a lot of money. It is a strange alliance but they could see the problems that might follow – without support there is no incentive to remain within the legal system, and this creates a problem of control.
>
> (Immigration lawyer 1, Bremen)

This is a further example of the intimate relationship between rights and controls, again in the form of a measure which could exacerbate the problem it seeks to contain. In the event the decision was to reduce (but not necessarily eliminate) support for those who are disguising their identity or not co-operating with their return. This means a rate of support, delivered in kind, below the already reduced rate for asylum seekers (*Migration News Sheet*, July 1998) – an attempt to drive out the relatively small number thought to be actively resisting departure.[17] This reduction of support thus becomes a formal marker of one of the distinctions already apparent within the *duldung* category, which can contain those deemed in need of protection and those required but unable to leave.

The plan to abandon the use of a tolerated status is linked to attempts to improve expulsion, as the unlawful stay of failed asylum seekers is already a problem for the system. Asylum applications which end with a *duldung* are still tied to the local area and any erosion of support inevitably increases the incentive to drop out of the legal system entirely. For those confined to remote areas with minimal support there must be a considerable temptation to abandon all claims to a legal status and move to a large city in which the possibility of 'black' work and an underground existence are stronger:

> If they are in Mecklenburg say, and have friends in Berlin and find black work, they will try to stay there. I always strongly encourage them to stay in touch with the foreigners' police in their area and I have experienced different practices. Some insist that they live in the area where they are registered and will only renew the *duldung* if they are there every night, others say they don't mind, that if they are not in the area at least they don't take the social support.
>
> (Adviser, Red Cross, Berlin)

Without recognition as a refugee under the Constitution the only possibility of upward progression from *duldung* and *gestattung* has been through humanitarian leave (*befugnis*), granted for two years at a time and renewable indefinitely. After eight years of *befugnis* the holder becomes eligible for an unlimited residence permit, after which they have rights of family unification and can later graduate to the right of abode. In principle, someone who has held a *duldung* for two years is eligible for transition to *befugnis*, but this is extremely rare:

> Actually I've never heard of anyone making this transition. The other way around is more likely now. They are beginning to see that *befugnis* was a big mistake, because from there you can get a permanent stay, and that was not the intention.
> (Social workers, refugee housing scheme, Hamburg)

> There are no clear rules for transition from *duldung* to *befugnis*. It is not like other transitions which can be made as of right because it is a humanitarian status. A lot depends on the reasons for having *duldung* and the probable length of the stay. If you have been co-operating with the authorities over trying to get back home you are more likely to have a chance. Also if you have work, it doesn't guarantee the move but it certainly helps.
> (Social Office, Hamburg)

Although there are no guaranteed conditions for transition to *befugnis*, again we see the centrality of employment and the restrictive nature of the right to work. The right is withheld from those in the weakest status, but if they can remain in the system for long enough they may have a small chance:

> If they rigorously apply a work requirement for *befugnis* it becomes almost impossible to make the transition. People with *duldung* have been barred from work, and then have only the restricted permit and it is almost impossible to get a job this way. After someone has been in the country for six years, and if at that time they have a *befugnis*, then they qualify for the full permit. Sometimes I have been able to persuade the Foreigners' Office that they have found a job and if they will agree the transition to *befugnis* they will then qualify for a work permit and will be able to move off welfare. We really have to struggle with the authorities to tell them this because the ideology in Germany is we will give foreigners no rights.
> (Social worker for asylum seekers, Oldenburg)

> It is almost impossible for an asylum seeker or someone with *duldung* to work. So the chances of getting and keeping *befugnis* are getting smaller, and that is a deliberate policy. There are people here with families, ten years or more, with children born here, but they can't get a *befugnis*. It is possible according to the law, but they don't want to give it.
> (Adviser, asylum support organisation, Hamburg)

Thus, while it is possible to see the range of immigration statuses as representing a hierarchy of rights through which an individual migrant can 'earn' progression, there remains the question of how the law is applied. For asylum seekers the *befugnis* category has been the fragile link from one side of the divide to the other, and the comments above suggest the development of a binary division between those statuses from which a migrant can progress to security, and those from which such a move is debarred. It remains to be seen how the planned use of a temporary residence status would operate in this respect, but the abolition of *duldung* certainly threatens to increase the size of the population with no lawful basis for presence and almost totally lacking in rights. This would to some extent be offset by the use instead of a *bescheinigung* (certificate), and also by the parallel decision to intensify efforts at removal. With the 2002 law it seems likely that the division between those who can progress to security and those who cannot will be more firmly drawn, which could trap not only the non-removables but also perhaps those granted subsidiary protection.

Stratified rights and citizenship theory

It has been argued here that with the growing separation of rights from 'belonging' (see Smith, 1995) the study of citizenship must broaden its focus to take in the granting and withholding of rights more generally. Indeed, the literature on citizenship has increasingly been attuned to the varying degrees of inclusion and exclusion, gain and deficit in relation to civic rights, with citizenship representing an idealised position of 'full' inclusion. In Marshall's (1950) model this full inclusion is guaranteed by social provisions, conditional for the able-bodied on being available and willing to work. In the system outlined above, however, and in contrast to Marshall's model, the right to seek and accept employment has itself been treated as a resource to which access is strictly controlled. In the German case, the close interaction between social rights, employment rights and residence permits has provided the means by which decisions have been made about who can and cannot progress through the system of statuses, and on what terms. Thus for the management of migration, while stratified rights may represent an incremental path to inclusion in Marshall's sense, the rights are granted or denied according to a broader set of concerns. Central amongst these are job protection, welfare protection, surveillance and deterrence, albeit in the context of trans-national obligations.

For the original guestworker population the route to security has rested on the ability to be self-maintaining under conditions which posed no challenge to indigenous labour. A similar set of conditions has applied to their claims to the right to family life through family unification, and even in establishing secure residence for the second generation. For those who have emerged from this process of selection, German acceptance of their full formal integration is now signalled by the 1999 Nationality Law. The subsequent intake of temporary workers has been under terms designed to prevent a repetition of this history, with strictly time-limited employment opportunities and no social supports. For asylum seekers, a more complex set of constraints has applied – to honour human rights obligations without encouraging entry or settlement, to minimise the welfare costs without facilitating employment and to withhold residence status without forcing clandestinity.

The 2002 law suggests that Germany is now set to enter a new phase of the management of migration in its search for highly skilled labour. Without future immigration Munz (2001) notes that the population is projected to fall from 82 million today to 58 million in 2050, and the proportion aged over 60 to rise from 23 per cent to 40 per cent. Germany must therefore compete for migrants on the world market, and this recognition has begun to shake the oft-cited assertion that Germany is 'not a country of immigration'. There are therefore plans to expand labour recruitment and improve access to the labour market for family members, as well as proposals to consolidate the rights that accompany subsidiary protection. At the same time, however, we find proposals to tighten restrictions on family unification for children, to emphasise the temporary nature of humanitarian protection and to intensify expulsion. While expanding possibilities in one area, the system itself seems set to become more rigid.

It is relevant here to recall Marshall's (1950) view that status differences are legitimate 'provided they do not cut too deep, but occur within a population united in a single civilisation'. The extension of citizenship rights and the struggle for a genuinely multi-cultural society is part of the process of creating that 'single civilisation'. In this context it is instructive to ask of civic stratification the questions conventionally asked of occupation-based inequality in relation to class formation and social mobility within and across generations. Insofar as foreign residents feel at least the realistic chance of betterment for themselves or their offspring then perhaps Marshall's conditions for legitimate status difference have been met. This may now apply to the descendants of the original guestworker population, but for others, as we have noted, betterment is debarred or made prohibitively difficult. It remains to be seen if imminent changes manage to tackle the problem of long-term partial membership, but they contain no promise to address the situation of those present for many years in the marginal status of *duldung* (to be replaced with *bescheinigung*) and no prospect of regularisation for those unlawfully present over a long period.

This account of the German system of foreigners' rights endorses an expanded remit for thinking on citizenship, to take in the full continuum of rights – an approach which, we will see, has growing relevance elsewhere. While qualifying conditions have always been present to some degree in the delivery of rights, most notably in relation to welfare (see Morris, 1994), the material above demonstrates their central role in the management of migration. In the German system, the fulfilment of certain conditions has been a pre-requisite for the acquisition of further rights, and has therefore served as the basis for selection in the route to long-term security and, ultimately, citizenship. So, for example, full employment rights have been granted only after a period of self-maintenance, while a claim for social support, though permissible, eliminates the claimant from achieving the next stage of security. Such a process highlights the sometimes ambivalent nature of rights and their close association with mechanisms of control. In the case of asylum seekers, the restriction placed on certain rights – whether to social welfare, housing or employment – and, crucially, their mutual interactions has so far served to hold many in a marginal position.

A strategy based on the denial of rights, however, runs the risk of driving the most marginal into an underground existence. If these latter groups remain present in the longer term – as many of them do – but with their rights severely curtailed and denied the prospects of betterment, there will be attendant problems not only of social justice, but of social cohesion and social control. This is precisely what the dual objective of the 1990 Foreigners' Law sought to avoid, by offering prospects of improvement for those legally resident, but securing the removal of those with undocumented or temporary status. The pending 2002 law promises to revise the system of statuses and reassert these two key objectives. The first aim is at least in sight for the original guestworker population and their families, and perhaps for a new generation of economic migrants. It remains to be seen if the second aim is fully achievable, or whether the presence of a group with minimal rights and poor prospects of improvement is inevitable. This possibility stands as a caution against too optimistic an assertion of the emergence of a post-national society, even at a time when the migrants of forty years ago have achieved at least the possibility of formal inclusion for their offspring.

3 The ambiguous terrain of rights
Italy's emergent immigration regime

In the previous chapter we discussed Germany's immigration and asylum regime in terms of a bureaucratised and formalised hierarchy of rights, linked to various aspects of control. Italy differs from Germany in several fundamental respects, most notable of which are that it has only relatively recently become a receiving rather than a sending country, migration has been a largely spontaneous phenomenon and the outcome is extremely varied both in terms of the circumstances and origins of the migrants. The legal regime of statuses and rights is fairly newly established, but more importantly, it operates alongside a variety of informal practices which prejudice access to formally established rights, or grant them only on the basis of discretion. Claims that we are entering an era of post-national rights have always been subject to qualification through the notion of 'implementation deficit', and this is amply illustrated by the Italian system. However, there is a further element of informality which characterises the position of migrants in Italy, and that is the role of voluntary sector organisations in offering a variety of supports outside the structure of formal provisions. There are thus two aspects of 'deficit' which are prominent in the Italian system – the difficulties of meeting requisite conditions for formally held rights, and the centrality of provisions which by their nature fall short of full entitlement.

We have already highlighted the link between rights and controls, and the driving logic of immigration policy tends to be that effective controls are a precondition of rights, while the delivery of rights can itself offer an opportunity for selection, surveillance and control,[1] underlined by the qualified nature of some ostensibly 'universal rights'.[2] The linkage between rights and obligations is a now-familiar refrain of policy makers more generally[3] but has a particular relevance with respect to immigration law and the policing of terms and conditions of presence on national territory. However, while the machinery of formal rights expands the scope for such devices of 'governmentality' (Foucault, 1991), the role of non-state organs in this exercise remains ambiguous. Offering provisions which may not be available as rights, they may also evade the practice of control. Taken together, these issues make for considerable ambiguity in the terrain of rights, in which a discourse of transparency and ethical certainty meets a practice of negotiated pragmatism. This ambiguity is made manifest in Italy through the construction and limitation of migrants' rights, their implicit linkage with the process of control and their ambivalent relationship with non-state supports.

An emergent hybrid system

Such tensions are played out in the broader context of a developing EU immigration policy described in Chapter 1 as a set of contradictory pressures with respect to the elaboration of trans-national rights and the enhancement of controls. However, while there are growing forces for convergence within the EU, the way in which the 'management' of these contradictions is achieved still shows considerable national variation. Key points of difference are the history, nature and scale of immigration; the features of the national welfare system; the functioning of the labour market; and the nature and extent of internal control – all of which make Italy an interesting case. In countries of the north, labour immigration, national protectionism and the assertion of human rights represent distinct chronological phases in the development of current immigration regimes (see Zolberg, 1989), and a new phase of labour recruitment is currently emerging. For Italy the process has been telescoped, and despite its history of emigration Italy today faces some of the same dilemmas and contradictions as the original immigration countries of Europe, albeit on a lesser scale, but compounded by a geographical vulnerability to clandestine entry.

This chapter is based on seventy interviews conducted principally in Milan and Rome in the summer of 1999 and spring of 2001. These interviews were conducted with immigration lawyers, local and state officials and a variety of voluntary and religious support organisations. The inclusion of both cities was intended to capture something of the variation in experience for migrants in the north and the south, captured by the difference between the two cities, which are the principal destination points for migrants into Italy. There are, for example, somewhat higher chances of achieving a formalised or 'regular' status in Milan, while in Rome the presence of voluntary and religious support organisations is particularly strong. The difference is one of degree rather than of kind, however, and it is still possible to identify the principal features of the Italian immigration and asylum regime overall.

Since ratification of the ILO Convention on Migrant Workers and Their Families in 1981, there have been five regularisations (*sanatoria*) for foreigners present without permission (FPWP) and three immigration laws in 1986, 1990 and 1998 (see Sciortino, 1991, 1999; Information and Studies on Multiethnicity, 1996; Calvita, 1994) with a fourth now pending. The incremental logic of these laws has meant an elaboration of immigration control, initially with a view to alignment with the Schengen accord[4] (Pastore, 1998), a gradual consolidation of migrants' rights, and attempts to establish a system of immigration quotas for migrant workers (both in 1990 and 1998). Italy's first asylum law is pending, having narrowly failed passage in the spring of 2001, and amendments to the 1998 law are now under debate (Statewatch, 2001b). Thus, in the period of less than twenty years since immigration was first recognised as a significant issue,

Italy has struggled to establish both a system for the protection of migrants' rights and a system of immigration control, while more recently emerging as a country of asylum.[5]

This rapid development of immigration law has provided the basis for a bureaucratised system of stratified statuses already familiar elsewhere. The prescribed route to secure residence is through a permit of two years, thereafter doubled to four, with the possibility of unlimited residence after five years[6] – a status only recently coming into operation – and naturalisation after ten.[7] To these statuses have been added a variety of forms of humanitarian protection and an increasingly complex classification of irregular presence, with the resultant schema grafted onto a pre-existing system of informality, irregularity and *ad hoc* supports. This chapter will consider the hybrid system which emerges, together with its associated ambiguities with respect to the framing and delivery of migrants' rights, and the stratified picture it produces.

The process of regularisation

In the unfolding and application of the laws governing residence and rights, one set of problems flows from the structure of the labour market and the position of non-EU migrants. It has been argued by several writers that labour immigration into Italy has, from the start, differed from earlier North European models. With the exception of small-scale manufacturing in the north-east, employment has been more service-oriented, with domestic and caring work particularly prominent, and street trade increasingly evident. Temporary work in construction and agriculture is also quite common. Recruitment has been organised on a small scale and even individual basis, the employment is often insecure and the boundary with informal employment practices is somewhat blurred (Pugliese, 1993; Mingione and Quassoli, 1998). In a country with minimal welfare provision for those outside secure employment this presents a problem, as does the role so far played by employment in achieving a regular status and, ultimately, secure residence.

The linkage between employment and residence is apparent in a number of aspects of immigration law and is a key element of the passage through a hierarchy of statuses to secure residence. To date, the critical transition for FPWPs has been to a regularised status, and this transition is even argued to be a necessary dimension of control:

> A *sanatoria* is necessary before you can even embark on a system of control. You cannot pretend that you can expel everybody and so first you have to make a *sanatoria* – always believing that this one is the last.
> (Immigration lawyer 1, Turin)

Italy is unusual in the scale and frequency of its *sanatoria*, which have featured in 1982, 1986, 1990, 1995 and 1998, with another now under discussion.[8] They have regularised progressively larger numbers,[9] with conditions of differing severity but a tendency towards less openness, which sits oddly with the 'clean sheet' logic underpinning the process. The 1998 *sanatoria* required official evidence of presence in Italy before 27 March 1998, proof of accommodation and a formal offer of employment, with the whole process serving as an instrument both for the regularisation of FPWP and as a means of promoting the formalisation of irregular work. But there have been inevitable problems of implementation:

> We do have some problems validating the evidence. For example, people manufacture the proof of their presence, and often the employer gives his agreement but then withdraws. He will come and sign a contract – and has probably been paid to do so, but doesn't take the second step of registering to pay the insurance contributions. In that case we give a 12-month permit to search for work.
>
> (Head of Foreigners' Office, Questura, Rome)

While one general feature of *sanatoria* is the opportunity they present for formalising irregular employment (e.g. Reyneri, 1998b,c), a major source of dissatisfaction with the recent procedure has been that, in fact, it compels and condones the practice. This is because permission to work is withheld until the end of the regularisation process:

> What employer asks for a worker at the beginning of the year and is still waiting at the end of the year when the permit is released? Of course most of the people who have made their application are already working informally, but the problem is that when the time for the permit comes the offer of formal work has been withdrawn.
>
> (Adviser, Foreigners' Office, Comune Milan)

Certainly the last *sanatoria* seems likely to have masked continuing irregular employment which leaves workers vulnerable both in terms of their livelihood and security of residence. While regularisation under the *sanatoria* may be claimed as a right by those who can meet the conditions, the logic of the process assumes a pattern of employment relations which does not always pertain. A similar picture emerges in relation to housing: while the terms of the *sanatoria* require evidence of somewhere to live, it is now officially recognised that this condition was not realistic, and the response has been a characteristic bending of the rules:

> With housing in the big cities they have made an exception – an organisation can act as a point of reference and provide you with an address which will be accepted. As long as you have a job they will be more lenient – you will eventually find housing.
>
> (Housing support worker, Milan)

> Housing is difficult – there is a major shortage in Italian cities. Sometimes we give the permit and check the housing afterwards when it comes to renewal in two years time.
> (Head of Foreigners' Office, Questura, Rome)

Inevitably, some applicants do not meet the requirements for regularisation and it is widely acknowledged that these rejected applicants will not necessarily leave the country. Hence the argument in favour of an inclusive procedure, which points to the potential problems created by an officially expelled but clandestinely present population:

> They have to be regularised, because if you don't recognise them what are you going to do with them? This is also a political decision, because to remove them is a very difficult operation.
> (Member of the Religious and Voluntary Expert Advisory Group, Rome)

> Our organisation and many others try to push for the maximum acceptance because the alternative is ethnic reservoirs of clandestines, which is much more dangerous.
> (Migrants' Support Group, Rome)

Thus there is a set of requirements which, if met, grant the individual the right to a regularised status, but which are applied with differing degrees of rigour and widespread knowledge of fraudulent practice. We should also note that the possibilities of regularisation are likely to be higher in the north, where there is a concentration of industry which sometimes offers accommodation for migrant workers. Thus similar regulations can have a different impact according to local or regional context, though the conditions imposed by the *sanatoria* often fit only poorly with the reality of either the labour market or the housing market. In many cases the procedure itself almost compels a degree of clandestine employment, while the ultimate decision of how many to accept seems to be anyway at least partially political.

Quotas, *sanatoria* and establishment

For those who succeed with their applications, the *sanatoria* functions both as a regularisation of legal status in the territory and as a regularisation of employment status, but there is room for doubt about its guaranteed long-term effects:

> These migrants don't always maintain their regular position. We have research that shows that for each of the different *sanatorias* we have had many migrants go back to informal work. It is not true that there is a steady and irreversible relation between regularisation and an official position in the labour market.
> (Spokesperson, Ministry of Social Affairs, Rome)

Thus one point of emphasis in the 1998 law is that, the current *sanatoria* aside, the management of migration can be best addressed by more rigorous controls and enhanced possibilities of regular entry and stay. The principal vehicle for this is to be the annual entry quota for employment, though there has also been an easing of entry for family unification, increased flexibility for changes of status within the territory and even the possibility of sponsored job search.

The argument supporting the quota system is fashioned in terms of precision and control:

> A percentage of the quota will be reserved for countries with whom we have bilateral agreements for re-admission, and we have also introduced the possibility of seasonal workers. The *numbers* for the quota will be calculated according to the needs of the Italian labour market. There is a monitoring exercise by Provincial and Regional Offices looking at the level of demand in the most accurate possible way.
>
> (Official, Ministry of Labour, Rome)

However, greatly to the benefit of workers and employers, as of 1998 there is no requirement to check individual requests for entry against the availability of workers already present, as in Germany,[10] though there are now proposals to re-establish such checks. Nor is there a restriction of employment options beyond the initial two years, although in practice the marked segregation of the labour market limits competition with indigenous workers (Reyneri, 1999). Thus there may be cause to question claims to precision in the calculation of the quota, not least because of the difficulty of assessing labour demand where there is strong reliance on informal work. In fact, while the quota for the year 2000 was set at 63,000[11] a UN report provocatively estimates that Italy will need at least 300,000 new workers a year to replace its ageing population (United Nations, 2000). This leaves the whole system at present poised between two approaches based on radically distinct and competing logics: continuing migration drawn by informal work with retrospective formalisation through *sanatoria*, and the aim of a planned and calculated precision through the quotas. Hence the argument that control of entry through quotas is meaningless without tighter control of the labour market:

> We don't control the economy. This is a problem and it is a magnet for clandestine migration. I would like to know how many employers have been arrested for using irregular immigrant labour. Very few.
>
> (Spokesperson, Ministry of Social Affairs, Rome)

Under the 1998 law the aims of control and integration hinge upon the third aim of regulated entry, through which it is hoped to contain continuing immigration. This strategy is to function from the clean sheet supposedly achieved by the *sanatoria*, but raises a number of questions: will access to the quota accommodate the same groups who would otherwise seek clandestine entry; will the availability of informal work continue to draw clandestine migrants; and will those who acquire, or arrive with, a regular status remain in formal employment? The 1998 law may well prove a watershed in the move away from informal labour and clandestine migration towards controlled entry for formalised work. Conversely, this formalised system for entry and rights may operate simply as one layer in a more complex structure of irregular work, clandestinity and periodic *sanatoria*. One pressing question must be the probable stability of any of these regular statuses. The ostensible shift in policy away from *sanatoria* and in favour of enhanced legal entry will not necessarily escape this issue. We must therefore consider the conditions and prospects for renewal of a residence permit after its two-year (or less commonly one-year) duration.

Most accounts suggest that while the renewal of a residence permit is not itself a major problem, this does not necessarily mean a fully 'regular' existence and, as we shall see, this is one basis for the stratified nature of the migrant experience:

> When it comes to renewal it is all the same problems [as the *sanatoria*] again. They have to find a regular job, or invent something and pay again. For the renewal after two years if you have work you get four, and maybe you can go on for four years without a regular job then find something again at the last minute.
>
> (CGIL Foreigners' Office, Milan)

So between regular and irregular existance there is evidence of an indeterminate terrain. In the past repeated renewals have been possible even without proof of employment, but the 1998 law introduces a restriction of this possibility:

> Everyone gets a renewal – even if they lose their job they can renew as unemployed at least for one year. There have been people unemployed for ten years and who have never had a regular job. . . . But we are not so sure now how the new law will work. You will still get one year but they may not get another renewal if they cannot demonstrate an income.
>
> (Head of Foreigners' Office, Questura, Rome)

The proposed amendments are much stricter on this point. However, in practice it is income rather than regular employment which has seemed to be the critical issue, with some room for discretion:

> You have to show you have a job and the minimum conditions for living – equivalent to social security – and to have a house. There are problems for people who work in the black economy and cannot show their income, and you can see that in practice a lot depends on the judgement of the Questura. They can be flexible and probably they will, but if they want to be strict they have the law on their side.
>
> (Immigration lawyer 2, Turin)

An additional flexibility introduced by the 1998 law allows for a change of status — for example from worker to family member — without leaving and re-entering the country. In fact, this could also offer a solution to cases of marital breakdown or domestic violence, by offering the vulnerable party an alternative basis for residence. Stability in family life can, however, feature in other ways, and was a recurrent theme in relation to control, as we see later in this chapter:

> Yes there is discretion. It depends on the city, the influence of certain associations, the problem of public order in the city, and above all the family conditions of the person. If there is a family there is a tendency to tolerate formal irregularities such as a missing document or a late application, or if the person cannot demonstrate completely their income — because it is known that many work in the informal economy.
> (State Police functionary, Rome)

Thus while non-renewal may be rare, the response to an application can rest on discretionary judgements whose outcome is not entirely predictable. Discretion may often favour the migrant, but will always introduce an element of uncertainty with respect to legitimate rights.

Family life

As we have seen, family life is one of the factors which can help a renewal, either as a sign of integration and stability which will have a positive influence on discretionary judgements, or by offering an alternative legal status for residence. However, there are a number of impediments for non-EU migrants wishing to establish a family. For example, foreign children will face a set of constraints similar to the process of residence renewal on reaching majority, unless they were born in Italy and opt for Italian citizenship at the age of 18. This possibility, however, is only available if the child's birth was registered, which is unlikely if the parents themselves did not have a permission to be in the country. The right to citizenship by birth is therefore a right which may not always be easy to claim.

As in Germany, Italian citizens have an automatic right to be joined by a foreign spouse, while for EU workers, as we have seen, this right is part of Community law governing free movement. For the TCN population, however, the situation is more complex. Family unification is often taken as an indicator of stability and settlement in a migrant population, frequently cited as the 'second wave' of flows which began as labour migration (Zolberg, 1989), and certainly there has been a steady growth in the proportion of permits issued for family reasons.[12] In keeping with enhanced legal entry, a feature of the 1998 law, the rules for family unification have been simplified, and the new *carta di soggiorno* is also to be extended to spouse and dependent children.

> The best part of the law is family unification under the right to family life. There is no waiting period and the right may be claimed before an ordinary

judge. It moves very quickly, and if it has not been decided within 90 days then it may be assumed granted. Also, in the previous law there was a waiting period of one year before the partner could work, but in the new [1998] law that has been eliminated. It was just another way of feeding black work.

(Immigration lawyer, Milan)

However, new amendments are likely to make family unification more restrictive. Even at present problems arise in implementing the 90-day limit, with embassies proving recalcitrant in the issuing of visas, and applicants facing difficulties in meeting the basic conditions:

> The rules are now much better defined. The income is scaled by family size and is quite easy to reach.[13] Housing is the real problem. They have to meet a required minimum which is based on some idealised notion of public housing, but in fact there is very little public housing. In the regulations [of implementation] this is weakened. They just have to produce a declaration by the municipality that the apartment meets basic health requirements.
>
> (Legal adviser, Rome, Caritas)

Of course, proof of income may be a problem for those without a stable, regular position in the labour market and it may be significant in this respect that cases of family unification are varied by region.[14] But it is housing which is most commonly cited as a problem. Tosi (1995:46) notes that while the aim of many migrants may be to settle and bring their family, the rigidity of access to social housing prevents this. In fact with owner-occupation at higher than 70 per cent and a rental sector dominated by simulated contracts and high rents (Tosi, 1996), the housing situation for immigrants is quite severe.

> Housing is very difficult in the big towns in Italy. It is usually available at only very high rents, so you get several families sharing. This makes meeting the conditions for unification very difficult so like everything else in Italy it is done by some trick.
>
> (CISL Foreigners' Office, Rome)

> It is not stated in the law that they need a formal legal contract, but they must show the apartment is available to them – the owner should declare he is hosting these people, or lending the apartment – it is vague, very Italian. They may want to check – though mostly they don't – and there are lots of tricks to avoid the checks.
>
> (Researcher, Foreigners' Office, Comune, Milan)

Under the Martelli law (1990) most regions made it officially possible for foreigners to gain access to public sector housing, and the recent (1998) law has underlined equal treatment between Italian citizens and all resident foreigners who have a permit for at least 12 months. However, nationally the public rental stock is only 5 per cent of total housing stock and 20 per cent of rental housing, and though this is higher in large cities it is unsurprising that 46.7 per cent of migrants live in shared accommodation and 12.9 per cent in a shared room (Tosi and Ranci, 1999:41). While the right to housing is recognised in legislation in a number of regions there is a gap between the principle and the reality, and considerable regional variation in access (Tosi, 1995). In Milan, for example:

> Formally there is no discrimination in the system, but immigrants have problems because they cannot prove some things so easily – to prove you have been in shared accommodation for a year for example, if you have been with clandestines who will not admit this. Or you have been moving around so much, or you have been homeless which doesn't get you any points at all. The criteria are not logical; they don't think about the reality.
>
> (Housing Expert, Milan)

> The fundamental problem is the insufficient provision. In Milan there are 1,600 or 1,800 apartments, and 35,000 people have applied. Equality under the law is very important symbolically, but the real problem is the lack of co-ordination between the law and the social policy which has to sustain the law. If a right has no meaning in material terms then this is symbolic in another way.
>
> (Housing activist, CGIL, Milan)

Nevertheless, there is concern in Milan about high concentrations of migrants in public housing. In Rome the situation is rather different:

> In Rome there has been a political decision not to use public housing for immigrants. It may be against the content of the current law but they don't care. The problem of housing in Rome has always been very delicate and national politicians wouldn't even try to interfere. The accusation would be that they were doing things for foreigners that they were not doing for Italians.
>
> (Head of Foreigners' Office, Comune, Rome)

Thus housing figures as a key criterion at different stages of a migrant career (albeit with differing degrees of rigour) – for their initial entry or regularisation, for the renewal of their permission and for family unification. Yet these rules, being applied in the context of an urban housing crisis, are met with the informal responses which so typify the Italian system – the bending of rules, the fabrication of evidence, and/or benign inefficiency. In fact, in this and many other respects the immigration regime in Italy manifests a high degree of tolerance and accommodation, though not without some associated deficit by virtue of the lack of clear entitlement and consequent insecurity.[15]

Impediments to rights

So far, at least, it has been possible to secure a legal status and to remain in that status even if living on the fringes of the formal economy. From a rights perspective the problem is that too often the future is secured by a trick of some kind, or a concession, and is not then secured as of right. The granting and renewal of permits is one example. This system functions through a hierarchy of statuses – a formalised mode of civic stratification – which offers increasing degrees of security for those able to progress through the system. The main impediment to accumulating rights has been the centrality of regular employment in achieving security of residence, such that we also find an informalised mode of civic stratification, shaped by practices of informality in the labour market:

> There is a push for labour market flexibility but the standards which govern the situation of foreigners do not take this into account. They are the first to feel the effects of flexibility but for the two-year permit, which is the minimum to live without nightmares about the police, you have to have an indeterminate contract, which is becoming difficult to find. So there is a contradiction between the flexibility of the labour market and the rules governing residence.
> (Immigration lawyer 1, Turin)

Conversely, even those workers who hold a residence permit may be limited in their employment options:

> According to quite reliable data in Italy there are 5 million irregular workers and 21 million regular. This is a characteristic of the labour market and does not just apply to foreigners. But among the foreigners you can find many with a regular permission to stay, and only irregular employment.
> (Migrants' Support Organisation, Rome)

While regularly resident foreign workers enjoy parity of treatment with Italian workers, the predominance of informal employment, enforced by a strongly segregated labour market, operates as an effective barrier to formal rights for many migrants. Without more rigorous policing of terms and conditions of employment it is unlikely that the quota system will reverse the demand for informal labour, not least because the limit has arguably been set below the level of need (see *Migration News Sheet*, August 2000). For workers in the informal sector there are inevitable repercussions, as we saw in the case of family unification, where the absence of a formal income makes the required conditions difficult to meet, turning a right into a concession.

There is also a set of more narrowly employment-related rights which a number of trade unions endeavour to secure for those employed in the informal sector:

> There are national contracts for every area of work, which cover the level of

pay, a month's holiday, the thirteenth month – which is like a bonus if you have worked for 12 months – and in the case of irregular workers the employer won't recognise these things. This is what we try to obtain for all workers.

(CGIL Foreigners' Office, Milan)

There is a particular problem for clandestine workers wishing to make a claim against an employer. Although they have recognition as a person before the law, there can be a cost attached:

If there is an accident at work, if there are wages owing, we will take up their case, but for those without a residence permit the consequence may be expulsion. For this reason 90 per cent of our cases are people who have a permit but are in irregular work. The usual pattern is they lose the job and the next day they want to sue for what is owing to them.

(CISL Foreigners' Office, Rome)

In fact it is these 'denunciations' that the Ispettorato di Lavoro relies upon in the policing of employers. This, of course, is a limited strategy, for as we have seen, a FPWP will be very unlikely to bring a case to their attention:

We work by responding to calls about particular firms, usually from a past employee. We can also work from our own initiative but generally speaking we do not have enough staff. Once we get a request to intervene then this becomes the opportunity to check all the workers in the firm and there are two issues – do they have a residence permit and are they working irregularly.

(Ispettorato di Lavoro, Milan)

For the employer, to take a worker without a residence permit is a criminal offence which carries a high fine and possible imprisonment, while simply to employ someone without a formal contract is an administrative offence, with a lower fine. In the former case the worker has very little scope for action, and even in the latter case there are many obstacles to asserting their claim:

The employer sets great store by delay; by the amount of time involved. First we call the employer and try for a conciliation, and they claim not to know the worker. Then we go to the Provincial Labour Office and they call the employer – maybe three times, and each time he doesn't come. At this point, after 3 or 4 years, everything is passed to the judge. If they are called to court then they go, but they rely on the worker giving up or going back to their own country by then. Finally they will make a settlement before the case comes to court.

(UIL Immigration Office, Rome)

The predominance of informal employment and the difficulties of policing the labour market mean that there is a population of clandestine workers with very limited rights. There is a further problem of renewal for those who do have permits and a potential impact on their ability to claim family unification. Irregular workers are also debarred from the rights which attach to formal employment, the most important of which are full health and welfare rights. So again informal labour market practices play a key role in structuring rights by making conditions of access difficult to meet and thus introducing a deficit.

The welfare system in Italy, for example, is principally geared to employment and to the related system of insurance (Tosi et al., 1998), with standard unemployment benefit requiring two years of contributions for a benefit period which is limited to six months. Joining the unemployment list secures certain health rights, and for this reason there is a high premium placed on the *libretto di lavoro* which comes with the right to work[16] and allows a worker to register as unemployed. Without a record of formal employment there is no 'as of right' protection in cases of unemployment. Such social assistance as is available varies locally:

> We do not have a provision guaranteeing a minimum income – only some funds for cases of severe need. This office has a budget for foreigners, but only for those who have some sort of a problem which means they cannot work, and we discourage people from applying just in cases of unemployment. The reason for migration was work and you cannot give such economic protection to a population of workers.
> (Head of Foreigners' Office, Comune, Milan)

> There is no monetary provision for unemployed foreigners without insurance. There are only the support systems – emergency centres where social services will give you a voucher to go and eat, and voluntary agencies which also offer something. The most fortunate may get a place in one of the reception centres [*Centri di Accoglianza*].
> (Head of Foreigners' Office, Comune, Rome)

Hence access to and forms of social support become part of the system of stratified rights.

Reception centres as social support

The original conception of reception centres in the Martelli law was to give an initial reception and orientation to people entering Italy legally for employment (Tosi, 1995):

> The Martelli law on these centres gave a very optimistic vision of immigration – that someone could arrive in Italy, be given the first reception for 60 days, and in that time could find a job and a house and become established.
> (Spokesperson, Ministry of Social Affairs, Rome)

Although the idea was further developed to include second-stage centres as a step towards fuller integration, and the provision of 'reception facilities' is confirmed in the 1998 law, the idea was never fully or effectively implemented and there is considerable variation in the provision which has been made (Tosi, 1995). In so far as they still function, it is rather to fill the gap in welfare provisions by providing shelter and respite for foreigners legally present on the territory:

> They have usually lost their job, and therefore their homes, and they come to the centres to start again.
> (Head of Foreigners' Office, Comune, Rome)

The time in the centres is for a specified period (six months in Milan and nine months in Rome), sometimes for a minimal fee (in Milan but not in Rome), and provision is not as of right but according to availability. Funding comes from the municipality, with the associated condition that the centres are not open to FPWPs, who are confined to emergency or charitable provisions. The 1998 law introduces a mechanism for the channelling of national funds to local authorities which is expected to meet about one-third of the cost. Finally, the provision is made indirectly by the use of competitive tendering between voluntary organisations who then deliver the provision subject to a detailed contract with the local authority.

In both Milan and Rome the central support office for migrants is the source of all the funding and organisational arrangements, and the office which issues the contracts with voluntary groups. It is also the office which deals with access and referrals to these centres.

> Keep in mind that the people who come here every morning have no other possibilities. We do not need to go through a long procedure of assessment. We turn many people away. They are put on a waiting list and given an appointment for the following week, and probably they go away and sleep in abandoned buildings or in the park or on the street.
> (Head of Foreigners' Office, Comune, Rome)

From what has already been said about housing difficulties, as well as from the comments above, it is clear that the provision in reception centres is very far from adequate to meet housing need, not least because it has increasingly been given over to asylum seekers (discussed below, p. 74):

> 400 places in these centres is nothing. There are about 100,000 people in Rome without a home. Half of them are Italian, and of the foreigners probably half are regular and half are irregular. Some of them for sure could have refugee status and they are living on the street.
> (Voluntary organisation A, Rome)

It is equally clear that, given the requirement to confine public spending to regular migrants, the FPWPs must pose a considerable problem:

> From the point of view of the reception centres migrants without a permission simply don't exist. The police should remove them but they don't have the organisation or the resources to do it.
> (Head of Foreigners' Office, Comune, Rome)

So provision for FPWPs is a highly contested area, cross-cut by complex classifications of both people and practices which underlie a further dimension of stratified rights in the migrant population. Most provision is made by voluntary sector groups, but often in collaboration with the municipality, and one important issue is the nature of this collaboration and its associated constraints:

> Voluntary organisations are very important, especially in Rome because of the Church. In the past they substituted for the failure of public intervention, but now they have become a part of the third sector; they deliver services and the public administration pays. There is a part of the activity, however, which is purely voluntary. In the first case the public administration sets the rules and decides who gets access, and in the second case they are autonomous.
> (Head of Foreigners' Office, Comune, Rome)

These organisations are involved in a range of activities and while much of their work is funded through the local authority, a small but significant aspect is not. In rare cases they may be involved in running reception centres funded from their own resources which can therefore bypass the conditions imposed by the municipality:

> We run four reception centres – three funded by the municipality and here we have 62 places where we need 500, but we have one experimental centre with only 8 places which is for people without documents. To be without documents is the most vulnerable situation, so we make them a document. We take a photograph, have it stamped and signed with witnesses, and then go to the municipality and ask for an identity card. It is not official – but it is almost official.
> (Voluntary organisation A, Rome)

This is just a hint at the ambiguity surrounding the classification of marginal migrants and the practices of control, accommodation and contestation which surround them. One position is to refuse to make checks:

> Giving food to the poor without checking their status is somehow accepted, but for clandestines [undocumented] a place to sleep is the hardest thing to

get. We have a completely open policy. We do not ask for documents. We have a centre with 40 places. It is not a place to stay for a very long period but we don't fix the time. It is until they solve their problem. It is completely self-organised, without supervision, they have their own keys and there is no charge.

(Voluntary organisation B, Rome)

Numerically, the provision offered is all but insignificant, but symbolically it has several functions. In the first of the two comments cited above (organisation A) there is a challenge to the designation of 'undocumented', while in the second comment (organisation B) there is a challenge to the climate of distrust surrounding such people, and a refusal to treat them in terms of administrative categories. In fact, the law imposes a legal penalty for harbouring FPWPs, but grants exemption to voluntary groups:

In theory these people [FPWPs] shouldn't be accommodated, but the volunteer organisations, since they are not public agencies, can support them. In fact, it was at the request of these organisations that the new (1998) law states this is not a crime.

(Head of Foreigners' Office, Comune, Rome)

In addition, the voluntary organisations are involved in other activities which are numerically more significant, and which do receive considerable support from the municipality. However, here there is a distinction with respect to long-term and emergency provision, the former requiring a regular status and the latter being more open:

The majority of centres in Milan require a regular status.[17] Those that do not impose this condition are mostly for emergency intervention and just receive people for a very short time, usually 15 days.

(Voluntary sector co-operative, Milan)

We distinguish between provision for those for whom integration is possible, and this could include those who are not regular – perhaps they didn't renew their permit – but could become so. This provision is not intended as an emergency service. For the others (with no permit) there are hostels and eating places funded by the municipality where help is short term and given purely on the basis of need.

(Head of Foreigners' Office, Comune, Rome)

Emergency provisions and FPWPs

The two significant forms of emergency provision are therefore in providing free meals for the destitute and running dormitories for the homeless (as distinct from reception centres), which were estimated to offer 250 places in both Rome and Milan. With each type of provision there are questions of access which are linked to funding sources, insofar as municipal support is tied to some kind of proof of identity. The responses are varied, with some organisations stressing their independence:

> The most important hostel in Milan has about 200 places a night. There is no checking of documents; access is simply on the basis of need. There are also about ten places in Milan where people can go to eat for free. The most organised is San Francesco, where you do an interview and then they give you a badge to use the facilities for a month, and you have to agree a longer-term project for renewal. They do not take money from the municipality and so are completely independent in this respect.
> (Director, voluntary support agency, Milan)

Some system of membership is common among voluntary organisations, and may extend to an even fuller system of registration, assessment and monitoring. Indeed, a membership card will sometimes serve as an informal proof of identity, accepted during the *sanatoria* as proof of presence in Italy. However, the registration process itself may be dependent on production of an identity document of some kind, underlining the distinction between documented and undocumented migrants even within the category of FPWP. Inevitably, such practices raise questions about the nature of the relationship between provision and control. In Rome, the tradition of support provided by the Church has been particularly influential and here the variety of practices form part of an implicit debate on these questions.

> Some services are delivered under contract to the Comune and have to meet their terms, others are made by certain organisations from their own funds. With the contract arrangement people should have arrived regularly in Italy, though their current status may be irregular. So we have to be organised for this – to register people and send a list of names to the Comune. If a person is clandestine with no documents and we think it necessary to feed them or give them a bed then we do so, but from our own resources. They are not registered, they do not get a membership card and they do not get longer-term support.
> (Support worker, Rome Caritas)

Other organisations take a more assertive stance against checks on status:

> When we first made the agreement with Comune they wanted only regulars to come and eat, but we refused to sign, and so did other organisations. Eventually we reached a compromise – a formula which didn't create problems for either of us. We give food to immigrants who *entered* regularly, and most of them did, even if they are no longer regular. In fact

this is almost impossible to check and we don't pretend to do it. We will not ask to see documents.

(Voluntary organisation B, Rome)

Thus we find distinctions between long-term provision (reception centres) and emergency provision (dormitories and canteens), which respectively apply to those with and without a permit. Where emergency provision receives funds by the municipality it should require the presentation of an identity document, which is closely associated with a further (uncheckable) distinction between regular and irregular entry. While some organisations accept and work within these designations, others refuse.

We should also note that the 1998 law introduces certain statutory provisions in which rights override legal status, notably the requirement of basic education for all children, and 'essential' health care for all people present on the territory, regardless of residence status.[18] There have been some problems of implementation but it is nevertheless interesting to find this active provision for FPWPs in the context of legal developments which have emphasised and elaborated various aspects of control:

> The logic behind this provision was concern about public health. The key word was not control of health but promotion of health; no screening but access.
>
> (Doctor, Rome Caritas)[19]

Indeed, there are political limits to the exercise of control. The 1998 law, for example, contains an explicit ruling against the use of emergency health care as a vehicle for immigration checks, while there is implicit agreement about the activities of the voluntary sector:

> The questura know very well what these places [voluntary organisations] are about but they don't check. There is an understanding which is absolutely clear.
>
> (Voluntary sector co-operative, Milan)

> Most of the people who come here are irregular, but they feel completely secure. The police know that if they come here aggressively and destroy the sense of security we have created then all of the people we deal with will be out on the streets and spread all over Rome.
>
> (Rome Caritas)

> It would be very difficult for questura to act in this way. It would be within the law, but the political mentality won't permit it.
>
> (Border control, Ministry of the Interior, Rome)

Thus control has different dimensions, only one of which concerns the technicality of regular presence, and in this context it may be useful to distinguish between containment – in the form of survival supports for unlawful migrants – and control in the sense of policing of legal status on the territory.

Classification and control

It is apparent from the previous section, however, that within the category of FPWP there are other distinctions which are made – a further manifestation of the developing system of civic stratification. While for some provisions a regular residence status is the ostensible requirement, those who are irregular because of a failure to renew may also be included. Others will be confined to 'emergency' provision, but even here there may be a further distinction between documented and undocumented, a distinction used more or less interchangeably with irregular and clandestine. Technically there is no difference between these two categories:

> Whether someone becomes irregular or arrives irregular makes no difference. It may affect the execution of an expulsion, but the legal status is the same.
> (Border control, Ministry of Interior, Rome)

However, in terms of the practice of control and the perception of FPWPs the distinction is quite central, and associated with a further sub-division:

> In fact there *is* a difference between irregular and clandestine. An irregular could be someone who had a permission but has lost it. The law says they should be told to leave within two weeks [i.e. given an expulsion order], but if the police find that this foreigner is someone dangerous then the expulsion would be immediate, or they would be held in a *centro di permanenza temporanea* until this was possible – up to a maximum of 30 days.
> (Head of Foreigners' Office, Questura, Milan)

In the statement above the 'irregular' would have documents and the 'clandestine' would be undocumented. The principal point at issue is whether an expulsion order should be actively executed:

> The criteria are quite clearly specified – if they already had an expulsion order and didn't leave, if they have no documents, if they are involved in criminal activity such as drug trafficking or Mafia crime, or if there is a suspicion they won't comply with the law.
> (Border control, Ministry of the Interior, Rome)

Other commentators have added that national identity is also a factor. In practice, beyond the formal classification by legal status, further distinctions are brought into play which suggest that some FPWPs can be tolerated and others not. The idea of the 'dangerous' migrant is central:

> The first criterion is the dangerousness of the person, based on police information – if they have been reported for some crime, or been found more than once with criminal individuals. The second situation is if a person is without documents and has never had a permission to stay, even if they are not dangerous. They also get an immediate expulsion.
>
> (State Police functionary, Rome)

> A person is dangerous if he has committed a crime, he has no family, no work, no house, and so on. It is really a question of signs of integration. A person has to eat and to live somehow.
>
> (Head of Foreigners' Office, Questura, Rome)

The significance of a family is not simply a matter of integration, however. In this respect the practice of the law also represents an attempt to temper control issues with a recognition of family rights. In legal terms this protection more commonly stems from national than international guarantees, with lawyers reporting difficulty in drawing on the ECHR in Italian courts, where the culture of human rights is relatively under-developed.

Public officials involved in migrants' support activities are explicitly opposed to involvement in policing issues:

> In the extensive interpretation of the law a public official has the broad responsibility to uphold the law and report those who do not comply. The Ministry of the Interior has never made pressure to apply the law in this way, and we certainly refuse to act on this extensive interpretation.
>
> (Head of Foreigners' Office, Comune, Rome)

Detection is thus most likely to emerge from direct control activities, though even here there is discretion. In the activities of the Ispettorato di Lavoro the same key distinctions operate:

> We pursue the employer's offence by collecting the documentation and handing it over to a magistrate. If our check reveals a clandestine worker then we call the police and try to prevent the worker from leaving. The situation is different for a worker with no permission but with documents, because we have an identity and can just pass the information to the police. But if they have no documents at all then we have no identity to record.
>
> (Ispettorato di Lavoro, Milan)

> The workers status is not our concern. They don't necessarily have to have a permission to stay. If they have a passport, for example, we do not need to involve the questura. If they have no documents and are clandestine, then we would report them.
>
> (Ispettorato di Lavoro, Rome)

The question remains as to what these distinctions signify, and in part they reflect the fact that an irregular immigration status is not a criminal, but an administrative, offence and requires some further infringement to warrant active police concern. The distinction between documented and undocumented is assumed to be associated in some way with criminality, for example, with the fact that undocumented migrants are likely to have travelled through traffickers:

> It is rare for people to have no papers, and if they say so they are hiding something, and this is not something we want to encourage. So we say if you won't show your passport we will not blame or punish you, but we will not be sending you to our services.
>
> (Support worker, Rome Caritas)

So there is an assumption of criminal association, but combined with practical constraints, and showing a certain slippage between categories:

> The person with documents found in a street control is expressing a readiness to be expelled, because with a document they can be. Expulsion without documents is very expensive, so we reserve the places in the *centri di permanenca temporanea* for people who are really dangerous. Those with documents can already be expelled if necessary, so we deal with them more softly. We could apply an immediate expulsion if there were any indication that they were dangerous.
>
> (State Police functionary, Rome)

The set of assumptions operating here is that people with documents though without a legal permission do not of themselves warrant expulsion; active expulsion is largely a response to criminality, and criminality is assumed to occur more commonly among undocumented people. This suggests an implicit policy towards immigration in which the irregular presence is tolerated insofar as there is otherwise a general respect for the law. Certainly it seems that there are degrees of irregularity which range from the person with a permit but in irregular work through those who fail to renew their permit, those without a permission but with documents of some kind, and those who are completely undocumented.

This implicit philosophy is strongly dependent on the development of temporary holding centres (*centri di permanenca temporanea*, CPT), which were rapidly introduced with the passage of the 1998 immigration law. These centres themselves have a somewhat ambiguous role and encompass a variety of functions: some are dedicated to expulsion, and there is at least the possibility that active expulsions are subject to resource constraints:

> These centres are always full, but the problem is that they are very expensive – not just sending people back but actually running the places. This is not

official information, but they are slowing down the expulsion programme because it is too expensive.

(Director, voluntary sector co-operative, Milan)

New amendments propose to extend the use of detention by lengthening the maximum period of stay from thirty to sixty days. Nevertheless, despite a number of re-admission agreements with countries of origin to facilitate removal, the main problem is the absence of documents, and 6,773 of the 11,269 held in 1999 were released without repatriation (Statewatch, 2000a). Increasingly, however, many without documents will have requested asylum, which introduces a further complexity to classification, provision and control:

> Undocumented asylum seekers are a big problem without a solution I think, because there is a recommendation by the UNHCR that asylum seekers must give proof of nationality but there is also an executive committee decision of the UNHCR that you cannot send them back simply because they have no documents. More than half of the applications are without documents; it could be as much as 80 per cent.
> (Member, Central Commission for the Recognition of Refugees, Rome)

Asylum and humanitarian protection

A function of some CPTs is to filter clandestine entries, identifying potential asylum and temporary protection (TP)[20] cases and holding others for removal. This holding function will be enhanced once pre-examination for manifestly unfounded and Dublin Convention cases is introduced. Indeed, the failed asylum bill incorporated these issues. The work of filtering and classification has inevitably increased as forms of protection become more varied, and while these developments are part of a trend across Europe they have a particular impact in Italy:

> The practical problem is the mass nature of the exodus. When in 1991 and in 1997 over a few days you had thousands of people arriving on the beaches then it was hardly possible to make an individual landing procedure. This is particular to the geographical situation of Italy.
> (Consiglio Italiano per i Refugiati, Rome)

> Of course they enter clandestinely, and if they are politically persecuted as individuals they can get refugee status, while if they are simply fleeing civil war they cannot. But who now can distinguish between political and economic problems of Albanians, or Kurds from Turkey?
> (Immigration lawyer 3, Milan)

Hence there is scope for ambiguity and error in the sorting of these arrivals, which are likely to include groups accorded TP, as well as clandestine migrants and asylum seekers. There are fears that the latter two groups could be confused (Trucco, 1999), denying genuine asylum seekers access to the status-determination procedures, while it is also the case that TP may include some who would qualify for asylum:

> The decisions in the Centres or at the border can be very personalised. If I like you I let you in. If you are a young man who doesn't look so nice and is a bit arrogant or aggressive, you may be an asylum seeker in every sense but you will not get in.
> (Refugee and migrant support organisation, Rome)

Those granted TP by virtue of a group identity bypass status determination and are usually admitted for a period of one year, for review thereafter, though a subsequent application for asylum would be possible. Their initial reception is an additional function of the CPTs, albeit with some awareness of the ambiguity of this practice.[21] Under the TP arrangement arrivals receive no monetary payment but have mostly been allowed to take employment,[22] and in many cases a further ruling has allowed those with work to convert their permit to residence for the purpose of employment,[23] whereby they become indistinguishable from other non-EU migrants:

> There has only rarely been an active attempt to remove these people and anyway there was the Dini decree in 1995, and now the latest *sanatoria*, which has meant anyone with work could apply to regularise. Even some people who had applied for asylum took advantage of this. Always it is the *sanatoria* which saves the world.
> (Head of Foreigners' Office, Comune, Milan)

The treatment of individual applicants for asylum – who do go through a status determination procedure – is in transition and is currently fraught with ambiguity. Their numbers have fluctuated wildly over the last decade, largely related to conditions in countries of origin. The apparent tendency towards increase,[24] however, may be explained in part by the lifting of the geographical reservation on asylum (from 1990), and by the application of the Dublin Convention (from 1997). There has in the past been a common assumption that one reason for the low number of asylum applications in Italy has been the preference of asylum seekers for some other destination, and that many who might apply were simply in transit through Italy – most notably Kurds for Germany. However, under the Dublin Convention such people can be referred back to Italy to pursue their application there, as the point of entry into the EU.

There is a formal, albeit limited, right to support for asylum seekers, who receive a monetary payment of L33,000 per day for forty-five days, on the basis of need, then for a further ninety days if they receive a positive decision. They may be accommodated in municipal reception centres, not as of right, but according to availability, and though some expansion of provision is under way capacity is far from adequate to meet demand:

> Now 90 per cent of the people in our centres are asylum seekers, which means they have superseded the other groups, though that original need is still there. Even so there is not a place for every asylum seeker who comes. The others are literally on the streets.
>
> (Foreigners' Office, Comune, Rome)

A similar shift was reported in Milan. Ironically, many of these places are filled by people who have no wish to remain in Italy, and reception workers find particular difficulty in trying to support people who have been referred back to Italy under the Dublin Convention:

> Most of the people in our centre are here because of the Dublin Convention. They wanted to go to Germany or Holland, but the police there saw they had passed through Italy and they were sent back. This creates a big psychological problem because they do not invest in being in Italy. Their aim is to get regularised and then return to the country they originally wanted.
>
> (Centre worker, Rome)

We have already noted limits on the duration of stay in reception centres (six months in Milan and nine in Rome), but asylum seekers are not, at present, allowed to work. This could be a reason for an asylum seeker who qualifies for TP to request a change of status, and may also be a disincentive to change in the reverse direction. Nevertheless, centre staff repeatedly stressed that a major part of their job was to encourage asylum seekers out to search for employment, not least because there is a long delay before their money arrives, and also because a decision may take a year or more.

> So they need to find a job – an irregular job. I don't like this situation. We should not be forcing people to live irregularly, but as it is I have to teach people not to respect the law.
>
> (Centre worker, Milan)

> We have to push them to be self-sufficient. One family was with us for nine months, then for the tenth we stopped giving them food and just allowed them to sleep here. We have to create some sort of pressure, to push them to work.
>
> (Centre worker, Rome)

The failed 2001 bill had proposed a number of changes (Trucco, 1999). Notably, it required municipalities to make provision for asylum seekers, most probably in the form of reception centres for which they would receive reimbursement from the central state.[25] A further proposal was to grant permission to work if there has been no decision after six months, though support workers in the centres note the psychological and material need for work from the point of arrival. There will be some eventual impact from the movement of immigration matters to the first pillar of the Amsterdam Treaty, and one item of the five-year action programme[26] is to establish minimum standards of maintenance for asylum seekers. However:

> This could be a problem for a country like Italy where there is not a very fully developed welfare system. Asylum seekers may see that other countries are more generous in welfare terms, but Italians can complain if they are mistreated in comparison with foreigners. It is hard to give an alien more than you grant a citizen.
> (Spokesperson, Dublin Unit, Rome)

The outcome of status determination is set to expand. In addition to full recognition, the 1998 law incorporated the practice whereby, in accordance with the European Convention on Human Rights, an applicant for refugee status might instead be accorded the lesser status of humanitarian protection (Trucco, 1999):

> This means you undergo an individual procedure which may recommend humanitarian protection . . . with permission to work and access to higher studies. This was applied to thousands of Kurds from Iraq and Turkey who were not expelled but given this alternative protection.
> (CIR, Rome)

Humanitarian protection can also extend to a halt on expulsion for a variety of reasons under the ECHR, which may include precarious health and the need for treatment. As yet, however, the law does not explicitly accommodate this situation:

> This problem arises in the centres [CPTs]. It is recognised that if someone has a serious problem of health they cannot be sent out of the country, and the Questura can say they should not be expelled, but there is no clear path in the law.
> (Doctor, Rome Caritas)

> Such a person has no legal status. They are regular irregulars.
> (Refugee support organisation, Rome)

There are, however, indications of ambivalence about its use of humanitarian protection, and there has been at least a floating of the possibility of yet another status – currently in use in Germany, but now under review:

> For the Kurds now we are stopping humanitarian protection because we

78 *The ambiguous terrain of rights – Italy*

have many foreign people here in Italy. For those from Turkey at the moment it is easier, but people from Iraq cannot be sent back. We discussed in Brussels the possibility of 'toleration'. This is not a legal permission – [it would mean that] they can stay in the country but there are no legal grounds. They should be sent back, but they [would be] tolerated.

(Member of Central Committee for the Recognition
of Refugees, Rome)

The removal of failed asylum seekers has been given high priority in the proposed amendments to the immigration law.

Conclusion

Much of the classificatory detail noted above may appear as a bureaucratic gloss on a system which has anyway been characterised by considerable informal tolerance for FPWPs. This has included opportunities for irregular work, a certain amount of non-statutory support and periodic *sanatoria* which have included in their scope asylum seekers and protected persons as well as clandestine migrants. However, the Italian system is poised in a particular moment of transition and a number of questions remain as to its future shape. A central feature of this transition is the attempt to move from past reliance on *sanatoria* to a more rigorous and systematic process of classification and control. Workers should enter through formal channels and progress to security of residence; those who become unemployed should leave if they do not find work; asylum seekers should proceed through the formal mechanism of status determination and leave if not recognised; and CPTs should filter mass arrivals to eliminate those without a reasonable case.

Against this official picture there is a strong possibility that the demand for informal work will continue, which will encourage continuing clandestine entry and/or residence renewals based on fabricated or, at best, short-term formal contracts. If so, there will be a continuing presence of people without formal rights[27] and with precarious means of livelihood for whom the voluntary organisations and the municipalities attempt to make some basic provision. The active policing of this group is likely to be confined to those designated 'dangerous', or in active conflict with the law, while the rest will experience benign neglect, in which case a further regularisation procedure seems inevitable (and indeed is now under discussion). For the present we find a hybrid system: the official presence of regular immigrants dealt with through a bureaucratised framework of rights and controls; the permeation of this formal system with informal practices; and the continuing presence of irregulars for whom reasonable chances of clandestine employment and last resort provisions are the basis of a survival existence not rooted in formal rights, but subject to minimal formal control.

The general claim that we are witnessing the emergence of a post-national membership linked to the expanding terrain of trans-national rights and organisations (Soysal, 1994) must be seen as at least partly rhetorical. In practice the distinction between rights established in law and those claimed prospectively as 'natural' entitlements (Bobbio, 1995) demonstrates the ultimately political and negotiated nature of rights, nowhere more apparent than in the field of migration across national borders. The Italian regime, as we have seen, is at a relatively early stage in establishing migrants' rights and, like Germany, illustrates the significance of differing degrees of inclusion and exclusion. However, what is both interesting and problematic about the Italian system is the intersection of formalised rules and regulations with the all-pervasive informal practices. What this signals above all is that the formal criteria of access to rights do not correspond to the lived experience of many migrants. Hence the discretion and flexibility in the administration of the rules appears as a flaw in the formal system, but is a necessary tool for bridging the glaring discrepancy between assumptions embodied by the rules and the underlying informal reality.

4 The shifting contours of rights
Britain's asylum and immigration regime

Britain differs from both Germany and Italy by virtue of a colonial history which dominated early post-war immigration. This background, together with an inclusive approach to citizenship based on territory rather than blood,[1] meant that migrants' rights were more commonly addressed through concerns about 'race relations' than as part of immigration law. Britain also differs from Germany and Italy in having no written constitution – which has been one source of expansion for migrants' rights elsewhere (Guiraudon, 1998) – and in having no land border with the rest of Europe. Indeed, Britain's island geography and mentality have been apparent in its resistance to full involvement in the emergent EU asylum and immigration regime.

There have been some fundamental shifts in these traditions, most notably changes in citizenship law, the introduction of a Human Rights Act (2000), involvement in the European single market and the opening of the Channel Tunnel. However, any reading of the HRA and Community law as indicative of an expanding regime of rights must be tempered by recent aspects of British immigration law and the well-documented withdrawal of unconditional rights of entry from Commonwealth citizens (see Layton-Henry, 1992; Bhabha and Shutter, 1994; Dummett and Nicol, 1990; Joppke, 1999). Culminating in the 1971 Immigration Act,[2] this contraction occurred alongside the extension of free movement and associated rights to nationals of EU member states, rights which, as we have seen, have so far been withheld from third country nationals (non-EEA citizens). The outcome was a new and more complex system of stratified rights: free movement for EU (and later EEA) nationals, the residual rights of Commonwealth citizens and the growing presence of non-citizen, non-EU migrants and asylum seekers.

Since the early post-war arrivals of Commonwealth citizens there has been a variety of changes in the character of the British asylum and immigration regime. The contraction of citizenship has shifted attention and concern to the rights of non-citizens, and the impact of the HRA with respect to immigration and asylum is therefore of particular significance. Incorporation of a human rights regime into domestic law represents a potential change in the character of the British system, which has rested to a considerable degree on 'concessions' or formalised discretion. This is an interesting contrast with Germany, which relies on a complex formal hierarchy of statuses, and Italy where informal processes permeate the whole system. The picture has been further complicated by a huge growth in the number of requests for asylum, which Britain has sought to limit in a variety of ways. This involved a number of changes in the nature of support provided, which in turn have raised human rights questions of their own.

Despite the changes in citizenship law and attempts to deter asylum seekers, and quite apart from the exercise of free movement within the European Economic Area (EEA),[3] inward migration continues in a number of forms (Home Office, 1999a). There were 70,000 acceptances for settlement in 1998, an increase of 11,000 on the previous year, as well as the entry of 40,000 work permit holders (plus dependants), 34,000 family members, and 46,000 asylum seekers (rising to 76,000 in the year 2000). The latter two categories are of particular interest for the purposes of this research, being based on claims to human rights enshrined in international conventions.[4] The present chapter considers each of these forms of entry and, additionally, the position of those unlawfully present, with respect to the legal statuses they engage and their associated rights and constraints. It outlines the key formal structures of inclusion and exclusion, alongside a consideration of informal processes of gain or deficit, and in doing so also provides a basis for comment on the expansion and contraction of migrants' rights in a rapidly changing regime.

The research for this chapter combines documentary sources in the form of official publications, policy documents and recent legislation with fifty semi-structured, qualitative interviews with a variety of practitioners in the field of immigration, in the winter of 1997 and the summer of 2000. All these meetings were conducted in London, which has a very high concentration of immigration expertise, and included immigration lawyers, voluntary sector advisers, local authorities, the Refugee Council, the Department of Social Security and the Home Office.[5] The objective of these interviews – as in the other two case studies – was to delineate the key statuses in terms of formal entitlement to rights, to identify the associated conditions of eligibility, to explore the implications of recent legislation and to document problems commonly encountered by migrants as they attempt to negotiate the system.

Access to employment

Access to employment readily illustrates a stratified system of inclusion and exclusion, the best-known example being the right of EEA nationals to unrestricted work and residence in any member state, which can also include a period of work seeking while supported by benefits.[6] Britain has already taken a decision to opt out of any extension of such rights to TCNs. In Britain, non-EEA migrant workers require a work permit which is issued to the employer by Work Permits (UK) – part of the Immigration and Nationality Directorate – following a two-tier system of application, with specified skill requirements for each tier:

> The two-tier system is principally about meeting the needs of international labour and capital – to allow the internal market of these companies to operate without obstacle.
>
> (Immigration lawyer 2)

Thus the first tier, with a simplified process of application, deals with intra-company transfers, board-level posts and posts related to inward investment. It also includes a growing number of shortage occupations for which the employer need not demonstrate the absence of qualified resident workers – this being the basic condition for second tier permits:

> The system is very efficient and not administered in the same way as other aspects of inward migration. However, there is a floor of skill level, which of course favours particular types of migrants and therefore particular countries very strongly.
>
> (Immigration lawyer 1)

Official figures (Home Office, 1999a: table 3.1) are not broken down into tiers, but considering all work permit holders, the USA is by far the most significant source (17,500 entries in 1998), followed by India (5,000), Japan (3,500), Australia (2,500) and South Africa (2,000). A recent Home Office report has confirmed Britain's high level of dependence on these workers (*Migration News Sheet*, February 2001:4). They are granted an initial stay of up to five years, renewable if the job continues (www.workpermits.gov.uk) and with the possibility of 'indefinite leave to remain' (ILR or 'settlement') after four years. In fact, the number who do settle in this manner is rather small, totalling only 4,010 in 1998 (Home Office, 1999a:table 6.4). Within the work permit system there is as yet no possibility of a permit for low-skilled employment, though domestic workers were allowed entry by virtue of a concession in 1979, which is now to be formalised but tightened by the imposition of skill requirements (Anderson, 2000:90; Home Office, 1998:31).

The work permit system was, however, under review at the time of writing (*Guardian*, 3 October 2001) and the Home Secretary announced the exercise as both an attempt to address skill shortages and as a means to limit clandestine employment. As in Italy, it is hoped that a quota system for economic migration will serve to re-channel illegal entrants and to formalise employment relations, and as in Germany there is a growing need for highly skilled workers. The plan involves expanding the permit system to accommodate four different types of worker: those who are highly skilled; others in areas of specialist shortages; qualified students wishing to change their status; and temporary workers in agriculture and tourism. While the latter category incorporates the possibility of unskilled migration, it is intended to be time-limited, and any chance of settlement is thus withheld.

The formal criteria of inclusion and exclusion governing the entry of workers are only part of the picture with respect to employment rights. In addition to workers entering the UK in order to take up employment, there are those present in some other capacity but who, once here, are allowed to work, notably dependent relatives[7] and some asylum seekers. They may, however, experience a deficit in claiming this right, especially since it is conferred by the absence of a prohibition rather than as an explicitly stated right:

> You don't need a permission but rather no active prohibition, and proving that to an employer has got more difficult. In the past, if you were here unlawfully or as an overstayer there was nothing to stop you working, because there was no leave to attach a condition to. As a result of that the 1996 Act made it an offence to employ such a person.
> (Law Centre adviser 1)

The employer sanctions, introduced in the 1996 Asylum and Immigration Act, make those employing someone without leave to enter or remain in the UK, or without a valid and subsisting leave, guilty of a criminal offence and liable to a fine (of up to £5,000 per charge). Scarcely applied in practice, they are an interesting example of the interface between rights and controls, and have generated concern about the impact on those with a legitimate right to take employment who are excluded by over-cautious employers (NACAB, 2000; Home Office, 1998:31). Thus a Home Office leaflet to employers states:

> If you carry out checks only on the potential employees who by their appearance or accent seem to you to be other than British this too may constitute racial discrimination. . . . Remember that the population of the United Kingdom is ethnically diverse. Most people from ethnic minorities are British citizens. Many were born here. Most non-British citizens from ethnic minorities are entitled to work here.
> (Quoted in NACAB, 2000:9)

However, there have been instances of fully entitled people, settled and in long-term employment, being required to produce documents, and in some cases dismissed (NACAB, 2000):

> Employers' sanctions set up doubts in everybody's minds, and a lot of confusion about people's status and entitlement to work. It's effects tend to be hidden – it is very difficult to prove why someone doesn't get a job.
> (Refugee Council worker).

The position of asylum seekers is particularly fragile, and for them employment is only ever the result of a concession, though the present arrangement is more generous than in either Italy or Germany:

> If an asylum request has not been resolved within six months then the applicant can request permission to work. But this is wholly discretionary. There is no law in this at all.
> (Refugee Council worker)

Even awareness of the possibility tends to be by way of informal networks rather than any clear official guidance. Furthermore, the dependants of asylum seekers are not allowed to take employment, and a couple may not even nominate which of them should be the worker – in effect discriminating against women, who are not themselves common applicants for asylum (see Crawley, 1997). Once permission to work is granted there may be problems in acquiring a National Insurance (NI) number; many prospective employers will expect to see a NI number, but acquiring one may rest upon first having a job offer. Fees required of professional workers in order to practice can be prohibitive (see *Independent on Sunday*, 12 November 2000), while recognition of non-EEA qualifications can also pose a problem. However, if the worker has valued skills a rare change of status – not normally permitted – may be negotiated, and in the future could even be facilitated:

> The Home Office require a lot of persuasion and I would say are very selective. For example, there are asylum seekers here from Sierra Leone, who certainly won't be sent back, and are qualified nurses, but the Home Office has been very awkward.
>
> (Immigration lawyer 2)

Thus on the apparently straightforward issue of access to employment and activating the right to work we find, first, a formally stratified system in terms of ease and conditions of entry and of stay, with inclusion and exclusion operating through a mix of skill and nationality. Then, for those present in some other capacity to which the right to work attaches – most commonly of third world origin – there are deficits deriving from administrative hurdles and from the indirect effect of employer sanctions. Finally, while certain skills are being actively recruited through the work permit system – and there have been recent moves to facilitate overseas recruitment of such labour (*Observer*, 3 September 2000) – some already present and in possession of such skills are inhibited in their use.

Family unification

The area of family rights is potentially much more complex, engaging as it does a set of associated human rights and often being cited as an example of transnational obligations which override domestic control (e.g. Soysal, 1994:121). The HRA incorporates the ECHR into domestic law[8] and in doing so asserts (among other things) the right to respect for private and family life (Article 8). Even before the passing of the HRA, however, Britain had an obligation to protect the rights enshrined in the Convention, though Article 8 is a qualified right, allowing interference:

> such as . . . is necessary in a democratic society in the interests of national security, public safety or the economic well-being of the country.
>
> (Steiner and Alston, 1996: 1193)

The scope of this qualification is demonstrated by a history of gender discrimination in the granting of family unification (Bhabha and Shutter, 1994:76), resolved by imposing the same conditions on wives as on husbands, and thus removing the last remaining unconditional right to family unification in domestic law. Hence:

> There isn't currently a right to family life conferred by primary legislation. It is granted under the immigration rules.
>
> (Immigration Advisory Service)

Under the 1988 Immigration Act, all spouses seeking family unification, whether to join citizens or settled persons, must show the existence of the marriage, the intention to live together and adequate maintenance and accommodation without recourse to public funds[9] (Joint Council for the Welfare of Immigrants, 1997: 11). Until its abolition in 1997 there was a further requirement to prove that marriage had not been primarily to obtain settlement in the UK, which targeted any assumed to have an economic motivation:

> The sex discrimination in the rules was all about keeping out young men from the Indian sub-continent. That's why you got the primary purpose rule in 1980. The worry was a labour market issue – that the visa was replacing the dowry.
>
> (Immigration lawyer 1)

The gender alignment of qualifying conditions for family unification in domestic law nevertheless left a formal element of stratification with respect to family rights. Residents of Britain (including citizens) are in effect disadvantaged in relation to the more extensive rights of EEA workers who enter by virtue of their right to free movement.[10] Under Community law family rights are more generous in several respects: the family is defined more widely (Plender, 1999:379), and the only requirements are proof of the legal relationship[11] and the availability of adequate housing. In fact, this aspect of Community law has become a matter of concern for the present government, as it secures a right of entry and residence for the non-European spouses of EEA citizens (Home Office, 1998:14), thus granting family rights superior to those held by British citizens.

The group most disadvantaged in claiming family rights, however, are those non-EEA citizens with 'exceptional leave to remain' (ELR), a status commonly rooted in Article 3 of the ECHR:[12]

> Refugees get family unification immediately and without conditions and that is a major difference with ELR . . . you may well be fleeing your country because of civil war but the price of that is no family unification for four years.
>
> (Advice Centre lawyer 2)

> The family situation of people with ELR is quite horrendous. Most of the Somalis I see now have got that status and they have this terrible wait before they can get their family over, and all the time they are sending large sums of money out of their benefit to their families in Ethiopia or wherever, never quite knowing it will get there.
>
> (Citizens Advice Bureau worker)

People with ELR may now be granted settlement after four years (previously seven: Home Office 1998), and entitlement to family unification follows, but under the conditions imposed by the immigration rules.[13] Thus while family unification occurs on a considerable scale and family life is recognised as a universal right, stratified access illustrates its qualified and variable nature such that alongside Community law covering EEA workers, we see a continuing role for 'national interest' in the formal implementation of family rights.

We also find that other informal factors have an influence, and again some attention should be paid to potential deficits in what is anyway only a conditional right. There is continuing concern over the application of the conditions and some express scepticism about the underlying intent. Prior entry clearance has been compulsory since 1969 (Juss, 1997) and the considerable delay often involved in this process disproportionately affects New Commonwealth countries (NACAB, 1996:20; Home Office, 1999a:52). Furthermore:

> There's great scope for judgement as to whether conditions have been met, and I would say the policy works quite actively against black people. Primary purpose used to be the tool and now it is maintenance and accommodation.
>
> (Immigration lawyer 3)[14]

Common problems stem from the disadvantaged position of minorities in the labour market, and sometimes the reliance on undeclared earnings – without the flexible approach taken by Italian authorities in such situations. A number of practitioners commented on the rising onus of proof:

> Since the abolition of the primary purpose rule, entry clearance officers are asking for environmental reports on housing to check that it is not statutorily over-crowded . . . When it is a private landlord they want copies from the land registry to prove that they really do own the property, so it is terribly onerous, especially if the tenant is not on very good terms.
>
> (Law centre adviser 1)

> In a sense this area is not really rights based. Immigration law states that the entry clearance officer must be satisfied; that is, he can use his discretion. If you meet the conditions you can probably come in, and if you are refused you could probably win on appeal, but it doesn't have the nature of a clearly stated right.
>
> (Law centre adviser 2)

The issue of acceptable proof also arises for other family members: proof of dependency in the case of settlement for elderly family members, who are treated more generously under Community Law (EEC 1612/68), or proof of intention to return for family visitors. This situation is now under review (see Home Office, 2002, CM 5387).

Interpretation of the conditions for entry clearance has also caused confusion, as for example with precisely what is meant by no recourse to public funds:

> Clearance officers can be mock naive about this and you might get them saying that this person [the settled spouse] has recourse to public funds when that is not the issue. The settled person has their entitlement, which is unchanged. The question is do they need additional recourse to support the other person. This is also a difficult concept to explain to clients and they may think they are not entitled when in fact they are.
> (Law centre adviser 2; see also NACAB, 1996:15)

Another contentious area is the question of discrimination in access to family life, which could fall under Article 14 of the ECHR, and now the HRA: for instance, the case of a woman with children living on public funds, or of a disabled settled person who is unable to work.[15] Concessions are possible in such cases but do not constitute rights as properly understood, falling instead into the area of 'decisions outside the rules'. A recent expansionary example (Home Office 1998:31) is the extension of unification rights to cohabiting and same-sex couples, where the relationship has existed for at least two years. However, until concessions are incorporated into the immigration rules, as a 'right' they remain fragile and vulnerable to a change in policy.

Social support issues after entry

For many the public funds rule operates principally as a gateway effect, very rigorously applied on entry but with little significance thereafter. However, the provisions affected have been extended in recent years to include all means-tested and disability benefits, and (as of 1999) safety net Community Care and Social Services provisions:

> So you are to a degree alienated from normal society, and there can be a certain amount of hardship – sometimes unnecessary. Maybe the settled spouse qualifies for a bit of Family Credit or Housing Benefit because of low pay and they don't think they can claim it. Or because Child Benefit is listed as a public fund they think they can't claim, which they can. So why is it listed?
> (Advice Centre Lawyer 3)

As we noted in Chapter 2, such a reluctance to make a claim can constitute a deficit with respect to legal entitlement. After twelve months (the probationary year) a spouse can request settlement, which carries full social rights, but at the point of application the maintenance and accommodation conditions again apply. This raises the question of what happens if the settled spouse loses their income through unemployment and is dependent on public funds when the probationary years ends. In fact, there seems to have been a softening of practice:

> There are Home Office instructions now saying you shouldn't refuse someone on those grounds alone. But it's just a policy instruction – it doesn't mean this won't happen. If they have just started claiming towards the end of the first year this wouldn't be sufficient for a refusal. But it could start to be so again. These policies can shift very easily.
>
> (Law centre adviser 1)

However, the rules themselves can generate further difficulties which do not directly concern family rights but which raise broader questions about an even more uncertain area of entitlement, that is, social support. There is no reference in the ECHR (or HRA) to social and economic rights (other than education), and while there is a UN convention on social, economic and cultural rights, it has little direct impact on signatory countries. The obligation is to 'progressively promote' these rights, 'to the maximum of available resources' (Steiner and Alston, 1996: 1175), so there is no immediate effect, the rights are resource-governed and it is left to the state concerned to determine the treatment of non-settled populations.

One effect of the alignment of benefit regulations with immigration rules, and an expanding definition of public funds (discussed below), has been the almost exhaustive exclusions of 'no public funds' cases from safety net provisions. A group made particularly vulnerable are elderly relatives who have settlement on entry, but subject to a sponsorship agreement by relatives which precludes the possibility of a claim on public funds for a period of five years, unless the sponsor dies:

> We find very difficult cases where the sponsor hasn't died but has become too ill to work, or the relationship has broken down leaving the elderly relative destitute.
>
> (Advice centre lawyer 3)

A similar problem concerns the situation of spouses subject to domestic violence in the course of their probationary year. The 1997 white paper has restated the significance of the probationary year as a 'safeguard against abuse' (Home Office, 1998:31) and so, according to the rules, if the marriage breaks down before the end of the year settlement should be refused. Furthermore, given the public funds rule, there is the question of maintenance and accommodation in the meantime if the joining spouse does not have employment. This problem has been addressed by means of a concession which grants settlement 'outside of the immigration rules' (Home Office, 1998:31) so that the abused spouse is not forced to remain in the marriage in order to secure ILR:

But there is a heavy onus of proof – they have to show an injunction, a caution or a conviction. The standard of evidence and burden of proof is too high for most of our clients.

(Law centre adviser 1)

This may be reviewed but at present those not able to meet the requirements of the concession may face a choice between destitution and remaining in a violent marriage. In fact the probationary period is itself being reconsidered, and may be extended to two years, but removed for unions of five years or more (Home Office, 2002:100–1).

Thus while the right to family life is clearly an established right, upheld in the ECHR and the HRA, as well as in Community law, effective access to the right is stratified and reveals a range of inequalities and uncertainties. Not least of these is the definition of the family and the recognition of family responsibilities, which vary not only between domestic and Community law but also across cultures. As a qualified right, family life is granted only subject to definitions of the national interest, and there are a number of deficits which derive from practical problems in meeting associated conditions (some of which may be discriminatory in terms of gender, race and disability). There are also limitations stemming from both the understanding and interpretation of conditions, elements of which require the exercise of discretion. While there have been significant expansions, some at present remain concessionary and thus fall short of full rights. Finally, the conditions for establishing family life may result in some casualties of the public funds condition if the family relationship breaks down, potentially leaving the subject legally present but lacking all rights to social support.

Asylum

In Britain (unlike Germany and Italy) there is no constitutional right to asylum and state obligations to refugees derive from the 1951 Geneva Convention (GC) and its 1967 protocol, which define the status and set out contracting states' obligations not to return a refugee to persecution.[16] Those not recognised under the GC may still have a claim to a lesser status of ELR under the ECHR, notably through the right to life and freedom from inhuman and degrading treatment. Thus, as in Germany and Italy, there is an element of stratification in forms of protection.[17] The rights underpinning these protections are absolute and not open to qualification as in the case of family rights, but as Jack Straw has noted:[18]

> The [Geneva] Convention gives us the obligation to consider any claims made within our territory . . . but no obligation to facilitate the arrival on our territory of those who wish to make a claim.

As we have seen in earlier chapters, this absence has been exploited to the utmost through the joint effect of visa regimes, increasingly imposed on countries likely to generate asylum seekers (Joint Council for the Welfare of Immigrants,

1987; Glidewell Panel, 1996), and sanctions which impose fines on carriers of passengers lacking adequate documentation (Cruz, 1995). In fact, this device was pioneered by Britain where carriers' liability was first introduced in 1971 and extended thereafter, most recently in the 1999 Act to include lorry drivers. A ruling under the HRA (*Guardian*, 6 December 2001) has judged a fine of £2,000 for each clandestine stowaway to be 'legislative overkill', a judgement largely upheld on appeal by the government, citing national security concerns since 11 September 2001[19] in asserting the need for effective checks on illegal entrants. The overall effect of current practice has been to introduce a deficit with regard to the right to seek asylum. While the rights guaranteed in the GC remain intact, they have been indirectly eroded by the practical difficulties which stand as barriers to their realisation. This has of course been compounded by the implementation of the Dublin Convention, as of September 1997.

The devices noted above have been part of an attempt (common across Europe) to reduce the number of asylum seekers requesting protection, numbers which have risen in Britain from 3,998 in 1988 to 76,000 in 2000.[20] A further element in this exercise has been the withdrawal and/or deterioration of provisions for asylum seekers awaiting a decision on their case. The result has been a system of stratified rights of access to support, which raises questions about what is owed to asylum seekers and other non-settled migrants in terms of social and economic rights. In Britain the first step in this process, set in motion in 1995, is now well known and based on the assumption that access to benefits was a significant factor in the rise of asylum claims:

> The trouble is that our system almost invites people to claim asylum, to gain British benefits. Most people who claim asylum don't arrive here as refugees. They come as visitors, tourists or students. And they accept that they should support themselves. The problem is that if they later claim asylum, they can automatically claim benefits. That can't be right and we're going to stop it.
> (Social Security Advisory Committee, 1996:xiii)

The means adopted by the then Conservative government was the reclassification of asylum seekers into two groups, port applicants – who claimed on entry and who were deemed deserving of support – and in-country applicants – who claimed after entry and were not.[21] However, a Judicial Review[22] and the judgement on appeal[23] both upheld the recourse of dis-benefited asylum seekers to support under the 1948 National Assistance Act (NAA), as people 'at risk' and 'in need of care and attention', with Lord Justice Simon Brown stating:

> So basic are the human rights at issue that it cannot be necessary to resort to the ECHR to take note of them.[24]

And indeed the NAA pre-dates the ECHR (1950) and its entry into force (1953).

The distinction between asylum seekers was anyway reversed by the introduction of the National Asylum Support System (NASS) in the spring of 2000, but this involved a further contraction:

> The real issue is how to run an asylum system which serves the British people's wish to support genuine refugees whilst deterring abusive claimants.
> (Home Office, 1998:35-6)

To this end, welfare benefits were replaced by a predominantly non-cash system for all asylum seekers – seemingly borrowed from the German system – based on vouchers and geographical dispersal, with maintenance at 70 per cent of standard benefit levels. Thus a system of national support is re-established, but the nature of the support has been downgraded, so as to meet the demands of the judgements noted above and yet act as a possible deterrent:

> There was a perception that numbers were growing in an unreasonable way and we had to be made less attractive to economic migrants . . . It was clear we were out on a limb in terms of support. By the time the Immigration and Asylum Act [IAA, 1999] came through it was pretty rare to be giving out benefits in the same way as you handed out cash to unemployed citizens.
> (Home Office official)

There are a number of points of interest in this brief history: the use of a reclassification of asylum seekers in the attempt to exclude one category from basic support; the fact that the challenges were largely in terms of national legislation; the only fleeting reference to international conventions; and the recognition of what might be construed as 'self-evident' human rights. However, the reach of these self-evident rights is limited as the rulings upholding the right to support linked it quite closely to the status of asylum seeker, thus reducing any potential for application to other migrant groups. As we see below, this has created another category of exclusion with respect to social rights, confirmed and consolidated by the 1999 IAA (para. 116).

The National Asylum Support System

The introduction of NASS does constitute a return to the right to support for all asylum seekers, but compared to the standard benefit rights accorded before the 1996 restrictions, it represents a clear contraction of rights. NASS began as a largely cashless system, offering no choice as to location and with implicit surveillance methods built in. While the government conceded that this form of provision was in fact more 'cumbersome' to deliver than standard benefit entitlements, it was justified with a view to deterrence (Home Office, 1998:39). There was also a moral distinction in operation:

> People who have not established their right to be in the UK should not have

access to welfare provision on the same basis as those whose citizenship or status here gives them an entitlement to benefits when in need.

(Home Office, 1998:38)

Furthermore, while the dispersal element is not of itself punitive, it has generated considerable concern about the potential for racial harassment:

> The Home Office accepts that this shouldn't be a housing-led system [see Audit Commission, 2000:12] but on the other hand you have to send people where there is available accommodation. Then you have the question of access to advisers, vulnerability to social exclusion and the worry about racism and racist attacks.
>
> (Refugee Council worker)

Moving out of London has proved very threatening to many asylum seekers. One way of evading dispersal is by finding alternative accommodation, but this too brings its problems, as there is then no provision for housing costs:

> With NASS you can just get the support, but what will happen is that after a while friends and relatives get fed up — all sorts of tensions can arise. And to make it worse they are refused other benefits because they have a lodger, even though this lodger doesn't pay. There's a lot of confusion about these cases.
>
> (Advice centre lawyer 1)

> I think the majority will try not to be dispersed — they will live with friends and sleep on a floor. And you will get a drift back; people who come back and have nothing. I think there is going to be a hidden group of people who go further and further underground and have no statutory support.
>
> (Refugee Council worker)

This is indeed what appears to have happened (*Observer*, 31 December 2000).

While overtly designed to enable people to pursue their asylum claims, the nature of provision under NASS has raised some human rights issues of its own:

> For me the vouchers are the most worrying element of this — it makes out asylum seekers as different and makes them very visible — so you find people looking at anyone shopping with vouchers and checking what's in their shopping basket.
>
> (Refugee Council worker)

> I think the system will force people into illegality to get cash. There are lots of cases where people will exchange £10 of vouchers for £7 in cash to see their lawyer, or even to pay rent. There was a case of someone hauled up by the DSS because his vouchers were used to buy baby milk and he was a

single man. This is a documented case – it is just amazing that they are doing these checks.

(Advice centre lawyer)

Ministers eventually agreed to a review of the system, partly in response to a charge that the form of provision itself constitutes 'inhuman and degrading treatment', a reference to Article 3 of the ECHR (*Guardian*, 28 September 2000). It has also been suggested that both the voucher and dispersal systems are associated with stigma and control and by their nature constitute a failure of respect for private life, interfering with the formation or maintenance of normal relationships with others (see Seddon, 1999:19). Thus we have a form of provision whose function was to give effect to the right to seek asylum, but whose very nature has raised a set of other human rights concerns, even causing some to opt out of the scheme, leaving them legitimately present but without support.

The outcome of the review of NASS was announced in October 2001 (*Guardian*, 30 October 2001) – after less than two years in operation it is to be phased out. The voucher scheme is to be replaced by a system of reception centres, dispersed across the country and making provision in kind, with a small cash allowance, while those housed outside this system will again receive support in cash (*Migration News Sheet*, December 2001). Vouchers were replaced by cash in April 2002, but a transition to reception centres will take several years to achieve, and at present leaves a number of questions unanswered. The quality and location of the centres will be important in determining the character and overall success of new provisions, and difficulties are likely to stem from under-resourcing and problems securing planning permission. Unless the centres offer acceptable standards and are located in non-threatening areas, then drop-out from the system is likely to continue. The control element of the scheme rests on the assumption that provision of board and lodging will be sufficient to hold people into the formal system. It is not yet clear from the new proposals whether the flexibility which permitted people to opt for accommodation with family or friends while retaining the maintenance allowance will continue.

Exclusions from safety net support

NASS was in part a rationalisation of the fragmented provisions which had variously been brought into play to support asylum seekers. As such, it was accompanied by a number of exclusions from provisions under the National Assistance Act:

> I think the reason behind this is to prevent recourse back to NAA provision after a final negative decision. But what is beginning to emerge as an issue is if someone is vulnerable do you, or do you not, as a local authority, have a responsibility towards them?
>
> (London Borough social services worker)

The exclusions have made the NAA consistent with other benefits and aligned eligibility with the immigration rules, but in doing so, they have raised two further questions. The first of these concerns asylum seekers without children[25] who do not leave the country on receipt of a negative decision. Enforced removals and voluntary departures by no means account for all refused asylum seekers, and on the basis of 1998 data (Home Office, 1999a:13-14) between 11,000 and 14,000 remain unaccounted for, a figure which would now be much higher with increased applications. Some simply disappear, though a small number retain legitimate status by virtue of seeking a judicial review (JR) of their case, while others may be unable to leave because of illness or lack of documentation. The refusal of countries of origin to recognise and receive back their nationals, and the related problem of rejected asylum seekers disguising their identity and/or origins, is common to most receiving countries. Thus for a variety of reasons, there will be a number of asylum seekers who remain present in the country after a negative decision, but for whom there is no obvious means of support:

> It's really a matter of us trying to ensure that people respect the court decision, rather than hang on for every possible stage. So the ministerial decision was that the logical end to support is the end of the legal process.
> (Home Office official)

To accommodate deserving victims of this decision, the government has made available a system of 'hard cases' support administered by NASS, in the form of full-board accommodation outside London, subject to monthly reviews and proof of active efforts to enable themselves to leave.[26] The scheme has a fixed budget and commentators have observed that access is extremely limited:

> One of my clients was no longer an asylum seeker, having had a final negative decision, but had been granted permission for JR, which meant his case was recognised to have some merit. So we wrote to the hard cases fund at NASS explaining this. The reply was that there was no impediment to his removal and they refused to give assistance.
> (Immigration lawyer 4)

JR cases granted a full hearing totalled only 300 in 1998 (Home Office, 1999b: 11), but cases lacking documentation would be much higher, while exclusions from NAA provision have affected an even wider range of applicants. This introduces the second issue, and takes us back to a point raised earlier with respect the public funds condition:

> [After the NAA judgement] local authorities started getting more and more requests from people who were not asylum seekers – a sponsorship that has broken down so they have a housing problem, people who have HIV, or people experiencing domestic violence who don't have a confirmed

status because they are here as a spouse. Or we have people who have been here for a number of years and we don't know how they have supported themselves, but they develop a health problem and can no longer do so.

(Law centre adviser 3)

There was initial uncertainty as to whether those unlawfully present should be included in provision, though we have noted the frailty of claims to social support under human rights law. This issue was addressed in a JR case heard in January 1998[27] in which a Brazilian overstayer requested assistance under the NAA from Brent Council, who refused because he was unlawfully present. However, since he was suffering from AIDS, was destitute and too ill to travel, it was ruled that Brent did have a duty. The judgement makes reference to the 'law of humanity', citing R v *Inhabitants of Eastbourne 1803*, but rules out a similar argument for those unlawfully present without special needs, and therefore able to leave.

The 1999 IAA, among other things, defined the basis for exclusion from NAA provisions as need arising solely from destitution, implicitly raising the question of what other additional needs might be at play in any given case. Failing health and access to essential health care has increasingly been used as the basis for a claim to remain, under Articles 2 and 3 of the ECHR (now also the HRA). However, given the exclusions from the NAA referred to above, such claims raise questions about the right to social support for those awaiting a decision. For the local authorities who fund and administer this provision, refusals can be linked to a pressing resource issue – as a number of court cases attest – and may prove a source of deficit in terms of access to rights formally held:

I had a client who was here unlawfully and HIV positive with a young child. The Home Office were considering her case but the sense was that Social Services didn't want to take on the expense if they could avoid it, though in the end they agreed. I have noticed that local authorities are increasingly reluctant to support people under these provisions because it is eating up huge amounts of their budget.

(Immigration lawyer 5)

However, Lord Justice Simon Brown has recently ruled that while awaiting decision on a request to stay, assessment for NAA provisions should be made exclusively on the basis of urgent need (though not destitution), and that: 'Not even illegality should to my mind bar an applicant who otherwise qualifies for support'.[28] As with the earlier ruling on asylum seekers, the judgement rests on an interpretation of the NAA (here in combination with the IAA) rather than any supra-national human rights instrument, with reference again made to the Eastbourne case and the basic 'law of humanity'.

So over a period of roughly five years we have seen a series of exclusions, resulting in a stratified system of support. Alongside the national welfare system we have had dispersal and vouchers under NASS (to be replaced by reception centres), a small number of instances of 'hard cases' support and provisions of last resort for the vulnerable under the NAA. Excluded from any support are rejected asylum seekers who are legitimately present but who do not meet the 'hard cases' criteria, the able-bodied whose leave is conditional on 'no recourse to public funds', and those who are unlawfully present and simply destitute – until perhaps the conditions of their existence produce the vulnerability which might qualify them for help.

Detention and removal

One other issue related to provision for asylum seekers is that of detention, with a continuum running from relatively relaxed, dormitory style facilities, to high security prison, where detainees are subject to prison rules. This of course raises additional human rights questions with respect to the right to liberty and a fair trial, a point illustrated by the new facility at Oakington, which falls mid-way between a reception centre and a detention centre. Oakington is explicitly intended for cases on which it is deemed possible to arrive at a rapid first decision, that is, within seven days. While the government has rejected and abandoned the formal 'white list' of countries deemed to be safe, the selection of cases is strongly shaped by nationality:

> They take people at the start of the process, only from certain countries, Eastern Europe mostly, also China, and Pakistan has recently been added to the list. They are cases which are not complicated by being safe third country cases, and ones for which, on the basis of the initial port interview, the claim for asylum seemed not to be very strong. They are decided within seven days, but then are either released to appeal, or alternatively held in formal detention.
>
> (Detention Advisory Service worker)

> Oakington deals only with Dover cases – the growth of clandestine entry there was getting to unsustainable levels, and its origin was the need for a middle way between detention of the small percentage who were likely to abscond, and the general system of temporary admission out into the world. . . . A number of factors are considered, of which nationality is just one. Is this, on the surface, likely to be an unfounded case which can therefore be dealt with inside a week?
>
> (Home Office official)

Observers comment that the facilities there are very good, with legal representation provided on site, and reasonable freedoms, but only within the confines of the perimeter. This has made the facility the subject of a challenge under the HRA in which Mr Justice Collins ruled that holding four Iraqi Kurds with no evidence that they were likely to abscond was in breach of Article 5 of the

ECHR – the right to liberty. However, a government appeal against the decision was upheld in a judgement which nevertheless noted that detention for a 'significant length of time' would be objectionable (*Guardian*, 20 October 2001). In fact, the practice of detention without trial and with no specified limit is a particular characteristic of the British system of immigration control:

> In this country we have detention without charge, trial or time limit. About 1,000 asylum seekers are currently detained, and there are maybe 150 other immigration detainees. It is a very arbitrary process . . . Asylum seekers are most likely to be detained on entry if there is a worry about their identity or nationality, or some suspicion they will abscond.
> (Detention Advisory Service worker)

As we have seen, the prospect of unlimited detention without trial does engage human rights questions – notably, the right to freedom and security. However, this is a right which may be limited by a variety of specified circumstances, one of which is attempting to enter a country unlawfully:

> One of the rights contained in the HRA is the right to be detained only under judicial authority, which in the past has been contravened every day by the Immigration Service. To cover this the 1999 [Immigration and Asylum] Act brought in the right to two mandatory bail hearings – at ten days then at thirty days.
> (Immigration lawyer 4)

> According to the guidelines people are only locked up as a last resort. We think that detention is used very arbitrarily; it is numbers driven. They have 1,000 places and they want to use them. Bail can be requested after seven days, but you need advice, a solicitor and sureties. You are in a strange country, you do not speak the language, you are detained. How do you get sureties? It is scandalous. What we particularly object to is that the adjudicator is not required to consider the lawfulness of the detention in the first place. It is very much at his discretion.
> (UNHCR official)

There has, however, been no decision to limit the period of detention and practitioners interpret this as a psychological strategy of control:

> If there was a time limit people would be counting down – not reveal their true situation and resist removal until the time when they had to be released . . . There is a period – it is not public – but we notice in practice it is two years . . . The reason for detention is the prospect of removal. If you cannot be removed you cannot be detained, though it may take a High Court habeas corpus action to establish that.
> (Detention Advisory Service worker)

> Some documentation cases go on for a very long time and people may be released for that reason. They would be released on temporary admission but if we effectively give up [on attempts at removal] the only real option is ELR. In some cases where the history is considered to be one which shouldn't be rewarded, we just have to keep trying.
>
> (Home Office official)

While detention has until now been used more commonly on arrival than to ensure removal, there has been a recent change in this policy. There is a noticeable gap between the numbers of refused asylum seekers and the number who either leave voluntarily or are removed, and there are plans to intensify the policing of removal (as in both Germany and Italy), which to date has been surprisingly lax:

> Most will just get a letter saying they should leave and telling them date and time, from which port, where to check in and so on. The Immigration Service say they expect about 10 per cent to turn up and are surprised if more than that do so.
>
> (Immigration lawyer 4)

> There is going to be an expansion of the detention estate and the thinking now is that detention shouldn't be used so much at the outset but rather at the end of the process to facilitate removal . . . people won't be given the opportunity to just disappear.
>
> (Home Office official)

The latest review of asylum provisions has indeed led to an announced expansion of detention places, from 1,900 to 4,000 (*Guardian*, 30 October 2001), planned both to increase the number of deportations and to end the use of prison for asylum seekers. The new plans have caused alarm by catering for the possibility of holding whole families (and therefore children): a plan thought to be in danger of contravening the UN Convention on the Rights of the Child, which Britain ratified ten years ago (*Observer*, 4 November 2001). The Convention maintains that children should not be punished for the activities of their parents, but also that they should not be separated from their parents. Much rests on the duration of the detention period, but the fact that teaching facilities are to be provided suggests that some stays could be lengthy.

Unlawful presence

The continuing presence of rejected asylum seekers is only one source of unlawful presence. Other routes include clandestine entry, entry by deceit or overstaying. The purchase of trans-national obligations is weakest in such cases, and those unlawfully present are often absent or explicitly excluded from International Conventions (see Bosniak, 1991). There have, however, been a number of recent regularisation exercises (see Home Office, 1998), including long-standing asylum cases, domestic workers who may have been fleeing abuse and the granting of ILR after fourteen years' unlawful presence. While the Home Office is overtly opposed to the notion of immigration amnesties (Home Office, 1998:41), these exercises do suggest a concern about the creeping development of a hidden population of uncertain status. Without the possibility of regularisation, those unlawfully present remain largely outside the framework of rights, though the precise boundary of exclusion is still being tested, as we saw above (p. 95) with respect to social support.

We have already noted the significance of failing health as a basis for social support. It may also constitute exceptional grounds to remain under the ECHR. The key case[29] was that of a drug courier found to be suffering from AIDS who would have neither care and support nor medical treatment in his home country. He was allowed to remain by virtue of a ruling under Article 3 of the Convention – freedom from inhuman and degrading treatment. Human rights issues may also be invoked by those unlawfully present through the right to family life as a basis to remain, though the determining question is whether there are obstacles to the pursuit of family life elsewhere.[30] We commented earlier on the qualified nature of the right to family life, but there are a number of family-related concessions, as for example cases of removal which could be disruptive for a child:

> This is a policy which came in about the beginning of 1999, which says if a child has been here for seven years or more the family won't be removed. But the Home Office has made it very clear this is not something you can apply for. It is simply one of the factors they will take into account.
> (Law Centre adviser 1)

Marriage may also be a route to regularisation, though we should note the obligation imposed on registrars by the 1999 Immigration and Asylum Act to report suspected sham marriages. However, where there is a marriage to a settled person or British citizen, which has subsisted for at least two years, there is also a concession against removal.

The role of concessions, or policy outside the rules, is a contentious area. Their ultimately discretionary nature means that they fall short of constituting rights as properly understood, though the publication of 'policies' under the present government has enhanced access. Thus:

> It can now be argued more convincingly in the High Court that the Home Secretary should be seen to be following the guidelines of his own policy. In fact now they have been disclosed there is also the intention to bring them into the immigration rules.
> (Law Centre adviser 3)

Human rights issues have always featured in the constitution and exercise of policy, although the HRA only came into effect in October 2000. In fact concessions in the past have been used as a means of addressing ECHR issues not accommodated by the Immigration Rules (NACAB, 1996:67). Thus:

> You could raise these issues before the HRA, and have been able to do so for some time. The family rights issues in Home Office policy, for example, are designed to reflect Article 8 and in a lot of cases the practice is more generous than the minimum standards imposed by the Convention.
>
> (Immigration lawyer 2)

The human rights appeal can now be the basis for an appeal against the denial of a concession or other refusal outside the rules, but its impact remains to be seen. Some commentators fear that the implementation of the HRA will not necessarily mean an expansion of possibilities (see Webber, 1999:7):

> A lot of cases currently granted on compassionate grounds could be refused because they are not sufficiently human rights based. The immigration rules and policy at present give some leeway – like ties and age at arrival and removal, immigration history and so on. But these things don't meet the high standards of human rights under the Convention.
>
> (Law Centre adviser 3)

So, on the one hand, there is the fact that the HRA establishes in domestic law rights which have in the past often been granted outside the rules by means of concessions. On the other hand, there is a fear that defining rights may mean limiting possibilities, and that the flexibility and openness of policy concessions can be a good thing. In practice we have seen that concessions operate at the uncertain limit of rights, and may feature in both their expansion and contraction, thus underlining the essentially indeterminate nature of rights and the need for close scrutiny of their mutual interactions and combined effects.

Conclusion

This book began by suggesting that the concept of civic stratification could provide a means of advancing a potentially polarised debate in which the assertion of post-national rights is weighed against an emphasis on national closure. In the British case, the contraction of British citizenship notwithstanding, an examination of migrants' rights does reveal a number of adjustments over time to accommodate the presence of non-citizen populations. To this extent, we may speak of moves towards a post-national regime of rights. This is not, however, to be interpreted simply as the incremental extension of universal rights, but rather as a more cautious system of management and regulation which can equally involve a limitation or contraction of rights.

Overall the British system is hard to characterise. Certainly once entry has been negotiated the route to settlement is relatively simple, after a standard wait of four years, and (at present) one year only for spouses, who also have an immediate right to work. There has been some streamlining for refugees, who now get immediate settlement, and for those with ELR, whose waiting time has been reduced. In this respect the regime is quite generous and the move to inclusion is often both speedy and unambiguous. Correspondingly, the exclusions are quite firm and becoming more so, as we have seen in the alignment of social supports with the immigration rules, the deterrent nature of provision for asylum seekers and the prohibitively narrow framing of the hard cases fund. The resultant pattern of stratified rights does not, for most migrants, have long-lasting consequences, unlike some other systems such as that in Germany. The main exception is the apparently increasing number of those who are unlawfully present and in a position of almost total exclusion with respect to rights.

However, entitlement and access to rights cannot be read unproblematically from broad statements of recognition, but require a closer examination of the conditions and context of practice. We have shown, for example, the way in which formal schema of inclusion and exclusion operate to stratify access to rights, even when derived from instruments for the assertion of 'universals'. Hence family rights are limited by a set of formal (and variable) qualifying conditions, while we have also seen a number of possible deficits, which informally limit access to rights that are formally held. Deficits may be the result of qualifying conditions which some groups find hard to meet, as with family unification, or the indirect effects of related aspects of policy, as with employer sanctions and the right to work. But a deficit can also be the result of an orchestrated strategy, as seems to be the case with impediments to the right to seek asylum by virtue of obstacles to arrival on the territory.

Attention to the stratified nature of entitlement to rights, the classificatory schema by which this operates and the possible deficits in implementation provides a conceptual framework for the analysis of rights in practice and for the broad characterisation of immigration regimes. This mapping exercise need not be confined to a static picture of rights, however, but may be used to document the sometimes complex patterns of expansion and contraction, of particular interest when a system is in flux – as in Britain. An obvious area of contraction in Britain in the course of the 1990s was that of social rights. One outcome is the stratified system of support described above, whose outline has, in part, been determined by complex cases testing the boundary of eligibility. This has sometimes led to the reassertion of entitlement under national law, though the right of presence in such cases has often been ultimately determined by a supranational human rights imperative. There have also been some small expansions with respect to family life, both through concessions and through the abolition of the primary purpose rule. Again changes were initiated at national level.

Perhaps the most notable expansion has been the passing of the HRA, which incorporates the ECHR into domestic law, though even here some caution is needed in interpretation and we have drawn attention to the operation of a legitimate hierarchy of absolute, limited and qualified rights. It also seems that the HRA can tolerate certain contractions, such as the erosion of social support and restrictions of liberty for asylum seekers. It has even been suggested that too rigid a definition of rights can limit a more generous though less certain practice of concession. Since few rights are absolute, most are amenable to movement in either direction and the terrain of rights is therefore a shifting terrain. This has been particularly apparent in Britain, as it negotiates the move from a colonial to a European regime, and from a system characterised by discretion to one more centrally based on rights.

5 Stratified rights and the management of migration

National distinctiveness in Europe

The expansion of trans-national instruments for the protection and assertion of rights in the latter part of the twentieth century is beyond question, but our understanding of their significance for national regimes of rights and control with respect to immigration is far from complete. As previous chapters have shown, we must, for example distinguish between international conventions, which are built upon and respect national sovereignty, and legal systems – notably the legislative framework of the EU – which override it. Both developments leave room for national distinctiveness and, indeed, many international conventions permit a degree of discrimination in favour of nationals.[1] Furthermore, we have seen that even 'universal' human rights, such as those embraced by the European Convention on Human Rights (ECHR)[2] contain a hierarchy of absolute, limited and qualified rights, with flexible interpretation of even absolute rights and with qualified rights explicitly defined with reference to national interests.

While this is less the case for rights embodied in EU legislation, the focus of which has been free movement within Europe, it is well known that the right to work and reside is reserved for EEA citizens, with only limited purchase for third country nationals (TCNs) other than as family members (for review see Staples, 1999). The Commission proposal to extend free movement to TCNs would not do so on terms comparable to those of EU citizens, and would introduce yet a further distinction. To date, the position of TCNs within the context of the receiving society has (with notable exceptions) been strongly governed by domestic law and the overall outcome has been depicted in the present work in terms of stratified rights or 'civic stratification'. This concept has been used here to explore the differential granting of rights by the state with respect to an expanding range of immigration statuses and the role of partial membership as a device in the management of migration. Such a framework, which incorporates Community and domestic law, as well as the impact of International Conventions, offers the basis for a contribution to a sociology of rights which goes beyond a traditional citizenship framework in considering degrees of partial membership, but remains sensitive to national difference.

In fact, the study of civic stratification offers a potential foundation for the comparative analysis of migrants' rights. Such analysis provides a measure of degrees of formal integration into the receiving society, whilst also drawing attention to formal and informal discretion and processes of gain or deficit in the realisation of rights. However, the study of a differentiated system of rights also highlights a dimension of control associated with the granting and delivery of rights. So, for example, rules of transition between statuses necessarily involve an element of selection with respect to long-term settlement, as for example with the requirement of self-maintenance. The associated administrative machinery can therefore operate as a system of monitoring and surveillance, and in doing so relies on linkages with other official sources (see for example Council of the European Union, 1994b), most notably those concerned with social support. Furthermore, the denial or limitation of rights has increasingly been used as an intended deterrent against future arrivals, as we have seen in the erosion of rights for asylum seekers.

The member states of Europe share considerable common ground in the problems they are addressing – the balancing of labour supply, national resources and international obligations – but they nevertheless also show considerable national distinctiveness. The detailed functioning of systems of civic stratification in three different national regimes has been explored in the preceding chapters. The purpose of the present chapter is to review these accounts in comparative perspective, drawing together and commenting on the contrasts apparent in the material presented so far. Some reflection on the nature and range of such difference is particularly timely as the member states of the European Union review the steps necessary to meet the Tampere timetable for a harmonised immigration and asylum regime (Council of the European Union, 1998). If past attempts at harmonisation are any indication the end result may still permit a degree of variation at national level (see Peers, 2000; *Migration News Sheet*, December 2000), and without such flexibility the challenge of harmonisation is truly daunting.

We have so far considered a set of three case-studies at national level focusing on the position of TCNs in Germany, Italy and Britain. These countries were chosen for their differences on a variety of criteria: historically they represent a guestworker regime, a country of past emigration and an ex-colonial regime, while geographically they represent (for the moment) the easternmost land border of the EU, the southern coastal border of the EU and an island with no neighbouring sending countries. We have also noted that each country stands in a different position with respect to a harmonised Europe. With different labour market and welfare regimes, different immigration histories and different formal and informal structures for dealing with migrant populations, these three cases serve to highlight some of the difficulties confronting any attempt at harmonisation.

More significantly, they demand attention to national variation in the delivery of rights located outside citizenship, which poses a number of questions for our evaluation of claims about an emergent post-national society. We must at the very least consider the role of the nation state in the interpretation and implementation of its international obligations, as well as the range of variation in the delivery of rights conferred both under international and domestic law. The discussion to follow briefly considers the three national regimes included in this study side by side, with respect to the rights of TCNs in relation to employment, family unification, asylum and unlawful presence – issues which are inevitably cross-cut by considerations of residence and of social assistance. The review makes no claim to be exhaustive, but the features I have chosen to discuss may safely be viewed as indicative, that is to say, they reflect the character of each of the three regimes in question, which is summarised in the form of a tentative typology towards the end of the chapter.

Employment

With respect to entry for employment the three regimes share certain features, and indeed a Council Resolution in 1994 set out the parameters for admission of TCNs for employment, though its legal status remains somewhat ambiguous (see Peers, 2000). Member states agree to have regard to the principles espoused in any review of their legislation, but the principles themselves are not legally binding (Council of the European Union, 1994a). The guiding intent was the curtailment of 'permanent, legal immigration for economic, social and thus political reasons', but without prejudice to the position of EEA citizens, TCNs who arrive as their family members and those covered by Association Agreements. To this extent, the stratification of rights is both explicit and uniform across the EU. Exceptions may be made where vacancies cannot be filled by national, community or lawfully resident non-community 'manpower', for employees of service providers, for strictly controlled seasonal workers, skill shortages and corporate transferees.

Indeed, since the Resolution was published there has been a shift in the orientation of member states as skill shortages become apparent, as the need to compete in a global economy becomes more pressing and as countries become increasingly aware of the failure to replace their ageing populations.[3] This is reflected to some extent in the Commission's proposal for a Directive on the entry and stay of TCNs for employment as part of the harmonisation process (European Commission, 2001c). The 'new' proposals have been described as an amalgam of the pre-existing Resolution and joint actions, but incorporating some new practices from member state level (*Migration News Sheet*, August 2001). The Directive would lay down general principles – such as respect for the domestic labour market – but this would still leave considerable scope for continuing difference in the management of national labour markets.

Germany

Of the three countries considered Germany operates the most complex system of stratified access to employment. National labour market regulations sanction corporate transfers at the top end of the employment hierarchy (people who are in fact allowed to progress to unlimited residence) and considerable seasonal and temporary labour at the bottom end. There are also strictly time-limited admissions for skill shortages, confining workers to the employment for which they enter and suggestive of a re-run of the guestworker history. Hence the recent 'green card' scheme for IT workers, which at present limits their stay to five years, the point at which they would start to accrue the rights of long-term residence[4] (Federal Ministry of Labour and Social Affairs, 2000). However, we have seen that there are more far-reaching proposals embodied in the pending 2002 law which would introduce a selective system of skilled immigration for settlement.

A key feature of Germany's labour market management is the distinction between the full permit, which allows full access to the labour market, and the limited permit, which asserts the priority of EU, national and already resident foreigners (Federal Employment Service, 1995). Holders of the latter will only be permitted employment subject to an active search (of up to six weeks) for alternative labour – a requirement which could be simplified if the 2002 law comes into force. This distinction reaches far beyond the conditions imposed on arriving workers; it currently affects all incoming TCNs by granting only phased access to the labour market and expanding the reach of differentiated rights with respect to employment. TCNs, however, are further differentiated, with Turkish workers protected by the EC–Turkey agreement which secures residence after four years in the labour market.[5] This agreement is of greater significance for Germany than for other member states since Turkey was the principal source of its guestworkers.

A mark of the establishment of this original population has been the arrival of spouses for family unification, though the limits of integration are also revealed by continuing family unification requests from the second and third generations. Family members of German or EU citizens have full and immediate access to the labour market, in contrast to those of resident TCNs, who do not, though we have noted the 2002 law would grant labour market access on arrival, in accordance with the status of the primary family member. Recognised refugees have full access to the labour market, but other statuses with restricted employment rights are those with limited residence, who can wait up to five years for a full permit, those with the subsidiary protection of *befugnis*,[6] who are confined to a limited work permit for six years, and those with the lesser status of 'toleration' (*duldung*) and asylum seekers, who were banned from employment completely for some years, but now have a waiting period of twelve months before possible access to a limited permit (*Migration News Sheet*, January 2001). Some adjustment might follow when the replacement of *befugnis* with temporary residence goes ahead, but under present rules employment rights would continue to be limited.

Britain

In comparison with Germany, regulation of the British labour market is much less complex. The two countries have in common ease of access for corporate transferees and needed skills, though the list of such skills is much longer in

Britain. However, there is no active search among workers already present and existing availability is checked simply by advertising and by the stated needs of the employers (www.workpermits.gov.uk). While incoming workers are confined to one area of work for a period, their permits are usually renewable and after four years they may qualify for settlement. There is otherwise no significant system of phased access to the labour market and TCN spouses of both settled residents and citizens are allowed full and immediate access to employment rights, as are recognised refugees and those granted humanitarian leave (ELR). Asylum seekers may at present request the right to take any employment after six months and there is no equivalent to 'tolerated' status.

Formal stratification of the right to take employment is thus much less extensive than in the German case. However, Chapter 4 has shown that impediments to employment in the British system often arise indirectly. For many, the right to work is not held by virtue of an active permission, or as the corollary of a residence permit, but is simply the absence of a prohibition. This has meant that the introduction of sanctions against employers of unauthorised foreign labour has interfered with the legitimate right of some to take employment (NACAB, 2000). The effect may be construed as a deficit in the realisation of a formally held right which has created particular difficulties for asylum seekers but potentially affects any 'foreign-seeming' worker. In terms of formal rights, however, access to the labour market is much more immediate and direct than in the German case.

Italy

Italy stands out in a number of respects which follow from the continuing high demand for low-skilled labour, often confined to the informal sector of the labour market (Mingione and Quassoli, 1998). The concern in national policy has been less with corporate transfers and skill shortages, than with securing the emergence of this informal sector employment (Reyneri, 1999). Two devices have been used to achieve this aim – periodic regularisations which have granted residence permits to those unlawfully present who can show a formal contract of employment[7] and, more recently, the setting of employment quotas for the regular entry of TCNs in exchange for re-admission agreements. Active checking against the availability of national or EEA workers was suspended in 1998[8] because of the essentially segregated labour market system, which confines extra-communitari to low-skilled work (see Reyneri, 1999). This segregation lessens the impact of equal treatment guarantees, as in the Maghreb Agreements of 1976, the Euro-Mediterranean Agreements of 1995 (see Plender, 1999:633–44) and the equal treatment for all workers under domestic law, as of 1986 (Calvita, 1994). Of course, such guarantees have no purchase on informal sector employment and the stratification of employment status is dominated by degrees of 'regularity', extending from formally resident employees, possibly admitted through the quota system, to those reguarly present but irregularly employed and finally to completely clandestine workers.

Like Britain, Italy imposes no employment constraints on spouses of either citizens or TCNs arriving under family unification, and an earlier waiting period of one year was abandoned once revealed as a means of feeding the informal economy. Recognised refugees and those with humanitarian leave are also granted the right to work, but asylum seekers are not, though in fact a very large proportion take employment in the informal sector, as the support available is inadequate in both amount and duration (Trucco, 1999). The failed asylum bill of 2001 would have changed this situation by granting the right to work after a period of six months, as well as extending social provisions, but legislation in this field is still pending.

Comment

The Council Resolution notwithstanding, we find three very different national systems of civic stratification in the granting and management of employment rights for TCNs. The German labour market is most tightly protected, by virtue of its rigorous prioritising system, supplemented by phased access to the labour market which at present affects all TCNs. The British system is based on simpler checks for incoming workers, full and immediate employment rights for other resident groups and a delay only in the case of asylum seekers, though we have noted the deficit experienced by some in accessing this right. In Italy a relatively simple formal system of rights and controls governing rights of access to employment is undercut by a continuing demand for informal, unregulated labour, which it is hoped a system of quota recruitment will redress.[9] Finally, we should note that the Commission's proposal on the status of long-term resident TCNs (European Commission, 2001c) would extend the right of free movement across the member states – though not with all the attendant rights conferred on EEA nationals. If accepted this would have implications for employment practice. Britain, as we have seen, has already signalled an intention to remain outside this Directive, despite a campaign demonstrating the considerable benefits it would extend to settled minority groups (Immigration Law Practitioners' Association, 2001b).

Family unification

Though family life is embraced as a universal right in the ECHR, we have seen how it may be legitimately qualified with reference to national interests, which often translate into resource constraints. There is also a potential for the layering of rights by virtue of the differing statuses of EU citizen, national citizen and TCNs. Certainly none of the three countries considered defines the family as broadly as EU legislation (Plender, 1999: 379), while the conditions of unification for EEA workers require only that adequate housing is available. Community law aside, there is again considerable scope for national difference, and this is reflected in the 1993 Resolution on family unification (Bunyan, 1997: 98), which reads more like a list of acceptable variation than a basis for harmonisation.

Germany

There are clearly stratified rights to family unification in operation, with distinctions between German citizens, EEA citizens and TCNs, the latter group being further sub-divided. Germany defines the family quite narrowly, requiring cohabitation for spouses, permitting children only under the age of 16,[10] and parents only in exceptional circumstances. However, same-sex couples have recently been recognised for purposes of unification and, indeed, can now marry (*Guardian*, 2 August 2001). Proof of a 'shared living community' is the only condition for German citizens who wish to bring a foreign spouse in contrast with TCNs who must also show adequate income and housing. There is an additional residence requirement for the second generation (Foreigners' Law, 1997, para. 18, 4(3)).[11] For recognised refugees, whose conditions of stay are largely governed by the Geneva Convention, the age limit for children is higher (at 18) and though family unification is granted in principle under conditions of self-maintenance, this can be waved at the discretion of the admitting authorities (ZDWF, 1996), and would be established as a right under the 2002 law. Those with humanitarian leave are not permitted family unification until they achieve a residence title (possible after eight years), and it is then subject to the usual conditions. Those with a toleration have no unification rights and only a slim chance of making this transition.

The EC–Turkey agreement has not been interpreted as conferring a right to family unification, and before a family member meets the conditions of the agreement for access to the labour market[12] their entry, residence and employment is subject to domestic law.[13] Here, the transitions between residence statuses are a key element of control, as we saw in Chapter 2. There is some variation between Länder but, typically, the incoming spouse of a TCN will have a limited residence permit for one year, renewed for a further two, before an unlimited permit is granted. This is a crucial transition, and one which may be denied if there is a reliance on means-tested social support (*Sozial Hilfe*). The commonest cause of problems is unemployment for the settled spouse, and we should note that unemployment stands at 22 per cent for the Turkish population in Germany (Wilpert, 1999), exacerbated to date by limitations on employment for the joining spouse, now to be ameliorated. In cases of welfare dependency, renewal of the residence permit will not necessarily be denied, but a transition to unlimited residence certainly will. The right of abode is the most secure status, requiring eight years prior residence and five years payment into a pension fund, which to a degree discriminates against women.[14] It is to be subsumed under a new 'settlement' status.

We should note that despite the emphasis on self-maintenance in qualifying for transitions, the incoming family member is not actually denied access to support, but a claim can count against the grant of more secure residence. Divorce can pose a particular problem for incoming spouses (whether of TCNs or of German nationals) as the transition to independent residence status requires four years of marriage and even cases of special hardship involve a two-year probationary period (*Migration News Sheet*, May 2000).

Britain

Family unification is more broadly defined in Britain than in Germany, with a higher maximum age for children (18) and dependent parents over 65 permitted on condition of a signed undertaking on maintenance, though this is still less generous than in EU legislation. A recent concession has extended family unification to same-sex or cohabiting couples of two years' standing (Home Office, 1998:31). In contrast to Germany (where unification rules distinguish not only between citizens and TCNs, but also between first and second generation), British citizens and TCNs are all subject to the same conditions for family unification: adequate accommodation and maintenance. This policy was adopted as the only means of limiting family rights for second-generation immigrants, many of whom have British citizenship by birth. However, the primary purpose condition (that the marriage should not have been primarily to obtain settlement) was abolished in 1997, since it discriminated against UK citizens as compared with other EU citizens resident in Britain (Home Office, 1998:18). Practitioners now remark that attention has turned instead to a more rigorous interpretation of the accommodation and maintenance requirements. Recognised refugees are granted family unification without conditions, but those with humanitarian leave must wait until settlement (after four years, which is much faster than in Germany) and fulfil the normal conditions.

The requirement to be self-maintaining means that spouses are admitted on condition of having no recourse to public funds, although settlement (and therefore full social rights) is granted after only one year (likely to be extended to two, and again subject to a maintenance and accommodation test). Unlike Germany, however, persons from abroad (who include non-settled TCN spouses) have actually been written out of entitlement in the benefit regulations, in a drive to achieve alignment with immigration rules. An early break-up of marriage for reasons of domestic violence means that (as of July 1998) settlement can be granted immediately – a more generous solution than in Germany. The residual problem here is for those spouses who separate within the first year but cannot meet the very high burden of proof, and may be trapped in a vulnerable position with no entitlement to support.[15]

Italy

Italy has the broadest definition of the family of all three countries, allowing unification for spouses who have not been legally separated, children up to the age of 18 and dependent parents, though with no recognition of same-sex partnerships. As in Germany, family unification is unconditional for national citizens and the incoming spouse can be granted an unlimited stay. TCNs seeking family unity must meet maintenance and accommodation conditions, and here the difficulty is often one of proof, insofar as even those regularly present can be dependent on informal employment for their income, a problem which is likely to recur at renewal of the permit. The spouse of a non-citizen will be granted an initial permit for two years, with the possibility of renewal for four. Although there was no formal waiting period, delay in the processing of applications has, in the past, had the same effect, and hence the 1998 law confers automatic permission if there has been no decision after ninety days, though some problems of implementation remain. Five years' residence (likely to be raised to six) will qualify TCNs for the new unlimited residence card, which anyway incorporates the whole family. On divorce a spouse may remain, but must convert to an independent permit for which there will eventually be an income test. Refugees have family unification rights without the accommodation and maintenance conditions, but the family rights of those with humanitarian status – as yet little used – remain unclear (Trucco, 1999).

In contrast to Germany and Britain, reliance on social support is scarcely an issue in Italy, since the system of means-tested provision is very limited and TCNs are anyway unlikely to qualify, unless in some sense vulnerable. Control therefore depends on the income and housing test, and the second layer of control available in Germany and Britain through the exchange of data between benefit officials and immigration officials is of little effect. There is provision of last resort made by charitable organisations, sometimes supported with municipal funds, for which immigration checks have not been politically acceptable.

Comment

As with access to employment, the issue of family rights shows Germany applying a more elaborate system of control, with phased steps to security which interact with employment and welfare constraints to pose something of a challenge to families of TCNs in the early years. While the controls in Britain are similar to those in Germany, British citizens are disadvantaged in relation to their German counterparts, but security for family members nevertheless comes much more quickly and unambiguously. In this respect the Italian system is closer to the British than the German, but as with employment both rights and controls are undercut by the role of the informal sector as well as the absence of a fully fledged system of social support.

The Commission Draft Directive on family unification (European Commission, 1999; amended by document 500PC0624), like the 1993 Resolution, contains sufficient leeway to permit some continuing variation between member states. However, in its present form, as yet to be agreed, the draft would have a particular impact on Germany, and challenges a number of its more restrictive practices. Changes embodied in the 2002 German law would bring only minimal conformity[16] and have been seen as rather provocative (Statewatch, 2001). Furthermore, the draft Directive retains the housing and maintenance conditions for the unification of TCN families, but would eliminate the distinction between national and EU citizens apparent in Britain, though the British government has already expressed its intention to opt out.[17] An earlier version included family rights for those with subsidiary protection, which at present in Germany could include some granted only a toleration,[18] but

112 *National distinctiveness in Europe*

this clause has now been dropped.[19] Nevertheless, it is thought that the draft is unlikely to pass without further amendment (see Immigration Law Practitioners' Association, 2001a).

Asylum

Sharp national contrasts are to be found in the case of asylum and humanitarian protection, and though all three countries show degrees of civic stratification in statuses of protection, they manifest significant differences in their definitions of a refugee, the types of protection available and the provisions for support during status determination.

Germany

One distinctive feature of the German asylum system has been the restriction of recognition to cases involving state agents of persecution (European Council on Refugees and Exiles, 2000), which significantly reduces the potential sources of refugee populations. Germany also operates two levels of recognition – protection under Article 16a of the Constitution, which grants unlimited residence, and protection under the Geneva Convention for those who pass through a safe third country, to which they cannot be returned. As we saw in Chapter 2, this group receives a *befugnis* or humanitarian leave, which has often also been granted (on a time-limited basis) to those seeking temporary protection from civil war situations. Asylum seekers who are denied recognition may still qualify under Article 3 of the ECHR,[20] but again only in cases of state agents of persecution. The resultant gap is filled by protection against danger to life, limb or freedom (Heinhold, 2000:82), which has been judged adequate by the European Court of Human Rights (ECtHR).[21] Those qualifying for these subsidiary protections may spend years in the temporary status of toleration; while long-term need should qualify them for *befugnis* (Heinhold, 2000:84), this transition has been notoriously difficult to achieve. Improvement of their position would, among other things, require self-maintenance but their employment options (as we saw above) are extremely limited. Likewise those granted *befugnis* as a subsidiary protection are tied to the restricted work permit for six years, and vulnerable to loss of this status if they do not progress to unlimited residence (possible only after eight years' presence). The 2002 law could significantly change the situation by consolidating the rights accompanying subsidiary protection – though asserting its temporary nature – and extending GC recognition to victims of non-state agents and of gender persecution. It remains to be seen if this law will be implemented.

Britain

Again the British system is less complex, transitions more immediate and direct. There are two statuses of protection – full recognition under the Geneva

Convention and exceptional leave to remain (ELR), which encompasses ECHR protection. Most importantly, Britain does (at the time of writing) recognise non-state agents of persecution[22] and for this reason – the ECtHR judgement notwithstanding – British courts have ruled Germany an unsafe country for the return of some asylum seekers (*Migration News Sheet*, June 1999; UNHCR, 2000). As we have noted, there is no equivalent to toleration, and those granted ELR can progress to settlement and therefore the full array of rights after four years, though this was recently made conditional on a test of self-maintenance. Civil war victims have been admitted under the status of temporary refuge for an initial period of six months, though this is often extended by the grant of a time-limited ELR.

Italy

Italy falls mid-way between Germany and Britain in terms of recognition, in that protection against non-state agents of persecution is not routine but is possible (European Parliament, 2000). Italy has only recently emerged as a country of asylum and application figures have shifted erratically in the past decade. Arrivals seeking some form of temporary protection have dominated the picture here, largely because of geographical proximity to Albania and ex-Yugoslavia. They have been dealt with by country-specific decrees, which have usually permitted employment and often the eventual possibility of conversion to a standard form of residence on proof of a formal contract of work.[23] There has, however been a rise in individual asylum applications, in part with the operation of the Dublin Convention and the return of asylum seekers who have passed through Italy. The use of a lesser humanitarian status is relatively recent, but is on the basis of renewable residence permits with the possibility of employment. As in Germany, the Italian Constitution also offers protection against persecution, but has not been used until the very recent case of Ocalan, who was offered constitutional asylum in 2001.

Comment

While all three countries have developed differing statuses of protection such as to constitute a sub-system of civic stratification, again we find that Germany operates a more complex and elaborate regime, especially with respect to the use of the very limited status of toleration, now to be replaced. Furthermore, there are important differences in the criteria of recognition, which have affected the feasibility of the Dublin Convention (for establishing a single EU asylum regime) both in principle and in practice. Clearly the major challenge for a truly harmonised regime is uniform definition of refugee status, and though this is included in the Tampere Action Plan (Council of the European Union, 1998) under measures to be undertaken within two years, the issue has yet to be resolved. It is simply noted as a 'longer-term' objective in the proposal on minimum standards of reception (European Commission, 2001a), but a change in the German system will remove one of the barriers to agreement in this area, though other aspects of the new legislation in Germany are inconsistent with the draft directives on asylum (Statewatch, 2001a).

Additional difficulties for establishing a common system derive from the nature and conditions of the social support available to asylum seekers. The aim to date is simply to agree minimum standards. The attempt to build deterrence into systems of provision is now quite common, one result of which, in separating provision from the national welfare system, has been to introduce yet another example of stratified rights. There are further distinctions between groups according to the outcome of their application, with rejected but non-removable asylum seekers posing a particular problem.

Social support for asylum seekers

Germany

Of the three countries under consideration Germany provides the most organised and controlled system of provision, although there is some variation between Länder. The key to the system is the compulsory dispersal of asylum seekers between local districts according to a strict quota. The asylum seekers do not have freedom of movement beyond the confines of the district, and accommodation and maintenance in the first three months is by means of reception centres which provide support in kind, with a small payment for pocket money. After these first months housing is usually in some form of communal unit or in shared apartments, with provision either by vouchers (the tendency in the north) or food packs (more common in the south) and very rarely monetary payments (for example in Hamburg). All make an allowance for pocket money. The level of provision is at about 70–80 per cent of standard social assistance rates.

The same system of support applies to rejected asylum seekers who cannot be returned – including some who are protected under the ECHR – who remain at this level of support for three years (indefinitely under the 2002 legislation). There is a further reduction of support to vouchers or food packages only for those rejected asylum seekers who are felt not to be co-operating in their own removal (*Migration News Sheet*, August 1998). A proposal to withdraw support entirely from this group was considered and rejected in 1998, though there has been some variation in practice between Länder.

Britain

Britain's recently revised system borrowed substantially from the German model, as do other proposed changes, but there are nevertheless significant differences. There is no initial reception period (except for those taken into a secure unit – a practice which has been challenged, though tentatively upheld, under the Human Rights Act), but asylum seekers are immediately dispersed on the basis of a 'cluster' system, which it is hoped will guard against isolation and racial victimisation (Audit Commission, 2000). As we saw in Chapter 4, accommodation was provided with maintenance in the form of vouchers and pocket money at 70 per cent of the standard level of means-tested benefit. While vouchers could only be collected from a specified local issuing point, the asylum seekers were not denied free movement, and one problem the system seems to have generated is a drift back to London by people who are then cut off from their means of support. (*Observer*, 31 December 2000). There was, however, a degree of flexibility in that people who could make their own accommodation arrangements – with family or friends, for example – could claim the maintenance only and live wherever they have support available, which would in turn generate its own problems. Though the system is less than two years old vouchers have been abandoned and there are now plans for reception centres making provision in kind.

The denial of support on refusal seems harsher than in Germany. The 'hard cases' fund, intended to support those for whom removal is not practicable, is run on a cash-limited budget and has so far proved extremely difficult to access.[24] We have seen, for example, that some people granted permission to proceed to judicial review – with a legitimate reason therefore to remain, have been denied support. The general philosophy underlying the use of this fund is that the end of the asylum procedure should mark the end of all support. For this reason the last resort support previously possible under the National Assistance Act has, since 1999, excluded recourse purely on the grounds of destitution (1999 Asylum and Immigration Act)

Italy

The system of support in Italy is less fully developed, being faced with much smaller numbers. All asylum applicants receive one monetary payment (L35,000 per day for forty-five days), but, as we noted, are forbidden to work. Municipalities run a system of reception centres, originally intended for incoming workers but now largely dedicated to asylum seekers. In some cases there is a small charge but in others this provision is free. There is insufficient accommodation, however, and many asylum seekers are left to fend for themselves in the informal economy. As well as permitting employment after the first six months, the recent bill had proposed to extend the monetary payment for the whole status-determination period, and require municipalities to provide accommodation, for which they would be reimbursed by central government (Trucco, 1999). Though the bill did not pass, some action in this area will eventually be required by the harmonisation process.

Comment

Again we find a picture of bureaucratised control and graduated provisions in Germany, to some extent mirrored in Britain but with both more flexibility and firmer exclusion on termination of the procedure. Much of this flexibility could be lost, however, with the move to provision in reception centres, depending on whether an opt-out is permitted. One factor behind the shift of policy in Britain has been the charge that support in the form of vouchers constitutes 'inhuman and degrading treatment', thus contravening the ECHR/HRA. The Commission's proposed Directive on minimum standards of reception embraces as an objective a dignified standard of living for asylum applicants, though it in fact endorses the use of vouchers as an acceptable mode of provision. Other objectives are to limit the secondary movement of asylum seekers within Europe, assumed to be influenced by differential conditions of reception and inconsistent with the Dublin Convention. Concern with deterrence has clearly been uppermost in both Germany and Britain, while the Italian system of support is still evolving and is at present much more limited and *ad hoc* than in the other two countries. One likely constraint on what is politically feasible here is the very limited nature of non-contributory social assistance in the Italian welfare system. The Tampere timetable for achievement within five years simply specifies minimum standards of reception, which again leaves room for national variation but nevertheless poses a significant challenge for Italy. However, the Commission's proposal leaves open the possibility of access to the labour market as a substitute for social provisions and in fact requires some degree of access to the labour market after six months, which neither Germany nor Italy at present permit.

Unlawful presence

The weakest position in any hierarchy of statuses must, of course, be that of unlawful presence, which provides an interesting test both of the reach of human rights and of the steps countries are independently prepared to take to secure regularisation or expulsion. The continuing presence of rejected asylum seekers is one obvious source of migrants lacking a formal status, particularly in Britain where there is no 'tolerated' designation to hold them into the legal framework (as in Germany) and no broadly defined regularisation (as featured in Italy). It is no doubt a general concern about this possibility which has led all three countries to develop short-term holding centres for newly arrived asylum seekers, particularly geared to cases thought to be manifestly unfounded. Detention on arrival is otherwise much more characteristic of the British system, which is also unusual in having no official time limit on administrative detention for immigration offences. Unlawful presence is by no means restricted to asylum seekers in any of the three countries, with clandestine entry and overstaying offering other significant sources of people whose presence falls outside the legal framework. Information on this issue is inevitably incomplete but, detention aside, there are some interesting points to be made about each of the countries under consideration in terms of minimum rights and the scope for regularisation.

Germany

In Germany regularisation *per se* scarcely exists, except in the form of old cases rulings, as for example the ruling in March 1996 (www.proasyl.de/haertef.htm)

in granting limited permits to asylum seekers present since before January 1987 (or in the case of families with children, since before July 1990). A more recent ruling in November 2000 offered residence permits to a variety of vulnerable groups, including traumatised Bosnians. While it is also within the scope of the law to grant regular status on an individual basis for humanitarian reasons, this is said to be rare. In addition to provision for asylum seekers, Germany does offer certain human rights protections by virtue of its Constitution, which includes strong support for family life, and also through incorporation of the ECHR into domestic law.

Though respect for private and family life is a commonly cited human right, we should note that its application is rather narrowly drawn, and will only have real purchase on legal presence where family life cannot be pursued elsewhere.[25] The protections against expulsion are strongest where there is a German child involved and the expellee can demonstrate a continuing and significant role in the child's care. Protection may also be offered in cases of ill health[26] or mental breakdown, but is likely to be limited to tolerated presence. The social rights of those unlawfully present are similarly limited. While anyone present on German territory and in need is eligible for the minimal form of support granted asylum seekers, without a case for toleration any attempt to claim would be likely to result in expulsion. However, despite the German reputation for strong control there are opportunities in the informal sector of the economy (Wilpert, 1999). In addition to asylum seekers without the right to work, one source of this labour has been the system of time-limited employment through which workers establish the know-how and connections to return or to remain, surviving through unofficial employment and clandestine presence.

Britain

In Britain as in Germany, regularisation of unlawful status is not extensive and has been offered only to address particular problems, such as the unlawful status of domestic workers fleeing abuse by their employers (Home Office, 1998:31), or very long-term unlawful presence.[27] Old cases regularisations have also been used as a means of reducing the asylum backlog for those applying before July 1993, who were granted settlement (in contrast to Germany's granting of limited residence), and those applying between July 1993 and December 1995, invited to make a case for limited leave (Home Office, 1998:41).

Until the entry into operation of the Human Rights Act in October 2000 (see Blake, 1999) there was no human rights guarantee in domestic law, except in the form of the 1993 Asylum Law. Britain had, of course, assumed other obligations as a signatory of the ECHR, which now also provides the substance for the HRA. In the past, issues such as requests to stay on the grounds of family ties and for other compassionate reasons have been dealt with through concessions granted outside the law, a key and continuing feature of the British system. We have, for example, noted the recent concession which protects parents from deportation where a child present for seven years or more is involved. Many such concessions are now backed up by the right of redress through domestic courts by virtue of the HRA, though practitioners fear that the overall result could be a scaling down of concessions to meet the human rights minimum required by the law, rather than more broadly defined compassionate grounds.

Any possible source of social support for those unlawfully present has been eliminated in recent years by the alignment of benefit rules with the immigration rules, in particular the denial of last resort provision for reasons of destitution alone. Exceptions to these exclusions are families with dependent children, who can claim support under the 1989 Children Act, and those with some additional vulnerability, who might also qualify for protection from expulsion under the ECHR.[28]

Italy

Italy, like Germany, has constitutional guarantees which protect family life, and the law includes protection from deportation for the custodial parent of an Italian minor. However, lawyers comment that there is as yet no fully developed culture or practice of human rights and the major opportunity offered to those unlawfully present has been via the recurrent regularisation exercises (five since 1986). The difficulty of establishing a secure formal contract of employment inevitably means a degree of insecurity and produces some movement in and out of regular status (Reyneri, 1999). In addition to possibilities of regularisation, at least to date, the system of policing immigration status is in effect selective, i.e. attention is focused on those unlawfully present who are deemed in some sense 'dangerous'. Something of a parallel to this in Germany and Britain is the selective enforced removal of rejected asylum seekers who are deemed likely to abscond.

There is no formal source of social support for those unlawfully present, and indeed little for those with a regular status outside contributory schemes. However, there is survival level provision available in the form of free canteens, and sometimes hostel accommodation, which is secure from police scrutiny and virtually free of any qualifying criteria in terms of immigration status. There is a tacit recognition here of the role of supports of this kind in the social containment of a population whose presence cannot anyway be fully policed. One can detect a similar logic at work in the provisions made for the 'tolerated' category in Germany, but there is no obvious parallel in Britain.

A typology

Overall, we find some marked differences between the three countries reviewed in terms of both the structure and underlying logic of their respective systems of stratified rights. This is by no means surprising given their immigration histories, and rights are in this sense contextual, negotiating both the past and the political present. What follows is a tentative categorisation of the three countries in 'ideal type' terms.

Germany: graduated selection

The German system is based on bureaucratised management through a graduated system of statuses for dealing with both regular migrants and those seeking humanitarian protection. It stands out from the other two countries both in the number and the complexity of statuses, compounded by a related system of phased access to the labour market – both of which should be simplified if the 2002 law is implemented. The graduated transition to secure residence has grown, in part, out of a guestworker history and the eventual need for incorporation of both the workers and their families outside what was a very restrictive system of blood-based citizenship. Although this system has been liberalised to some degree (*Migration News Sheet*, February 1999), the main impact of the changes will not be felt until a new generation reaches adulthood. One notable effect is the differential rules for family unification which disadvantage long-term residents in relation to German and EU citizens, illustrating the qualified nature of the right to family life, and also long-term presence which falls short of full membership.

In addition to its guestworker history, Germany has historically had very high numbers of asylum seekers and the right to seek asylum has now been limited as a result of changes to the Constitutional guarantee. A further aspect of management is the variety of statuses of protection with differing degrees of security, the weakest of which offers no firm basis for a long-term stay. These distinctions are mirrored by a differential system of social supports which grants the tolerated group minimal provision and only poor prospects of employment. The most negative effect of this system is the long-term lawful presence of a group with very limited rights, and more generally the proliferation of statuses of partial membership which are not necessarily either temporary or transitional. The 2002 law should somewhat simplify the system of statuses, could improve access to protection under the GC and also improve the rights of subsidiary protection. The temporary nature of all protection will be reasserted, however, reproducing long-term, partial membership, but on somewhat improved terms. The overall effect could be to move Germany somewhat closer towards the distinctive features of the British system.

Britain: inclusion and exclusion

Britain is much less a system of graduated control. Historically the challenge was not the incorporation of non-citizen guestworkers, but the stemming of the arrival of Commonwealth immigrants who held full citizenship. The history has thus been partly one of the removal, rather than the expansion, of rights (see Layton-Henry, 1992), extending even to the family unification rights of British citizens. Like the family rights of long-term residents, these are conditional – in contrast to the privilege that both Italy and Germany grant their own citizens. Family members do, however, have full and immediate access to the labour market and can achieve independent security of stay after only one year (under review). The path to settlement for economic migrants and those granted humanitarian protection is also relatively quick and simple, with secure settlement possible for some who in Germany could at present be trapped with a toleration – a situation the 2002 law could ameliorate. The British system in general seems designed to avoid the very outcome which the German system has produced, that is, the long-term lawful presence of people with only partial membership. The resultant system of stratification is thus less extensive and allows for more rapid transitions between statuses.

Britain has principally relied on external controls, being aided in this by its island geography – now somewhat undermined by the Channel Tunnel (see *Independent on Sunday*, 25 Feburary 2001). There has, however, been a creeping expansion of internal controls (Morris, 1998), which function in tandem with exclusions from social support. These are now quite fierce and arguably increasing, as we have seen in the case of last resort social support and the very restrictive functioning of the hard cases fund. The decisions on inclusion and exclusion from rights are more severe and conclusive in the British case, and the negative result of this could be the growth of an underground population with very few rights whatsoever, fuelled by overstayers, clandestine presence and, in particular, the non-removal of rejected asylum seekers.

Italy: informal toleration

As a relatively recent country of immigration, Italy is still developing its legal framework and is unusual in operating a quota system for the entry of migrant workers outside the designation of specialist skills. The system has only recently included a formal status of long-term residence, through the introduction in the 1998 law of a *carta di soggiorno*. Like Britain, Italy offers open access to the labour market for family members, but has so far denied formal employment for asylum seekers. This has been one aspect of contradiction in the system, which to date has not provided adequate social support for asylum seekers and has therefore all but enforced a practice of irregular employment. Indeed, the whole immigration and asylum regime seems to incorporate two parallel systems.

The formal system of rights and controls operates alongside informal systems of employment, social support and, to some extent, toleration. The major difficulty for migrants is the fact that their claim to formal rights often rests upon secure establishment through formal employment, but this is undercut by the continuing tradition of informality in the Italian economy. Italy is currently poised at a critical moment and the future pattern of immigration and migrants' rights will depend on whether there is continuing informal acceptance and periodic regularisation, or the enforcement of more rigorous policing and formalised entry, or indeed whether these two possibilities will continue to run in parallel, with the key transition being that from irregular to regular status.

In all three countries citizenship by birth on the territory to settled parents should ensure security and a degree of integration for the next generations, though in both Germany and Italy the child must chose its sole citizenship at majority. Both these regimes also set more demanding conditions for naturalisation than Britain (another area of proposed change), though all three systems privilege the spouse of a national. Citizenship aside, the issues of rights and controls which have been raised here will continue as long as there is an inflow of migrants, whether as workers, as family members or as asylum seekers. In many areas – citizenship, asylum and work permits, for example – there have been some signs of convergence, but there are also strong indications of continuing differences likely to persist for quite some time to come.

Conclusion

This chapter opened with a comment on the scope for national distinctivenss with respect to migrants' rights, within the context of a single European market. This distinctiveness is manifest even in the implementation of international conventions which the national regimes in question hold in common, and is often shaped by domestic constraints. A potentially polarised debate which weighs national closure against post-national rights, is not, therefore, the most helpful way to address the issues at stake. I have rather suggested an approach that examines the management of contradictory forces shaping migration by means of a system of stratified rights whose details differ according to national context. With respect to employment, we have found contrasting approaches to the management of national labour markets, ranging from Germany's protective system of phased access, through Britain's simpler system of inclusion and exclusion, to Italy's informal demand, periodic regularisation and immigration quotas. We have also noted the privileged position of corporate transferees and a revival of the active recruitment of skilled labour.

The functioning of trans-national rights requires further comment in two respects. Despite the fact that all three countries considered are signatories of the ECHR and the GC, there are significant differences in their delivery of the rights that these Conventions endorse. Family rights, for example, are differently defined in each system, differently again in Community law, and only fully understood in interaction with employment and residence rights and restrictions. More notable are the national approaches to asylum and the contrasting provisions for subsidiary protection, which show very marked differences despite their derivation from the same trans-national guarantees, though there are now some signs of convergence.

While Community law – unlike international conventions – overrides domestic law, the projected harmonisation of immigration and asylum regimes in the EU requires the reconciling of some quite sharp distinctions. We have noted that attempts so far have tended to establish an acceptable range of difference, rather than seek to impose uniformity, and it seems likely that on some significant matters this will continue to be the case. Commissioner Vitorino, for example, has admitted to considerable difficulties in the harmonisation process, noting that the Council had reached agreement on only two out of eleven proposals (*Migration News Sheet*, August 2001). Thus while impact of trans-national forces on nationally governed societies is undeniable they must pass through the prism of national interests and national distinctiveness. The means by which this mediation is achieved is argued here to be the national regimes of civic stratification.

6 Gender, race and the embodiment of rights

The argument of this book has been organised around the concept of civic stratification, that is, the system of inequality generated through the differential granting of rights by the state. For migrants this system finds formal expression in the range of immigration statuses and the associated rules of transition which govern duration and security of stay. I have so far explored three different national systems of civic stratification or stratified rights with respect to migration. As we have seen, the questions posed in the course of such work and the material they have generated connect very closely with the related literature on citizenship, thus providing a starting point for discussion of the gendered and racialised dimensions of migrants' rights.

The citizenship literature has traditionally explored the nature of membership of a national community, be it in terms of participation (Marshall, 1950) or closure (Brubaker, 1992), but Turner (1988) notes a further significant aspect of citizenship, namely the introduction of the principle of social equality to the terrain of rights. The result has been an expansion of what he terms 'status politics', with particular groups increasingly seeking state compensation for what are perceived as *de facto* disadvantages and perhaps mobilising around claims to particular needs. This argument is indirectly supported by the view that even the construction and practice of rights which profess universality are in fact particularist in content. That is to say, they have been constructed around a set of assumptions about the content of social life, the model for which is – at least implicitly – the white heterosexual male (Phillips, 1992).

As a result, a further important development within the literature on citizenship has been a focus on the embodiment of rights, the way in which rights translate into lived experience with respect to diversity. Notable examples are the way in which differences of gender and sexuality (see Bhabha, 1996; Richardson, 1998) shape access to rights, though such analysis may be readily extended to race (Anthias and Yuval-Davis, 1992). An exploration of this issue invites attention to the way in which formal status equality and its associated rights are shaped by normative prescriptions and expectations which implicitly deny particularist needs. Examples are the failure to accommodate women's reproductive role, or the absence of recognition for the cultural expression of minority citizens. The process of access to rights, or the machinery for their delivery, may furthermore incorporate informal systems of social esteem related to such particularisms, as with judgements which seek to identify the deserving and undeserving.

In shaping or constraining access to rights, processes of stereotyping, prescription and devaluation are argued to function in close interaction with class-based disadvantage, and this position is captured by Fraser (1995) in her analysis of redistribution and recognition. The former concept relates principally to material distinctions of class and/or welfare divisions, and the latter to cultural or normative distinctions which generate differing degrees of social esteem. A similar configuration of influences may be found in Turner's (1988) model of three dimensions of stratification – class, entitlement and culture. These insights apply not simply in relation to the rights of citizenship *per se*, but to the analysis of the terrain of rights more generally, and are deployed below in an account of access to migrants' rights from the perspective of gender and race, with particular attention to formal status difference.

Gender and rights

Literature on gender and citizenship has challenged the construction of rights by virtue of their confinement to the public sphere (e.g. Lister, 1997). Since this issue largely cuts across national difference in immigration regimes the account below is organised by reference to different types and aspects of migration, rather than country by country, though national differences are noted where relevant. The broad argument is that both formal entitlement and the active realisation of public rights may be shaped by constraints which derive from the private sphere (Pateman, 1989). In this respect, gender functions as a status in two ways: in the ascription of features which dictate the distribution of private obligations of caring, and by the associated allocation of esteem, which devalues the private sphere (Fraser, 1995). Both these aspects of a gendered status regime limit access to the public sphere and therefore to certain rights.

There has been some reaction against such arguments, one view being that generalised structures of disadvantage (as in the case of gender difference) cannot be addressed by a focus on individual rights (see Cook, 1993: 233), while other criticisms go further, and wish to challenge any unitary category of 'woman' (e.g. Brah, 1993). This complicates, rather than invalidates, a gender focus, however, and certainly cannot undermine the claim that some such generalised view of 'woman' has to date structured access to a variety of rights. Certainly a historical account of gender and citizenship (Lister, 1997) reveals that perceptions of women held by legislators and interpreters have been impediments to equal treatment. We also find that where formal equality has been established, informal assumptions and expectations can produce a deficit in its active attainment. Yet a gender-blind approach can also produce discrimination through a failure to take account of the circumstances most common to women's lives. These arguments can be illustrated by an examination of the experience of women migrants, in which the patterns of civic stratification already described are further differentiated with respect to gender.

Literature on gender and migration (e.g. Kofman *et al.*, 2000) has convincingly challenged a gendered analysis of migration which attributes to women the passive role of 'follower' as against the active male role of initiator. Although we will see that there is some continuing basis for this assertion, insofar as women are disproportionately represented in cases of migration for the purpose of family unification, the distinction disguises a more complex and changing reality. While there are indeed gendered patterns of migration, their detail varies over time and between countries, and their reading requires a more subtle understanding of agency than is permitted by the active/passive distinction. Here I will briefly consider three principal modes of migration from a gendered perspective: employment, family unification and asylum. Although the absence of official statistics which consistently offer a gendered analysis is something of an impediment to this task, and I by no means claim to achieve an exhaustive account, it is possible to highlight some of the principal features of a gendered immigration regime, drawing on material from the three countries in this study (and occasionally from elsewhere).

Gender and employment

Certainly post-war labour migration included women among its recruits, and they featured as guestworkers for a variety of industries in Germany, particularly in the later years (Castles and Miller, 1998:71), with family members initially migrating as workers in the absence of other means of family unification. Women also featured prominently among the migrant workers to Britain from a variety of Commonwealth countries, but in particular from the West Indies, for a mixture of service and manufacturing jobs (see Bhabha and Shutter, 1994). Italy at this stage was a sending rather than receiving country, but the pattern in the north of Europe was anyway soon to change, with severe restrictions on recruitment from 1973 limiting migration opportunities from outside Europe to those with needed skills. Given common patterns of male privilege both in terms of the definition of, and access to, occupational skills, this inevitably militated against women's opportunities as migrant workers.

There has been recent talk of the 'feminisation of professional migration' (Kofman *et al.*, 2000:64), and in Britain this refers to a rise from 16 per cent of work permits issued in the mid-1980's to only 20 per cent a decade later. To date, men retain the advantage, and much of women's 'professional' recruitment continues to be in nursing, though domestic work remains a possibility for those without formal skills. This pattern can be read in two ways. While it provides a clear example of women's association with the private domain, and a concentration of employment in those areas traditionally constructed as 'female', one outcome has been a protected employment niche for women. Certainly private domestic work is one of the few areas of low-skilled employment which has been a continuing means of migration since labour recruitment ceased in the mid-1970s. The opportunity has considerable costs attached, however, though the detail varies between the three countries considered.

In Britain, as of 1972, work permits for unskilled workers from outside the EU were ended, and with them most migration opportunities for unskilled male workers (Bhabha and Shutter, 1994: 174–5). Exceptions were made for the hotel and catering industry and for resident domestic workers, thus favouring women, but recruitment was restricted to a small quota which was progressively reduced and phased out completely by the end of 1979. The effect was a marked fall in the proportion of women entering Britain to work, reflecting a shift at the time 'towards professional and highly skilled occupations in which female workers form a comparatively small proportion' (Department of Employment, 1982). This left nursing within the National Health Service as the only significant route of entry, and Kofman *et al.* (2000:109) note the clustering of overseas workers in the 'less desirable' areas of such work.[1]

However, there was a now notorious concession made in 1979, which allowed employers entering the country to bring domestic workers as members of their household (Anderson, 2000:89). This concession perfectly illustrates the vulnerabilities which can be associated with domestic work, and one of its principal effects was unlawful status for women who left their employer, in some cases fleeing abuse. The plight of these women captures the ambiguity of live-in domestic work, whereby the distinction between worker and household member becomes blurred, with a consequent loss of both rights and privacy. The problem in Britain was finally addressed in July 1998 by a change in the rules (imposing a skill requirement and formalising entry) and an exercise to regularise workers who had fled from abusive employers (Anderson, 2000:90; CM 4018:31). Though domestic work remains a possible route to settlement, it has been considerably restricted as a basis for formal entry.

Germany echoes some of these tendencies, with a shift from manufacturing to service work for women migrants, recruitment from overseas into nursing and the growing significance of domestic work as an option for female migrants (Kofman *et al.*, 2000:131). Anderson (2000:82) comments on illegal placement agencies bringing women from Latin America but notes that Poland has emerged as the principle source country and that live-in work is not the norm in Germany. This is related to the possibility of visa-free travel as tourists for a three-month period, during which Polish women find work informally, sometimes in systems of co-operative rotation with other workers (Morokvasic, 1991). Perhaps the most striking aspect of the domestic market in Germany is its still increasing significance for women from Eastern Europe and the Ukraine. Friese (1995) has documented the pattern whereby professional women are finding that their most marketable skills are domestic, and that their best hope of maintaining their own family is by working in child or elder care in Germany. Recent proposals have recognised this situation by arguing for a three-year residence permit to accommodate the pattern (*Migration News Sheet*, December 2001).

The situation in Italy is distinctive because of the prospect of legal entry through the quota system, but more significant to date has been the recurrent possibility of regularisation. The opportunities are also more extensive, given the relative underdevelopment of the welfare system and consequent demand for child care and elder care in the home. Such work usually requires some basic qualifications, and Chell (1997) reports a pattern of upward mobility from domestic to care work. There is also a common wish to progress from live-in to live-out, and from irregular to regular status. In this respect women have a rare advantage over men, insofar as domestic work offers the cheapest form of regularisation in terms of insurance payments, and is an area of work in which men have yet to win full acceptance. The opportunities for low-skilled men tend to be in insecure and temporary work such as agriculture, construction and restaurant work in which employers are less ready to offer a formalised contract.

Thus with respect to migration opportunities we find that while women have generally been disadvantaged in terms of the acquisition of skill, their association with the private sphere and with the work of caring has secured for them a disadvantaged but protected area of employment. However, given that domestic work is still often irregular, women's association with the private sphere can take on a particular meaning, leaving them in extreme cases trapped in the home of their employer in conditions under which they have no legally enforceable rights. Furthermore, the boundaries between the formal and the informal are constantly shifting, so that the end of quotas for domestic workers in the UK shifted many domestic workers underground, while an end to regularisation in Italy would have the same effect. At present, however, the scope for variation is quite wide, ranging from the completely undocumented, to those legally present but working without permission, to those who can progress to regularised status (a narrow possibility in Britain and to date much stronger in Italy) and finally to those recruited through formal channels. There are racialised overtones to this hierarchy, not least by virtue of the professional classes of the (white) developed world harnessing the domestic labour of the second and third worlds, as well as patterns of advantage and disadvantage between different national groups. At the bottom of this hierarchy, however, the situation of clandestine domestic workers overlaps to some extent with that of clandestine sex worker.

Sex work

Sex work, even more than domestic work, is a case of the embodiment of a status. However, it is an area of activity which echoes the vulnerabilities of domestic work insofar as the fringes of both domestic and sex work can involve trafficking, debt and captivity, while each area of work carries gendered and racialised overtones. The potential for overlap is illustrated by the fact that domestic work can itself become 'sexualised', as Anderson notes with respect to the domestic workers in Berlin who specify 'no sex' when advertising their services. The flight from abuse of some workers admitted to Britain under the concession arrangement almost certainly included some cases of sexual abuse (Healy, quoted in Anderson, 2000:92). This, however, is something apart from the large-scale, highly organised, international underground sex industry:

According to international estimates, traffickers in human beings abduct up to 700,000 women and children every year; approximately 9 million human beings worldwide are living in conditions akin to slavery. The Commission estimates that 120,000 women and children a year are lured from the countries of Central and Eastern Europe alone to the European Union.

(European Parliament, 2001)

The accounts of this trade are more familiar from the frequent press reports (e.g. *Observer*, 1999, 2000, 2001; *Guardian*, 30 May 2000; *Independent on Sunday*, 11 March 2001) than from fully researched academic literature, but the same picture emerges with a repetitive clarity. Women from third world countries, and increasingly from Eastern Europe and the ex-Soviet Republic, are being driven by poverty, coaxed by persuasion or coerced by deceit or violence into a contract to offer sexual services in exchange for passage into Europe. Reports cover a variety of situations from women who have independently made their way into Europe to set themselves up as prostitutes, to those who willingly agreed to sex work to pay off the debt incurred in their passage, to those captured or sold unwillingly into sex-slavery. They are then reportedly held in safe houses, without documents, and required to work to pay off not only their debt but the charge for accommodation and other related services (*Guardian*, 30 May 2000). Source countries are typically central and south America, east and west Africa, south-east Asia, and the former Soviet Bloc and Balkan region; the women are often marketed under some label of exoticism.

While professional Western women can buy their way out of the indigenous gender order by purchasing foreign female labour, Western men can buy their way out of the sex order by purchasing 'exotic' sex. In part, national distinctions between European countries turn on whether prostitution is legal, in which case a two-tier system develops with state-recognised brothels offering safe sex and underground brothels offering unprotected sex. This has been construed as another case of first world women making gains at the cost of third world women (Leidholt, 1996). Where prostitution is not legal, undocumented women seem to account for an increasing section of the industry, estimated at 70 per cent in London's Soho (*Guardian*, 30 May 2000). The academic debates surrounding this phenomenon have two principal concerns: one relates to agency and empowerment, the other to rights.

Despite the existence of a Council of Europe Convention for Suppression of the Traffic in Persons and of the Exploitation of the Prostitution of Others, dating back to 1949, sexual trafficking of women has come for many to represent a major human rights crisis. What may be taken for common prostitution is only the surface appearance of a form of sex-slavery, characterised by social isolation, indebtedness and *de facto* captivity. Even where women have entered knowingly into the work, it is argued often to be on the basis of misleading information about the conditions and financial rewards (*Guardian*, 30 May 2000; Leidholt, 1996). However, the 1949 Convention targeted both the trafficker and the trafficked person, each of whom should be subject to a penalty

(Truong and del Rosario, 1995), and the resultant vulnerability of the trafficked person poses some practical problems.

Their unlawful presence in the destination country means that they have no support should they wish to denounce the trafficker, and indeed can be easily disposed of if troublesome. Thus deportation action against the 'victim' has been much more feasible than action to trace the agents (Truong and del Rosario, 1995) and lack of support for the women can serve as an aid to the trafficker. Many women are also left vulnerable under the Convention by a definition of trafficking which rests on violence and coercion, and by an interpretation of debt and indentureship as indicative of a voluntary arrangement. More recently, in 1989, the European Parliament (EP) passed a Resolution on the exploitation of prostitution and trafficking which condemns prostitution as a violation of human rights and argues, among other things, for assistance to victims of trafficking, especially in prosecuting their agents.

A key problem in the related complex of argument and positioning is that of agency and context. Murray (1998), for example, argues that much of the campaign against trafficking underestimates the active agency of the alleged 'victims'. In doing so, she also highlights certain contradictions, citing attempts to 'rescue' the women and return them to the repression and poverty from which they were fleeing. Murray's argument is that the coercive side of trafficking has been overestimated, to the neglect of the active strategising of the women involved, and that anti-trafficking campaigns have in practice increased their problems by encouraging racism within the sex industry. However, there has been some recent change in the framing of the problem, as for example in amendments made by the EP to a Commission proposal to combat trafficking in human beings (European Parliament, 2001).

One key aspect of the amendments has been the recognition that trafficking may involve the consent of the 'victim', and there is an emphasis on the role of vulnerability and inducement. Drawing on the additional Protocol to the UN Convention against organised trans-national crime (conference in Palermo, 2000), the EP report extends the conception of trafficking to include inducement (and therefore consent), and 'the abuse and deception of vulnerable persons', where that vulnerability may arise from poverty and lack of opportunity, and irrespective of the individual's consent. By implication then, consent does not imply full agency where the surrounding circumstances are sufficiently constraining. The report also calls for financial support, as well as job search and training assistance for victims of trafficking, with the possibility of voluntary return, though none of these positions as yet has any legal force.

Central to the broader debate surrounding the issue of trafficking is the question of whether prostitution *per se*, or simply coercion, is the target. For many women prostitution can offer the quickest and surest route out of poverty. Some argue they would be best assisted by its legalisation and improvements in the conditions under which they work (Murray, 1998:63). Others, for example the EP Committee on Women's Rights, see legalisation as exacerbating women's vulnerability and enhancing 'men's self instated right to buy bodies (human beings) for their own amusement' (European Parliament, 2001). This position connects with the view that any campaign against trafficking which leaves the dominant gender order and the surrounding legitimate sex industry intact is addressing the symptoms, rather than the cause, of women's problems (Truong and del Rosario, 1995; Leidholt, 1996). The notion of the embodiment of rights thus acquires a particular salience, in the context of debate about the right to commodify one's own body as weighed against assertions of the integrity of the human person – but in circumstances which make that commodification feasible and often profitable.

The right to family life

A set of related issues is raised by aspects of the law on family life and the specific phenomenon of mail-order brides which shades over into aspects of trafficking and the sex industry. Indeed, the EP report cited above includes marriage under false pretences in its conception of trafficking of persons for sexual exploitation. This is the case where traffickers use marriage as a loophole in immigration restrictions, but much of what is termed 'mail-order marriage' is rather more ambiguous (Tanton, 2000) and may reflect the genuine search for a partner (Truong and del Rosario, 1995), though again some difficult questions arise concerning agency and rights.

For many women in the less developed world, marriage to a European man represents escape from poverty or possible gender oppression and involves a high degree of informed strategic action (Tanton, 2000). For the men, however, it represents an opportunity to restore what they view as the proper arrangement between the sexes (Kofman et al., 2000), or to coerce a version of the marital relationship which they find acceptable (Truong and del Rosario, 1995). This is possible because of the dependence enforced by the conditions for family unification, and/or the restrictions placed on the spouse in the early years of their stay. Thus recognition of the human right to family life is granted under conditions which impose a degree of dependency on the incoming partner. Of course this pattern is ostensibly gender-blind, insofar as it applies whether the joining partner is a husband or a wife, but in fact family unification figures show arriving spouses to be disproportionately made up of women.[2]

We saw in earlier chapters how national regimes differ in their treatment of incoming family members, with implications for all cases of family unification, not just mail-order marriage. The situation in Germany, where Kofman et al. (2000:70) note that mail-order marriage is particularly prevalent, is among the more extreme. Indeed, the entry of foreign wives of German husbands has more than doubled since 1996 to account for almost one-third of all spousal unification.[3] German citizens are under no requirement to demonstrate an ability to house and maintain the incoming spouse, though this spouse will not at first have full access to the labour market. Since they are not granted independent residence until after four years of marriage, they remain in a dependent and vulnerable situation during this waiting period. There has been concern about the potential for abuse in such a situation and, as we have seen a recent ruling grants independent residence in cases of proven 'special hardship' after two years (*Migration News Sheet*, May 2000). The same rules apply to spouses of foreign residents, who must also demonstrate an ability to house and maintain the arriving family member, again creating a rather precarious situation of dependency.

In contrast, we have seen that independent settlement is granted after only twelve months in Britain. However, campaigns have finally produced a special concession which permits immediate settlement in cases of documented abuse, though we noted the difficulty for some in meeting the threshold of proof. Those who flee a marriage under such circumstances have only limited leave to remain and no entitlement to social assistance, but, unlike the corresponding situation in Germany, they would have full access to the labour market from the point of arrival. Nevertheless, deportation on the breakdown of marriage is still an active policy (Kofman *et al.*, 2000: 87) and the need for the probationary year has recently been reasserted and the period may be extended. In Italy there is a degree of toleration of marital breakdown in such circumstances, partly by virtue of the change of status clause in the 1998 law, but long-term settlement would eventually require an independent income test.

It is, of course, open to ask why such rules and regulations which are gender-blind should be cited as evidence of disadvantage for women. In part it is their very gender-blindness which causes the problem, if one accepts the case that women are more physically and culturally vulnerable to abuse, a case that is hard to deny given the flourishing forms of sex-exploitation cited above. However, even as principal migrants seeking unification with a family member, women are more likely to find themselves in a situation of disadvantage which stems from their weak position in the labour market. Inadequate income, or perhaps more significantly, inadequate housing, can be a barrier to family rights, and given women's predominance in domestic work, much of which is live-in, the accommodation requirement can be difficult to meet. Marriage is not always the key relationship in such cases, and there is considerable ethnographic evidence of domestic workers leaving children at home in the care of other relatives (Chell, 1997).

There is one other area in which women are perhaps more vulnerable, and that is in cases of forced marriage, which are more likely to feature in securing a male route to immigration than a female route. This has been a sensitive area for many of those committed to respect for diversity but concerned about individual freedoms. Where cultural dictates override the individual this poses Western liberalism with some difficult questions (for full discussion see Kymlicka, 1989). In Britain a Home Office working group has only very recently condemned the practice (*Guardian*, 3 June 2000), but current proposals stop short of a ban.

The implementation of the right to family life thus raises a number of problems in practice, and here I have noted those most relevant to gender disadvantage. However, with the theme of 'embodiment' in mind, we should recognise that a similar analysis could be conducted with respect to other divisions such as sexuality, disability and age. Some of the evidence presented in earlier chapters has a bearing on this diversity – the barriers to family unification for homosexuals have only recently been reduced, the disabled who are state-dependent have great difficulty in claiming family rights and the elderly who join relatives on the condition of full maintenance can find themselves vulnerable if the relationship breaks down. I have only touched the surface here of how a genuine entitlement to rights must deal with embodied diversity, but there are other aspects of this issues which must be considered in the context of asylum.

Asylum

Citing a 1985 UN conference report, Castel (1992:39) states 'it is estimated that two-thirds of the world's ten million refugees are women and young girls', yet it is generally accepted that women find it harder than men to meet the legal criteria for recognition (Castel, 1992; Crawley, 1997). Gender has become a focus for interest and concern in relation to asylum principally because of its absence from the Geneva Convention as an enumerated basis for persecution (Indra, 1987). Thus under the Convention someone qualifies as a refugee if they have a well-founded fear of persecution on the grounds of race, religion, nationality, membership of a particular social group or political opinion – but not gender. The key criticism of this definition is that it contains a notion of the political which has been drawn up around the public sphere activities of men, to the neglect of the private. However, it has also been argued that the best corrective to this does not necessarily lie with an addition or amendment to the framing of the Convention, but rather with its interpretation in practice (Greatbatch, 1989).

Kelly (1994) identifies two gender-related aspects of a claim for asylum, both of which highlight the potentially embodied nature of rights but more importantly of vulnerabilities, by virtue of the greater capacity of men to dominate women physically, culturally and/or psychologically. Thus, the type of harm threatened or perpetrated may be gender-specific, as for example with rape, genital mutilation, denial of reproductive rights, etc., while the reason for the persecution may be a woman's gender, as with the coercion to comply with social and cultural norms. In arguing a case, however, reference must be made to political opinion and/or membership of a social group and this is where the scope for interpretation lies. We can see this in the question of what constitutes persecution and of whether various gender-specific forms of physical harm fall under the definition, rape and sexual assault being particularly problematic.

Castel's (1992) account of two Canadian judgements[4] illustrates this point. She shows that relevant issues concern both the identity of the attacker – as either an agent of the government, or of a group of political/military insurgents – and their motivation. For rape to be viewed as more than an individually motivated act it has to be linked to an intention to punish or humiliate (rather than sexual gratification), and to the imputation of a political opinion. However, that political opinion need not be narrowly defined but could extend to the issue of the gender order itself, and the question of men's rights of disposal over women's bodies. Thus rape may be viewed as persecution by virtue of political intent, and has been cited as a method of torture inflicted on female detainees, and as retaliation between warring factions in situations of civil war. Interpretation of the meaning of the act is then linked to other interpretive problems over what constitutes political activity or political opinion.

In one case cited by Castel,[5] resistance to the rape itself was considered political – a challenge to the gender order which legitimated the act. In other cases it is women's association with the more overt political activities of male relatives which leaves them vulnerable (Kelly, 1994:529). Their relationships of care or support for these men can thus render women 'political' regardless of their own personal opinions, and we begin to see that distinctions between the public and private spheres are vulnerable to challenge. This is important because although a claim to persecution may be sustained by virtue of a threat to life or freedom, or other serious violation of human rights (Greatbatch, 1989), a link with the five grounds cited by the Convention must also be made. Thus the cases of apparent persecution of women because they are women must be linked either to their political opinion (real or imputed) or to their membership of a social group.

Much also rests on the relationship of the violation to the state, either by virtue of a state agent or of a state-endorsed action. Bhabha (1996: 4) cites cases[6] in which 'private' behaviour may clash with state interest in public morals and demography, and which therefore raise additional questions about the scope of legitimate interference in state sovereignty. Pursuing this issue in relation to Iran she shows how a challenge to cultural and religious mores, such as prescribed dress, can be viewed by the state as dissidence. She detects a shift over time in the response of Western governments to this plea, which is thought to reflect a 'gradual but growing judicial acceptance of gender persecution as a valid ground for the grant of refugee status' (p. 19), an issue which has recently received recognition in Germany (*Migration News Sheet*, November 2001).

There would be much greater difficulty in establishing a claim to asylum in cases of domestic violence, where the state is involved only by default, through the failure to protect. Domestic violence is the prime example of injury associated with women's relegation to the private sphere, and not one in which governments can be easily held accountable. Although this is arguably a human rights issue, it must be shown to be a generic (rather than incidental) problem before an argument about the absence of equal protection could be made (Thomas and Beasley, 1993). Even then, for asylum to be granted domestic violence must be convincingly portrayed as a form of persecution linked to the five grounds specified above, and there has been a recent decision of the House of Lords on two such cases as conjoined appeals.

Both cases involve Pakistani women[7] forced by their husbands to leave their homes, being falsely accused of adultery and at risk of criminal proceedings and flogging or stoning to death (see *International Journal of Refugee Law*, 1999). Both women had been granted exceptional leave to remain but were pursuing requests for full refugee status. Much of the deliberation on the case concerned the definition of membership of a particular social group, the counsel for the applicants arguing that 'three characteristics set the appellants apart from the rest of the society viz gender, the suspicion of adultery and their unprotected status in Pakistan' (IJRL, 1999:503). Other possible definitions considered included 'women perceived to have transgressed Islamic mores', and an analogy was made with homosexuals who, due to their vulnerability in some countries, may be recognised as a social group for Convention reasons.

The appeals of the women were upheld by the House of Lords, on the grounds of membership of the social group 'women in Pakistan', who as such were unprotected by state and public authorities if under a suspicion of adultery. In the course of the judgement the point was made that the defining feature of the persecution in this case – as opposed to other cases of domestic violence – was the fact that the state was unwilling or unable to offer protection. However, a minority dissenting view (Lord Millett) argued that the social norms allegedly transgressed were not a pretext for persecution, but are 'deeply embedded in the society in which the appellants have been brought up and in which they live' (IJRL, 1999:527), i.e. that established cultural practice cannot be viewed as persecution. For both the upholding and the dissenting argument the social and cultural context was vital in giving meaning to the nature of the threat confronting the women, though producing two differing conclusions.

Finally, we should note the likelihood of some ambiguity in the case of women's claims to persecution, whether it be the 'personalised' form of persecution, the informal or familial basis of their political affiliation, the supportive and domestic nature of the political involvement, etc. For this reason, it has been argued that women are much more likely to be granted some form of subsidiary protection than full refugee recognition – as in the initial judgement in the cases cited above. This then has an impact on the associated rights they can claim, and particularly weakens their position in relation to family unification, which for women leaving children at home has very damaging implications. We should also note that there is scope for considerable variation between countries in their response to gender-based cases, and that Germany's restrictive interpretation of state involvement in persecution (see European Council on Refugees and Exiles, 2000) could have a particular impact on women. This position is now likely to change after some disagreement as to whether an expansion of recognition to incorporate gender persecution should apply to protection under the Geneva Convention or only to subsidiary protection. It has, however, been ruled out of the Constitutional definition of asylum (*Migration News Sheet*, December 2001).

'Race' and the embodiment of rights

Race has in common with gender the fact of being a basis for social differentiation whose markers are borne on the body. Though race as a biological category which can directly account for social difference has long since been discredited, it nevertheless has a continuing significance as a system for 'the assignment of rights to individuals' (Rex, 1986:19). This significance also extends to ethnic differences based on the claim to common origins or a shared culture, whose manifestations may be in the form of cultural signals as much as literal physical characteristics. Finally, there are distinctions of nationality which may coincide with, or be cross-cut by, racial or ethnic difference (see Smith, 1995). A vast amount has been written on the relationship between race, ethnicity and immigration, and I will not attempt a review of this literature but confine myself to one very specific issue – the different ways in which race, ethnicity and immigration status correspond in the three countries I have considered.

Much of the debate addressed in this book has revolved around the question of 'membership' for racial, ethnic or national groups which do not possess the citizenship of the host community, and though there has been speculation about their incorporation into a post-national society this process is far from complete. Alexander (1988:83) notes that theorists of 'solidarity' have been infected by enlightenment thinking in proclaiming civic solidarity as the 'future' of the human race, and warns that there is no inevitable evolutionary logic at work here (cf. Turner, 1988:60). He also argues that civic integration is always unevenly attained, partly because national society will inevitably exhibit a historical core. Indeed, this is reflected in the emergence of stratified rights as a response to the presence of non-nationals. The device has been shown here to function as a further basis for differentiation as much as a foundation for inclusion, and in this process race, ethnicity and/or nationality can operate as a status in some respects comparable to gender. Thus we find both a formal restriction of rights, by virtue of the rules governing immigration status, or informal deficits in the claiming of rights, possibly linked to the broader dimension of esteem or belonging (cf. Fraser, 1995).

Documenting and understanding this process in relation to migration has become increasingly complex, with EU citizenship (or effectively EEA nationality) being the principal differentiator, but with significant differences within the EU and non-EU categories. In the latter case we find East Europeans with no notable physical distinctiveness but more subtle identifiers, some of whom carry formal advantages by virtue of the Association agreements, Turks, who have a unique position in Europe with regard to formal rights, and are distinguished by culture and religion, and other TCNs covering a wide variety of race and ethnicity and a range of possible civic statuses. The picture is further complicated, as we have seen, by variation between national systems of immigration and incorporation, and increasing racial and ethnic diversity linked to the widening range of countries of origin. Thus immigrant populations are classified by formal divisions of citizenship and immigration status, which may coincide with, or be cross-cut by, distinctions of race and ethnicity, as well as associated distinctions of 'esteem'.

A central question must therefore address the likely impact of status differentiation on racial or ethnic cohesiveness, and the distribution of racial and ethnic groupings across the status hierarchy. We have already noted the hierarchy implicit in the distinction between migrants exercising free movement within

Europe, based on the worker/non-worker distinction. The former group even on immediate arrival have many more rights — including some rights to social assistance — while for the latter initial residence is conditional on self-maintenance. The rights of both categories are addressed in European law, which is binding on all member states. To this degree the EU does indeed represent a post-national society. Of more interest, however, is the racialised pattern of stratification which emerges from each of the national immigration regimes, starting with rules for the acquisition of citizenship and extending to a number of other aspects of civic status. These issues are therefore addressed below on a country-by-country basis, for to a much greater extent than gender, racialised patterns of difference are country-specific.

Germany

The notion of the embodiment of rights takes on a particular significance when the right to citizenship is in the blood (see Brubaker, 1992). As we have seen, Germany has been noted for the exclusive nature of its citizenship rules: both its reliance on 'ethnic' or blood-based criteria and the prohibition on dual citizenship. Although there have been recent modifications — notably permitting those born in Germany of settled parents to hold dual citizenship until the age of 23 — the issue has not been resolved. The result is a very large non-citizen population (about 7.5 million, or 8.8 per cent of the total population[8]), with two key sources predominating: Turkey and ex-Yugoslavia. Non-citizen Turks account for about 2 million of this population, with ex-Yugoslavia accounting for over 700,000 (about 1 million if Bosnia and Croatia are included).

Turks not only for the most part lack the formal rights of citizenship but, being readily identifiable, are also easy targets for the conferment of a negative status, or the absence of 'esteem', which may be less of an issue (though not completely absent) for East Europeans. The Turkish population, however, does not occupy a homogeneous position in terms of formal status, but is divided across seven different immigration categories (excluding full citizenship). Even discounting the least significant of these (the *bewilligung* status for temporary workers, which includes only 7,000), this means there are significant subdivisions, with around 750,000 Turks currently (1999 figures) confined to a time-limited residence permit. Part, but by no means all, of this figure is accounted for by the probationary period for family members arriving under the rules for family unification. Others either have not sought or have not qualified for an unlimited stay. Smaller numbers are confined to the statuses associated with asylum — about 21,000 having humanitarian leave, 15,000 a tolerated status and 40,000 awaiting a decision.

The division between the asylum-related permits and the standard permits of residence goes beyond the associated rights they carry. It reflects a probable ethnic division within the national grouping, the likelihood being that the former groups are principally Kurdish. This kind of division is in sharper evidence for the ex-Yugoslav population, with almost as many holding a tolerated status as hold an unlimited stay (around 145,000 as compared with 160,000). In this case we have a population which, while not clearly distinct from Germans in 'racial' terms, is unified by past national origin but sharply divided along ethnic (now increasingly national) lines which are to some extent mirrored in the formal statuses they occupy. The most significant aspect of these divisions by formal status is the difficulty of progressing to secure residence from the two principal statuses of protection. This means that within one national (or ex-national) population there are ethnic concentrations of people locked into two statuses with significantly limited rights and no reliable route to a more secure status.

The other notable aspect of the German situation is that, in contrast to Britain, the same two national source countries head each of the principal formal status divisions in terms of numerical presence. Their rank order relative to each other is sometimes reversed, with ex-Yugoslavia predominating in the asylum statuses and Turkey in the residence statuses. Nevertheless, the picture is one in which the source countries of the early guestworkers are also the principal source countries of asylum seekers. Key countries of origin can shift quite rapidly, but according to 1999 figures the next two most numerous groups holding humanitarian protection were Afghanistan and Lebanon (with 18,000 and 15,000 respectively) and holding a toleration (*duldung*) Vietnam and Afghanistan (12,000 and 6,000 respectively). These countries rank with a number of others which generate small but significant numbers of long-term migrants whose presence falls short of full 'inclusion', key additional sources being Eastern Europe, Iran, Morocco and Sri Lanka. However, one striking aspect of this rather disparate list is the complete absence of any predominantly black source country.

We have already noted that a key feature of status distinctions operating in Germany is the associated pattern of phased access to the labour market. It is well established that certain minority groups are anyway disadvantaged in the search for employment, and that this disadvantage has been exacerbated by the informalisation of employment practices (Wilpert, 1999) so that about 40 per cent of the descendants of the original guestworkers are estimated to become downwardly mobile. This pattern is in some ways in interaction with the formally stratified pattern of access to the labour market which maps onto immigration statuses and to some extent mirrors ethnic distinctions. The waiting period before family members have full employment rights will most obviously affect the principal immigrant group – notably the marriage partners of the second and third generations – and is reflected in the very high number of Turks with a limited residence permit.

However, the limitations are of much longer duration for those with subsidiary protection such as *duldung* and *befugnis*. Here we find concentrations of particular ethnic groups, notably Kurds, Afghanis and Bosnians.[9] While the stratified system of statuses does not reflect an exclusive ethnic hierarchy, there are nevertheless fairly clear tendencies, so that informal deficits by virtue of ethnic identity will often be exacerbated, and in some sense confirmed, by formally stratified rights. Where this happens the formal and informal status systems operate together, and constructed disadvantage will both encourage and be amplified by an absence of esteem or 'recognition'. In addition to these distinctions there is a varied sub-stratum of clandestine workers in Germany, fed by visa-free travel from Poland, by rejected asylum seekers who have not left, by former Vietnamese contract workers from East Germany (see Wilpert, 1999) and of course by the domestic workers and sex workers referred to above.

Britain

As we noted in Chapter 4, Britain moved closer to a model of ethnic citizenship when it introduced an element of 'patriality' into the right of abode in the 1971 Act. The concept itself was later abandoned but the principle of inherited citizenship was incorporated into the 1983 British Nationality Act. This act also restricted the territorial basis of citizenship, and confined the automatic right by birth in Britain to children of a settled parent. A child born to parents during a temporary stay in Britain – an asylum seeker, for example – would no longer be British. The overall effect has been to make the civic/ethnic map of Britain extremely complex.

There are residents of Asian or Afro-Caribbean origin whose citizenship dates from before 1971. They retain this citizenship and pass it on to their children, so that there is a continuing British citizenry of Asian and Caribbean ancestry. There are also those who were born in the New Commonwealth but whose parents hold British citizenship, and who are therefore themselves British citizens with the right of abode, though they may have difficulty proving this. Indeed, for this population of ethnic minority British citizens the principal dimension of civic injustice operates by means of deficit, that is, the existence of informal constraints which may affect their access to formally held rights. These citizens have been a particular focus for concern in relation to the expansion of internal controls, as we saw in Chapter 4 with respect to employer sanctions and benefit entitlement (see Morris, 1998). While holding the formal status of entitlement these citizens are not granted what Fraser would term full esteem or recognition, and instead can easily become subject to various forms of scrutiny and suspicion.

Contemporary migration from ex-colonies is still quite common, and is the major (though not exclusive) source of settlement. In 1998 the main countries of origin were (by numerical significance) Pakistan and India, followed by USA and Bangladesh.[10] Family unification is the principal route, and if the incoming family member does not hold British citizenship then the hurdles are considerable and the initial status is probationary. As we have seen, British citizens are not privileged over settled persons in securing family unification, but many practitioners note the particular stringency with which applications from the Asian sub-continent were dealt with – another form of deficit. However, once present in the country, eligibility for settlement comes quite quickly (after one year) for the joining spouse, and if the principal family member has British citizenship then the incoming partner also has the possibility of citizenship after a further two years (Joint Council for the Welfare of Immigrants, 1997:339). This route to settlement has been a source of concern for some in relation to forced marriages (*Guardian*, 3 June 2000) and as noted above, the probationary period may be extended (Home Office, 2002).

One outcome in terms of civic/ethnic stratification is a multi-ethnic citizenry, with a particular concentration of Asian British, sub-divided between Pakistan, India and Bangladesh. Ostensible 'racial' divisions thus disguise significant ethnic sub-divisions. To these we must add the situation of the non-citizen ethnic minority population, who hold either limited leave or settlement. The relative ease of access to settlement, and even citizenship if desired, should mean that formal status divisions are short-lived, though they can be of particular importance in cases of marital breakdown and/or domestic violence, as we saw above. Divisions related to lack of esteem and deficits in access to rights are more enduring and are at least part of the source of disturbances such as those in the 1980s (see Scarman, 1981) and more recently.

This relatively simple picture of civic statuses and of rules of transition between them is made more complex by the growing presence of asylum seekers. Unlike Germany, the countries of origin show no obvious correspondence with the principal sources of settlement listed above, though there is a degree of overlap. Source countries with more then 4,000 applicants in the year 2000 were Iraq, Sri Lanka, Afghanistan, Iran, Somalia, ex-Yugoslavia and Turkey.[11] The long delay in processing applications, and the visibility of asylum seekers by virtue of the nature of provision and particularly the voucher system, has conferred on them a particular 'outsider' status, though they are ethnically rather diverse and have little internal cohesion. They occupy a position both of low formal status and of generally low social esteem. If refused, they are also likely to feed a growing clandestine population of undocumented workers with even fewer rights.

Something of the scale of this phenomenon is suggested by a report from the Greater London Authority which states that between 352,000 and 422,000 refugees and asylum seekers are resident in London, accounting for nearly 5 per cent of the capital's population. 75,000 are estimated to be unlawfully present (100,000 if dependants are included). The Home Office is reported to be aiming at 30,000 removals in the coming year, predicted to require 'regular forcible incursions into the heart of many of London's ethnic minority communities' (cited in *Guardian*, 11 July 2001). However, as we have seen, these asylum seekers are not notably from Britain's traditional source countries of immigration, and the relationship between asylum seekers and more established minorities is something about which little is known.

At the bottom of the civic/ethnic hierarchy are the undocumented clandestine workers, some but by no means all of whom are failed asylum seekers. The evidence of this phenomenon is largely anecdotal, but the picture is again of workers from a variety of source countries – with East Europeans featuring prominently – who find work in agriculture, construction, hotels and restaurants, or as domestic labour (*Guardian*, 23 May 2001). Like the asylum seekers, these clandestine workers are a clear outsider group with little internal homogeneity. Beyond their 'foreignness' they are ethnically divided. Thus in terms of origins and civic status, the greatest correspondence is found among the traditional ex-colonial migrants' groups, who inherited the tail end of citizenship of the UK and Colonies or who have been able to settle through family ties or, more rarely, employment opportunities. They make up the black and Asian citizenry, and settled population. Below them are a more diverse and shifting population of asylum seekers and below them clandestine workers, of similarly diverse racial and ethnic origins, united only by the absence of rights and limited prospects of improvement.

Italy

Italy of course differs from Britain and Germany in both the timing and the scale of its immigration. Having been a receiving country for only about twenty years, and with its first immigration law in 1986, the pattern is not comparable to the larger-scale labour immigration and active recruitment of the post-war years. Instead immigration has grown piecemeal, largely feeding small-scale enterprise or service work, and has come from multiple sources. There is therefore no ethnic concentration equivalent to either Britain's Asian or Germany's Turkish populations. The most common source country is Morocco (which accounts for 11.7 per cent of foreigners, followed by Albania (9.2 per cent) and the Philippines (5 per cent), while non-EU countries which contribute more than 3 per cent to the foreign population include ex-Yugoslavia, Romania, USA, China, Tunisia and Senegal (Caritas di Roma, 2000).

One result is that no obvious association can be made between immigration and race or ethnicity in Italy, though this is less the case if we look at the regional pattern of residence. In some towns one ethnic or national group (usually Moroccans) may account for about one-third of all foreigners, as for example in Modena, Bergamo and Bologna. Conversely, in Milan and Rome – the two cities with the highest number of foreigners – the most numerous groups account for only a relatively small proportion of all foreign residents: 13 per cent for the Chinese in Milan, and 9 per cent for the Albanians in Rome (Caritas di Roma, 2000).

Although there are clear patterns of employment by national origin – Moroccans often working in construction, Chinese in small business and textiles, Filipinas and Latin Americans in domestic service, Senegalese as street sellers, etc. – there is no fully developed hierarchy according to civic status. This is partly because the legal system itself is still developing, so that the introduction of a long-term residence permit is very recent and asylum seeking is only just becoming a numerically significant issue. More significantly, the principal distinction has to date been between the 'regular' and 'irregular' and there is no direct pattern of ethnic advantage here. As we have seen, the chance to regularise depends on an offer of formalised employment and insofar as there is a pattern of advantage it is regional, with the small and medium-sized enterprises of the north-east actively seeking foreign labour and being keen to regularise those workers who are unlawfully present.

Any distinctions by ethnicity or nationality exist by virtue of established niches of opportunity, like the oft-cited example of Indians in the dairy industry and pig farming (Reyneri, 1998b). This turns into an ethnic advantage in terms of the chances of sustaining a 'regularised' position. Reyneri (1998c), for example, reports that those groups least likely to return to the underground economy are those involved in domestic and care work (Filipinas and Peruvians), those accommodated by their own communities (Chinese) and others who have achieved a degree of 'integration' (Egyptians, Somalis, Poles and Romanians). Among those most vulnerable to losing regularised status are the Moroccans and Senegalese, despite being groups with long-established presence in Italy, and they can become vulnerable to another distinction which operates in the context of immigration control. We saw in Chapter 3 that enforcement agencies tend to distinguish between those termed 'dangerous', which was defined as isolation, absence of a family life, lacking signs of integration and so on, and others. This translates into a focus on single males and in practice will often mean Moroccans, Albanians and Senegalese.

The Italian picture then is one of a kaleidescopic variety of ethnic and racial groups and, insofar as their prospects of secure settlement are pre-determined, it seems to be by the functioning of ethnic niches in the labour market, some of which provide a more certain route to regular status than others. To this extent, it is ethnic identity via networks of recruitment rather than immigration status *per se* which has shaped a migrant's prospects, and this could continue to be the case as the quota system becomes established. There is still likely to be a powerful role for networks from the point of view of both the migrant, in terms of migration decisions, and the employer, in terms of recruitment. This process is something of a contrast with the German system, where at least in the early years many migrants have their prospects formally shaped by restrictions on the work they can accept, while the same effect in Italy occurs by means of informal processes. As far as clandestine employment goes, all three countries seem to share the highly varied ethnic and racial mix, this being a feature of contemporary migration with source countries having become more diversified (Salt *et al.*, 1994) Since all migration into Italy is relatively recent, this diversity is apparent across the whole range of migrants, and is not concentrated among the clandestine group. Of course, the repeated regularisations have meant that almost any migrant could have begun their stay in a clandestine capacity.

A racialised system of rights?

Immigration statuses in practice represent a system of social structural division in terms of rights, raising the question of how this structure is 'embodied' in terms of race and/or ethnic divisions. The question of how far different status positions correspond to an ethnic or racial identity is important in terms of the potential for social cohesion. So too is the related question of the potential for movement through the system of statuses for any given individual. These questions have different answers in each of the three countries considered above.

In the UK, despite the limitations of the British Nationality Act, the now defunct citizenship of the UK and Colonies has had its continuing effects in laying the foundations for the consolidation of an Afro-Caribbean and Asian citizenry, though these effects are undermined somewhat by lingering deficits in the implementation and delivery of rights. Relative ease of settlement (once entry has been achieved) has also been important in offering security not only to the narrowly defined migrants group, but to many occupying the lesser statuses of protection. In fact, the major stigma and exclusion seems to be moving from ethnic identity *per se* to civic status, with asylum seekers and clandestine migrants viewed as the foreign 'outsider' group, though with no single unifying racial or ethnic identity.

The picture in Germany is rather different, with a more graduated system of statuses characterised by the long-term presence of an original guestworker population which has not yet achieved full 'membership'. In terms of embodiment of rights the system is characterised by concentrations of migrants by national origin who are divided by civic statuses, which in turn correspond with ethnic divisions. Thus we find the Turkish population not only spread across limited and unlimited residence status and the right of abode, but extending into the different statuses of protection for Kurds, whose prospects of ultimate security are much more limited. The same picture emerges for the ex-Yugoslav population, with sharp contrasts to be found between the original guestworker population and the more recent ethnic groups present as civil war refugees.

In Italy we found no such clear correspondence of race and ethnicity with immigration status, as a result of the very varied range of source countries, the relatively short history of migration and the still emergent legal framework. Concentrations of advantage and disadvantage are much more the product of employment position and informal processes of recruitment than of formally structured statuses, with recurrent regularisation having played a significant role in creating an ethnically heterogeneous immigrant population. However, we have noted that the risk of falling back into irregular status is greater for some groups which are also the focus of overt mechanisms of control.

Conclusion

This chapter has addressed the way in which abstract systems of rights are mediated through 'embodied' distinctions of diversity, and the focus here has been on gender and race/ethnicity, though there are other features of diversity which could also be included. Drawing on Turner and Fraser, the argument has been that diversity affects the status order both in shaping formal standing in the context of immigration, and in shaping informal delivery of rights through judgements of 'esteem' or the process of 'recognition'.

For gender the precise dynamic occurs through women's association with the private sphere, which limits their employment options and often confines them to caring and/or domestic work. Although this serves to provide a protected employment niche, differential opportunities and gender norms also mean that women are more often the 'followers' of male migrants and therefore more vulnerable to the dependencies associated with this position. These distinctions are, however, symptomatic of a gender order in which heterosexual men assume a power of disposal over women's bodies, and this relationship has its most powerful manifestation in cases of mail-order marriage and, more overtly, sex work. Women's agency thus operates in a context which can lead them to commodify their bodies in circumstances of persuasion, coercion and sometimes captivity. Their rights may accordingly be restricted by virtue of the hidden or 'private' nature of their position, usually under the authority of a man, whether as householder, husband or pimp. Even access to full recognition as a refugee has been shown to be limited by women's association with the private sphere.

The impact of race/ethnicity in the embodiment of rights is rather different, and shows greater variation between national regimes. This is because it is built around historical patterns for the appropriation of foreign labour which vary between colonial and guestworker regimes. The result has been different patterns of correspondence between immigration status and race/ethnicity such that the enduring pattern of disadvantage can be formally expressed (as in the absence of full rights) and/or informally expressed (as in deficits in the claiming of formal rights). As the nature of migration flows have changed and asylum seeking has come to assume greater prominence, we have seen two tendencies – the emergence of more heterogeneous 'outsider' groups united and stigmatised by their civic status and limited rights (as in Britain) and the division between groups of shared national origin by virtue of the correspondence between ethnicity and civic status (as in Germany). Italy shows a much more varied picture as a result of both its mixed immigration history and its practice of regularisation, but even so, some patterns of ethnic disadvantage are apparent. Thus while racial and ethnic divisions are manifest as structures of inequality, the form they take varies according to historical context, the opportunity structure and formal and informal status regimes.

7 Managing contradiction
Civic stratification and migrants' rights

We opened this book with a comment on the growth of interest in the concept of globalisation, which has served to draw attention to the fact that many aspects of social life transcend the boundaries of the nation state. Ranking among them we find trans-national migration, multi-state collaboration and the growth of international conventions, all of which challenge any lingering assumptions about the bounded nature of 'society'. There has been a related challenge both to empirical orientations and to theoretical frameworks to take account of this by moving beyond what has been termed 'methodological nationalism'. The concept of globalisation alone, however, offers little detailed guidance as to how this is to be achieved, and indeed has been applied to a wide variety of transnational dynamics which require much more nuanced analysis. Such analysis has begun to develop in a variety of areas, most significantly for the present work in relation to trans-national migration and migrants' rights.

The late twentieth century has convincingly been described as both 'the age of migration' (Castles and Miller, 1998) and 'the age of rights' (Bobbio, 1995). Theoretical debate about the precise relation between these characterisations continues. As we have seen, political and academic interest in cross-national migration has generated two very different and potentially polarised positions. One perspective emphasises the enduring power of the nation state, manifest in its capacity for control over entry and rights and through the continuing symbolic and material significance of national citizenship (see for example Brubaker, 1989). The other view sees migration, and more specifically migrants' rights, as the manifestation of an emergent post-national society in which migrants can increasingly draw on trans-national rights located outside the nation state, rendering national citizenship redundant (see for example Soysal, 1994).

Mediating polarisation

Of course there is some validity in each of these opposing positions, which in their different ways attempt to grapple with the likely future of the nation state, but neither offers an adequate basis for a full understanding of either the migrant experience or the political responses it has provoked. However, while Brubaker (1992) emphasises the continuing significance of citizenship as the ultimate basis of belonging, he also notes the absence of a theory of partial or limited state membership (1989:5) and his observations on the *ad hoc* proliferation of lesser statuses open up the possibility of a broader perspective. Indeed, it has been argued here that this undertheorised phenomenon holds the key to a more nuanced understanding of migration and migrants' rights and may be viewed as the outcome of a set of contradictory dynamics – a view which provides the framework for this book

Taking Europe as an example, it was argued in Chapter 1 that while the national management of welfare and the labour market militate against a more open policy, labour demand and human rights commitments have meant continuing immigration. Thus despite a dominant discourse of closure at national and EU level, inward migration has taken a number of forms and in the face of these contradictory dynamics most member states have been developing strategies for the management of migration. The interesting question is not, therefore, how to weigh national closure as against post-national rights, but how the management of conflicting forces is being negotiated and with what additional implications and effects.

An exploration of this question requires some understanding of the granting and delivery of rights and their associated conditions of eligibility, yet as Turner (1993) has noted, sociology as a discipline has no obvious foundation for a contemporary theory of rights. While citizenship has to some extent filled this void, usually with reference to the work of T. H. Marshall (1950), a number of writers have noted his failure to address the essentially exclusionary nature of citizenship and its inevitable creation of an outsider group. Others (Soysal, 1994) have argued that citizenship has anyway been superseded by residence status, which grants much the same social and economic rights as citizenship, though we should note that non-citizens are denied full political rights and many do not hold full rights of residence. In fact, it is the increasing diversity of 'outsider' status which is most in need of analysis.

One response to the limitations of the concept of citizenship has been to seek a foundation for claims to universal membership (or 'personhood') by drawing on human rights discourse (Turner, 1993; Soysal, 1994) and even to see human rights as a possible fourth phase of rights, following on from the gradual unfolding of civil, political and social rights (Parry, 1991). This solution, however, offers no obvious means of addressing the different legal statuses occupied by non-citizens, or the stratified nature of their rights. Others writers are more cautious about universalist pretensions. Bobbio (1995), for example, distinguishes between rights established in law and those claimed prospectively as 'natural' entitlements, highlighting the ultimately political and negotiated nature of rights (see also Waters, 1996).

An alternative approach, then, requires us to focus on the political and social construction of rights and the underlying principles of control, as well as critically examining the reach of trans-national forces. A potential framework for such analysis has been explored in the course of this book and is based on the concept of 'civic stratification' (Lockwood, 1996), which focuses on both the formal inclusions and exclusions which operate with respect to eligibility, and the informal gains and deficits which shape delivery. However, this framework also invites attention to the expansion and contraction of rights over time, with respect to either a particular area of rights or a particular subject group. Such an approach addresses some of the limitations of a traditional citizenship framework (e.g. Marshall, 1950) by considering the position of non-citizens, but remains cautious with respect to claims about universal, trans-national rights.

The trans-national dimension of rights

It is the existence of trans-national instruments for the protection and assertion of rights which has fuelled much of the post-national speculation (e.g. Sassen, 1998). We have seen that from a European perspective there are two sources of trans-national expansion: international conventions, which secure the rights of non-citizens (sometimes selectively) and operate through national sovereignty; and the Treaty on European Union (and later the Amsterdam Treaty), whose underpinning rationale is the creation of a single market and whose legal framework overrides national sovereignty. However, we should note that constraints confronting national regimes by virtue of their international obligations are largely self-imposed, i.e. the state concerned must first opt in to the convention or treaty in question. The pressure to do so may be moral and/or political (as with human rights issues), or more overt national self-interest (as with membership of the EU).

The fact of international conventions *per se* does not of itself make for a compelling case. Their effect can be limited in a variety of ways, not necessarily mutually exclusive – by granting protection only to citizens of countries which are party to the convention;[1] by addressing the needs of a specific group such as children, women, workers etc.;[2] by dealing with a specific area of rights, such as social and economic rights, or employment rights;[3] or by limiting rights to those migrants who are lawfully present in a national territory.[4] While it might be assumed that conventions explicitly asserting human rights would be the most inclusive, they contain no challenge to the right of a state to govern the entry and stay of aliens. We have also noted a degree of flexibility in the implementation of certain human rights – as in the European Convention of Human Rights (ECHR) – which leaves room for significant national differences in recognition and delivery.

The principal significance of the European Union with respect to migrants' rights is similarly limited, as we have seen, and lies in the extension of the right to work and reside to all citizens of EEA countries. While Community law offers some purchase for TCNs, it is generally agreed that the introduction of this new level of differentiation, symbolised by European Citizenship, has been of much greater significance (Martinello, 1994). Even proposals to extend the right of free movement to long-term resident TCNs would do so on terms less favourable than for EEA nationals. Indeed, taken together, the effects of trans-national influence on migrants' rights is less an assertion of 'universal personhood' (Soysal,

1994:1) than the introduction of a rather complex set of refinements and distinctions which variously shape the prospects of different categories of migrant.

For a full understanding we must therefore examine the forces at play in the granting and withholding of rights, the qualifying conditions of access and the nature of the interplay between domestic, trans-national and supra-national law. Thus while national systems for the granting of rights are cross-cut by rights conferred under Community law and by virtue of other international obligations, we have seen in earlier chapters that the impact of such law must be read with close reference to the domestic setting. We have also introduced a further dimension to our discussion: rights as governance. The granting of rights to non-citizens involves, in Foucauldian terms, the development of 'political rationalities' for inclusion or exclusion, while also extending the available 'technologies of government' through the institutional framework for their delivery (see Rose and Miller, 1992). In other words, the elaboration of rights for categories of non-citizen also provides the opportunity and the means for exercising surveillance and control. We have seen this played out in aspects of civic stratification.

Civic stratification

Classification of migrant statuses

A key component in Lockwood's approach to civic stratification is the construction of formal devices of inclusion and exclusion with respect to rights. The foundation for such a system in Europe is well known, and is to be found in the different legal statuses of belonging, the most obvious being national citizenship, citizenship of an EEA country and TCN status. The nature of the distinctions between these three categories vary between member states, but they represent the clearest formal markers of inclusion and exclusion with respect to key rights – free movement in the case of EEA citizenship and voting and absolute security of residence in the case of national citizenship. In addition to these formal citizenship distinctions, TCNs fall into a variety of sub-groups, some of which derive from Community law, by virtue of various Association agreements (see Staples, 1999; Guild, 1992), and could be expanded by rights of free movement for long-term residents. Others are rooted in international conventions such as the Geneva Convention (GC) and the ECHR, which offer varying forms of protection.

Further distinctions between TCNs are elaborated at national level, being largely determined by purpose of entry (see Brubaker, 1989). Central in this respect are entry for employment, family unification and asylum seeking, while there is a further category of unlawful status, resulting either from overstaying or from clandestine entry. These distinctions are significant both in defining legitimate access to rights and in setting out a prospective trajectory for establishing security of residence. While it is not routinely possible to change status with respect to the purpose of stay – except by marriage – it may be possible to progress from a time-limited and insecure status to indefinite residence, or even from an unlawful to a lawful status. We have seen how these passages are governed by rules of transition (Baubock, 1991) which are nationally variable but which serve as markers of the basis and scope for inclusion and exclusion.

For migrants in the early stages of this process the key issues are security of residence and social and employment rights. Those who wish to remain in a country for an indefinite stay must generally demonstrate a capacity to be self-maintaining, though some countries (e.g. Germany and Italy) exclude family members of their own nationals from this requirement and particular arrangements are usually made for asylum seekers. Once achieved, residence status confers full social rights – one foundation for the claim that citizenship has been superseded by residence status. Prior to this point, however, the requirement of self-maintenance may be enforced (as in the case of Britain) by the denial of recourse to public funds. In other cases there is no explicit exclusion from access to social rights, but a claim for support may affect subsequent prospects of a secure stay (as in Germany).

This connection between public funds and security of residence opens up the possibility that delivery of social rights can be harnessed as a vehicle of control and as a means of monitoring those lawfully present. Indeed, there are clearly established links for data exchange between the agencies of the state in both Germany (para. 71 *Sozialgesetzbuch*) and Britain (see Morris, 1998). These links can be brought to bear in checking the status of claimants, in validating transitions to a secure status and as a possible means of detecting those unlawfully present, thus complicating the role of service delivery. However, while self-maintenance acts as the key criterion of residence, there is a prior dimension of inclusion/exclusion which operates by virtue of control over the right to work and, in some cases, the degree of labour market access granted. This, of course, can affect prospects of security, though the denial of transition to a more secure status does not necessarily mean the denial of a status. Thus TCNs can find themselves locked into a position with reduced rights, while remaining present in a country for significant periods of time (a feature of the German system that the 2002 law is attempting to address).

Informal deficit and formal rights

The operation of inclusions and exclusions and their associated rules of transition is revealing with respect to the informal dimensions of civic stratification, gain and deficit, whereby rights which are formally held can be enhanced or restricted in practice. While the criteria of formal citizenship status are set out in primary legislation, other aspects of the granting and administration of rights may be less clear cut. This is especially the case where there is any role for discretion or interpretation in the application of criteria of eligibility, where prestige factors,[5] classically race or wealth, can positively or negatively affect a decision. Acceptable proof of self-maintenance can also pose difficulties for those whose income comes partly or wholly from the informal sector, a problem characteristic of, but not exclusive to, those countries in which major sectors of the economy do not conform to official requirements. In Italy, in particular, the difficulties affect not only renewals of temporary residence but also the key transition from unlawful to lawful presence by virtue of regularisation, when formal employment may be the central requirement (see Reyneri, 1998a).

Stratified rights themselves create a climate of suspicion and surveillance, as for example with realising the formal right to take employment, which has proved a problem in Britain with the sanctions imposed on employers who recruit unauthorised workers (NACAB, 2000). While these sanctions in theory serve to protect the terms and conditions of employment for legitimate workers, they can have the indirect effect of impeding some in the realisation of their right to take work, hence creating a deficit. A similar dynamic is to be found with respect to social support, whereby the introduction of formal exclusions, as in Britain in the course of the 1990s (Bolderson and Roberts, 1995), created a climate of suspicion surrounding any foreign-seeming claimant (Allbeson, 1996). This can act as a deterrent to claiming even where a legitimate rights exists. It has also led to uncertainty about the boundary of entitlement.

In countries where there is no formal exclusion (as in Germany), the possible impact on future security is itself a deterrent. Further, there is still a possible role for status difference – in the sense of 'prestige' – which may operate through moral judgements about claimants, as in the case of the deserving and undeserving poor (see Barbalet, 1988). In countries such as Italy, with under-developed systems of formal welfare, the dynamic is different. There is considerable support available by virtue of charitable organisations which escape formal control and surveillance by the state, but which fall short of formal rights as they are properly understood.

Residence and maintenance as trans-national rights

In some cases basic rights of residence and social support can be conferred by virtue of Community law, and international conventions may also have some limited impact, but the effect is to introduce additional distinctions between migrants and thus contribute to civic stratification. The most secure position for TCNs comes under Community law, from marriage to an EEA worker, which confers associated residence, free movement and social rights. However, these are derived rights, and early divorce (i.e. before establishing independent residence) can mean their curtailment.[6] Community law in the form of the EC–Turkey agreement also secures residence for workers who have become established in the labour market,[7] prior to which they are subject to domestic law. There are related protections for spouses and children, but again only when specified conditions have been met (see Staples 1999: 253). Entry and residence may also be secured by virtue of the right of establishment under the Association Agreements with countries of Eastern Europe.[8]

International conventions deal with security of residence and social rights only in the context of certain qualifications and limitations, by virtue of their respect for state control over entry and stay. So, for example, while the International Convention on Social and Economic Rights has a minimal core of expectations whereby individuals should not be deprived of essential foodstuffs and basic care (Dent, 1998:7), this does not imply a right to residence or protection from removal. Under the ECHR the right to life and freedom from inhuman and degrading treatment (Articles 2 and 3) can be a basis for protection and support, but only for those with no feasible alternative, as for example in cases of failing health.[9] Other conventions secure more substantive rights for specific groups. For example, the European Convention on Social and Medical Assistance grants equal treatment in social security for contracting parties and prohibits repatriation on the sole ground of need for assistance. This prohibition only applies, however, after five years of continuous residence (Plender, 1999: 269). Thus with respect to social rights, those granted on the basis of 'universal personhood' are strictly limited, and this discourse of 'universality' applies more to aspirational efforts than to legally established entitlements.

Family life

These limitations have implications for the universal right to family life, which is commonly cited as a principal source of continuing immigration and is one over which nation states have little control (e.g. Soysal, 1994:121). Family rights do offer the basis of a claim for residence under the ECHR, but there is an inherent ambiguity in operation. The Convention accepts interference with this right (only) 'in the interests of national security, public safety or the economic well-being of the country'.[10] Distinctions are again to be found between national citizens, EEA citizens and TCNs. While some countries grant nationals unconditional unification rights,[11] for TCNs this 'right' is usually subject to a test of the original migrant's ability to house and maintain additional family members. This in effect excludes them from social rights for a transitional period, the duration of which is nationally variable. Family unification is not, therefore, established as a direct right, but may be made subject to a set of qualifying criteria which can themselves be open to interpretation and which may change with national circumstances.

Far from being an absolute right, the legal entitlement to family unification has seen a number of pragmatic shifts. Both Germany and Britain, for example, have sought to reduce the family rights of second-generation migrants. In Britain this meant removing unconditional family unification rights from all British citizens (Bhabha and Shutter, 1994) since this category included many migrant families. Conversely, in Germany, it meant establishing a distinction between German citizens, for whom the right is unconditional, as opposed to non-citizen migrants. While non-citizens there have always been required to meet certain conditions, further distinctions have been introduced between first- and second-generation migrants (Joppke, 1999). We should also note that one challenge to establishing a Directive on Family Unification across the EU has been the fact that not all countries recognise this as a right *per se*. In Austria, for example, family unification has been dealt with as part of an immigration quota.¹²

Thus while the right to family life is established as a universal right, insofar it is asserted in the ECHR, it is subject to qualifications commonly dictated by a desire to control and limit immigration. Family unification is governed by different rules for different categories of migrant and there are common deficits in realising the right and meeting the associated conditions. This is especially the case where regulations leave scope for interpretation, as with the British requirement to satisfy the Immigration Officer (for discussion see Joint Council for the Welfare of Immigrants, 1997:149–50, 245). Again, a reliance on informal sector employment (as in Italy) can be an impediment to demonstrating self-maintenance, while low income may interfere with access to adequate housing in a competitive market. Where the conditions for family unification involve an exclusion from public funds for a specified period, this also has the effect of cutting families off from the supports available to others and even creating a reluctance to claim support to which they are in fact entitled. We have therefore seen how the (qualified) right to family life is formally stratified with respect to the conditions of entitlement (inclusion and exclusion), but informally stratified with respect to its delivery in practice (gain and deficit).

Absolute rights and civic stratification

The principal examples of absolute rights are international obligations with respect to recognised refugees and a variety of other statuses of protection. Under the GC the central obligation of receiving states is that of *non-refoulement* – a commitment not to return the asylum seeker to a situation which threatens life and freedom. There is an implied guarantee of access to status determination procedures, but no obligation to facilitate the arrival of asylum seekers at national borders. Indeed, we have seen how the use of visas (Joint Council for the Welfare of Immmigrants, 1987) in combination with carrier sanctions (Cruz, 1995) has served to create a deficit in accessing the right to seek asylum. The same may be said of the Dublin Convention, now incorporated into the Amsterdam Treaty of the EU. The Dublin Convention has itself revealed certain ambiguities in the right to seek asylum and also in the lesser statuses of protection under the ECHR, in that member states vary as to their definitions of a refugee and in the forms of protection they offer.¹³

In fact, we have shown how the forms of protection available themselves constitute a sub-system of civic stratification, ranging from full recognition, through humanitarian leave to remain, to toleration or temporary protection. Despite being drawn from the same international instruments¹⁴ the nature of the protection offered, and specifically the security it carries, is nationally variable. In Germany, for example, protection under the ECHR has often meant only a toleration, which is technically just a deferral of removal (see Heinhold, 2000), though in practice it may last for many years. The use of this status should cease when and if the 2002 law is implemented (*Migration News Sheet*, April 2002), but debate has been couched in terms which emphasise the generally temporary nature of protection. Similar cases in Italy will receive a two-year renewable permit, and in Britain four years' permission with the possibility of settlement thereafter (European Parliament, 2000). This variation in practice with respect to the fulfilment of identical obligations is a further illustration of the fragile and negotiated nature even of absolute 'rights', though we are seeing some signs of conversion.

The treatment of asylum seekers also provides an example of the close interconnection between rights and controls, through the introduction of an element of stratification into systems of social support. Material support for asylum seekers has been endorsed by some courts as necessary for the pursuit of a claim to asylum,[15] and asylum seekers fall into a category for whom there is no clear option of departure from the receiving country. However, several countries have developed a system of provision which is explicitly linked to deterrence, variously using reception centres and cash-limited systems of support to discourage any who might (it is believed) be drawn by the availability of direct payments through the welfare system. The administration of such systems, requiring the collection of vouchers from a specified local issuing point, can provide a means of keeping track of claimants which all but ties them to a particular locality. This effect is, of course, enhanced where there is a compulsory system of dispersal (as in Britain and Germany), linked in the German case with an overt denial of freedom of movement outside the local district.

We have also seen how reliance on vouchers to be exchanged for goods in itself represents a deficit in the right to support, in that the nature of the support detracts from its value.[16] As with other aspects of welfare support, the accompanying stigmatisation also detracts from the essential worth of the rights. There has even been the threat of a challenge on human rights grounds, citing inhuman and degrading treatment (*Guardian*, 28 September 2000), and this is one of the factors which prompted a further change to the British system of support. Where there is no fully developed system of support (as in Italy, which currently operates a one-off financial payment, sometimes in tandem with municipal and/or charitable projects), the opportunities for tracking asylum seekers after the submission of an application is much reduced. Conversely in Germany, a proposal to remove support from failed asylum seekers was rejected – though the level of support was reduced – in part through an awareness that provision of support provided a possible basis of control, by tying recipients into the legal system. In Britain the cessation of support on final refusal is much more conclusive.

The relationship between stratified rights and controls is thrown into sharp relief by the punitive nature of much support for asylum seekers, and where overly harsh systems of provision mean substantial drop-out and a consequent loss of control. Though the legal status of asylum seekers is secured until they receive a final decision on their case, they may still become part of a floating population of people living on the margins of society outside any formal institutional system of support. This possibility is apparent in different ways in Britain, where some opt out rather than accept dispersal (*Observer*, 31 December 2000), in Italy, where there is insufficient capacity for all, and in Germany, where breaching the confinement to a local district can mean disqualification from support. A more extreme manifestation of a marginal population is the continuing presence of rejected asylum seekers who are one source of an apparently expanding phenomenon of unlawful presence.

Unlawful presence

The position of those unlawfully present in a national territory is the ultimate test of the reach of universal rights. In terms of civic stratification they occupy the clearest case of exclusion, though even here there are internal distinctions. Clandestine migrants are either absent, or explicitly excluded, from many international conventions. We have noted a major exception, the International Convention on Migrants Workers and their Families (Bosniak, 1991) which asserts the fundamental freedoms and dignity of all migrant workers, but has so far been signed by sending countries only. Those unlawfully present are not entirely lacking in rights, but claiming a right can jeopardise their presence in a country, a fact which is often exploited by unscrupulous employers. Clandestine migrants can, of course, stake a claim to absolute rights as contained in the ECHR, but they are rather few.

The key absolute rights affecting the position of those unlawfully present are Articles 2 and 3 of the ECHR, the right to life and protection from inhuman and degrading treatment, whose potential is perhaps greater than might at first appear. As well as offering protection from situations of civil war, recent interpretation of these rights has been the basis of permission to remain and to receive essential maintenance in some instances of poor and deteriorating health.[17] In such cases the right to life and/or freedom from inhuman and degrading treatment can override the absence of a lawful residence status. These rights do not, however, have the same purchase in the case of an able-bodied person who is in a position to leave the country. Similarly, those unlawfully present have only limited rights to family life, though family ties have sometimes been the basis for a claim to legitimate status,[18] subject to the question of whether family life could be pursued elsewhere.

Where an unlawfully present population exists in significant numbers the national government faces the dilemma of whether to tolerate their presence, thus accepting the existence of a stratum lacking the most basic of rights, or whether to offer a route to regularisation. In Germany those who cannot be removed have been granted a formal 'tolerated' status, from which it is prohibitively difficult to advance to greater security.[19] Britain has tended to avoid the creation or overt acceptance of long-term marginal statuses but has targeted some groups in rather limited regularisation exercises, including 'old cases' rulings on asylum seekers, a device also used in Germany.[20] In Italy, there is an implicit toleration of those not deemed 'dangerous', or who do not come to the attention of the police, and the use of regularisation has been much more extensive there, albeit with the familiar deficits associated with informal employment, which make the conditions hard to meet. In practice, it is often state concern about the governance of people present on national territory rather than the force of human rights which dictates the approach to regularisation and, as we saw above, in the case of unlawful presence human rights obligations have only limited effect.

Civic stratification, mobility and disadvantage

The concept of civic stratification opens up the question of the structured differentiation of non-citizen populations and invites attention to the scope for mobility through the system. The way in which civic stratification functions in practice cannot be addressed at a purely theoretical level, however, and rests on the rules of transition imposed in different national systems. Thus each national system of rights may produce a different 'shape' in terms of the rights, statuses and prospects of its non-citizen population. In Germany, for example, we noted the tight control over access to the labour market, which is often phased and can therefore impede the possibility of achieving security, while Britain grants both full labour market access and settlement more readily, once migrants have negotiated entry. In Italy, with its much shorter history of migration, the key transition has been from irregular to regular status, though there is some evidence of the reverse dynamic (Reyneri, 1998c).

The focus of policy concern in recent years has shifted away from migration and settlement *per se,* towards the treatment of asylum seekers. This is especially the case in Germany and Britain, which have experienced very high numbers[21] in contrast to Italy, where asylum seeking is still an emergent phenomenon. Aside from those whose application is rejected completely, many of whom may remain in an unlawful capacity, there are those granted some lesser status of protection with restricted rights and security – but with significant national differences. Again the possibility of settlement arrives more quickly and simply in Britain, albeit dependent on meeting the usual conditions of self-maintenance, while Germany has made more use of the tolerated status and offers generally weaker prospects of security. In Italy there has so far been more crisis management in the form of temporary protection, but less use of other forms. Eventual change of status has usually been permitted for those with employment.

As well as the formal structures of differentiation, it must of course be acknowledged that civic stratification is permeated with distinctions of race and gender, which can affect access to rights and the prospects of movement through the system. These issues were explored in Chapter 6 in the context of sociological work on citizenship (Richardson, 1998), which highlights the extent to which rights are 'embodied', that is, lived out through processes in which race and gender are deeply implicated. As feminist work on citizenship has shown (e.g. Lister, 1997), women's access to the public sphere of rights is significantly shaped by their association with the private domestic (or sexual) sphere. We need only consider the capacities in which many women migrate – as family members, as domestic workers, as care workers and as sex workers – to see the relevance of this distinction (see Kofman *et al.*, 2000).

Where there is an associated relationship of dependency – be it on a husband, a private householder or a pimp – this of course undermines women's access to rights and has exposed them to abuse and exploitation.[22] Furthermore, their generally disadvantaged position in the labour market can affect the prospects for a more independent status. Nevertheless, 'domesticity' can sometimes operate to women's advantage, albeit in rather limited ways. Domestic work, for example, has been a route to regularisation for undocumented women both in Britain and Italy, when men may have greater difficulty. The reverse is more often true for access to refugee status, and although women are increasingly recognised as a 'social group' for some purposes,[23] again their association with the private sphere and marginalisation from overt political roles can mean that they suffer from forms of persecution which are not readily recognised as 'political' (Crawley, 1997). If recognised at all, they are much more likely to be granted a lesser form of protection (Bhabha and Shutter, 1994).

As with gender, the impact of formal legal structures will vary for distinct national and ethnic groups, shaped by different histories of colonisation and immigration. The wide range of statuses these 'minority' groups occupy invites attention to the correspondence between civic stratification and degrees of membership, and 'racial', ethnic and cultural hierarchies. In host countries which recruited migrant labour in the immediate post-war period there is now a settled population living in relative security. This is most obvious in the UK, where the early Commonwealth immigrants arrived in possession of full citizenship. In the German guestworker regime, where citizenship has been more difficult to access (Brubaker, 1992), security is more likely to be through unlimited residence (or the right of abode) which we have noted denies full political rights. Of course there have since been significant changes in citizenship regimes on which we comment briefly below.

Voting aside, these more established groups are now less likely to experience overt exclusions than the problem of deficit in accessing formally held rights, as we have seen with the effects of internal controls on black British citizens (Allbeson, 1996; NACAB, 2000). Deficit can also arise, as for example in Germany, as a result of labour market disadvantage, which can undermine the stability of family life (Wilpert, 1999). Confinement to informal sector employment is of particular significance here, most obviously in the case of Italy, but by no means absent as an issue even in Germany, a country noted for the rigour of its controls. However, the overt denial of rights and long-term confinement to marginal status is now of growing significance for asylum seekers, or rather those granted a status which falls short of full recognition, or rejected asylum seekers who remain present. In so far as historical links with the host country affect their destination, we can find shared country of origin spread across a variety of legal statuses which may echo internal ethnic divisions, a pheonomeon particularly apparent in Germany.

Expansion and contraction

The final aspect of civic stratification which requires some comment is the expansion and contraction of rights. We have seen that in Lockwood's schema

(1996) expansion is counterposed to exclusion, but in fact is more appropriately viewed against contraction. This shifts the focus from classification by legal status and individual prospects for advancement to security, to the broader dynamic of a regime of rights. As Lockwood notes, this can apply either to the enhanced prospects of particular groups and positions over time, or to a change in the terrain of rights as new dimensions are acknowledged or 'discovered'. A key example he gives is the elaboration of human rights instruments in post-war Europe. However, it is particularly important that expansion be viewed not against individual exclusions, but against contractions in the overall regime of rights, as there is no guarantee of an irreversible expansionary dynamic in relation to rights.

Of course there are examples of incremental advance, and these provide the substantive basis for claims that we are witnessing the emergence of post-national society. The most obvious instance of expansion has been the gradual transformation of Germany's guestworkers into long-term residents with social rights and family rights (Joppke, 1999). There has also been an expansionary shift in terms of access to citizenship, which has moved away from blood-based belonging to incorporate an element of *jus soli*, together with a greater degree of toleration for dual citizenship. While access to citizenship in Britain is more generous than in Germany with respect to dual citizenship and naturalisation rules, the criteria governing conferment of citizenship have moved in the opposite direction (cf. Castles and Miller, 1998). The dynamic has been one of the removal of rights and the incorporation of aspects of *jus sanguinis* (as of 1971) to secure the now notorious removal of citizenship rights from New (and therefore black) Commonwealth citizens (Layton-Henry, 1992).

Despite a certain optimism surrounding the potential for human rights, particularly with respect to migrants' rights, the area of trans-national migration contains some of the most striking examples of contemporary contraction. This is one reason why the post-national argument does not entirely ring true. There have been several instances of contraction with respect to family rights, with examples from both Britain and Germany. Not all change has been negative, though, and in both countries growing recognition of same-sex relationships has been an area of expansion. In Italy, with a shorter history of immigration, rights are still in the early stages of establishment and family rights have recently been enhanced, at least in principle, but with notable deficits in practice. A contraction now seems likely.[24]

We have already noted a contraction in the right to seek asylum, by virtue of the deficit introduced by carrier sanctions and visa regulations operating in concert and the restriction of choice associated with the Dublin Convention. There have been proposals to revise the Geneva Convention in order to curtail the spontaneous arrival of asylum seekers,[25] and the expanding use of subsidiary protections have been viewed by some with caution. It is not clear how far their use represents an expansion of protection or an erosion of the right to full recognition. We have also seen contractions with respect to social support for asylum seekers, with countries which have traditionally received large numbers of applications seeking a means of deterrence. Countries in which the asylum phenomenon is less fully established, however, are faced with a need to improve their provisions, and changes here are likely to be expansionary. This will be with a view to achieving the common minimum standard specified as part of the drive towards harmonisation in Europe (Council of the European Union, 1998).

The position of asylum seekers raises more general questions about the nature of socio-economic rights in trans-national context. These rights represent a currently contested terrain and an issue which is implicated in the distinctions between genuine and bogus asylum seekers, and between refugees and economic migrants. If social rights are human rights then in principle this distinction should dissolve but, as we have seen, the right to survival support has generally been rather narrowly construed. While the language of rights promotes a sense of ethical certainty, the study of rights in context reveals a greater potential fragility. Hence the incorporation of expansion and contraction with respect to an understanding of migrants' rights serves to highlight the political and negotiated nature of rights. A regime of rights can expand and contract over time in relation to national circumstances, shifts in perception, changing priorities and trans-national pressures, all of which have implications for the national/post-national debate.

The national/post-national divide

One further point should be made with respect to the power of the nation state as related to its trans-national obligations. Although the state is ultimately bound only by agreements it has actively chosen to embrace, the interpretation of those agreements falls in the end to the courts rather than to the government. Even within the confines of national legislation there have certainly been decisions which have gone dramatically against the wishes and intentions of government.[26] This is one reason why the incorporation of international conventions into domestic law is important in terms of the individual's right of redress. Community law, of course, has its own court of reference in the form of the European Court of Justice, as does the ECHR through the European Court of Human Rights. The degree of power wielded by a national judiciary with respect to international conventions is to some degree within the gift of the legislature. The adoption of a charter of rights in domestic law, as in the UK Human Rights Act, 2000, for example, still leaves considerable room for manoeuvre as to the power of the courts. While the judiciary can rule on the interpretation of law with respect to specific cases, in neither Britain nor in Germany do they have the power to strike down legislation (*Guardian*, 11 September 2000). In Italy an active culture of human rights law has yet to develop.[27]

Overall, deliberation about how to weigh national closure against post-national rights seems wrongly framed and neither position significantly advances our understanding of the dynamic underpinning the position of migrant populations. A better focus would be the tools deployed in the management of migration, and I have argued here that civic stratification is central, representing both a formal system of differentiated rights and a parallel dynamic of gain and deficit, as well as a vehicle for the exercise of control. The structures of inclusion and exclusion generated by domestic law are cross-cut in a variety of ways by trans-national and supra-national forces. While domestic constraints are sometimes overturned in the process, the effect is often one of mediation at national level – hence the scope for national difference in the honouring of international obligations.

Unanswered questions

This book has given a detailed account of the asylum and immigration regimes in three different national contexts, considering the structure of legal statuses, the formal and informal dimension of rights and the scope for movement through the system. The varied outcomes have been presented in terms of a typology which attempts to capture the key features of each national system, with Germany characterised by graduated selection, Britain by more definitive rules of inclusion and exclusion and Italy by the significance of informal processes. The question remains as to how such differences have become established. Though a full answer would take us beyond the scope of the present work, some tentative observations can be made.

One approach to understanding the unfolding of these different national regimes would look at differences which are rooted in history – the connection between citizenship rules and patterns and sources of labour recruitment are clearly central. Germany's graduated system emerged from a traditionally exclusive, blood-based model of citizenship and the recruitment of workers who, for the most part, retained their 'foreigner' status. Their long term stay, resulting in part from employer demand and in part from a growing state acceptance of moral responsibility (see Joppke, 1999), yielded a system for the incremental accummulation of rights. Conversely, Germany's constitutional guarantee of the right to asylum has undergone a contraction in the face of growing numbers, though a broader interpretation of the GC seems now to be accepted.

In British history, the phenomenon of Commonwealth citizenship meant that early post-war migration was initially on the basis of full inclusion with respect to formal status. Though the status of Commowealth citizen has been eroded and finally abolished, the basic orientation of inclusion or exclusion retains its significance – in relation to both immigration and asylum. The British system therefore moves quite quickly either to full rights of settlement or to detention and/or removal, a lesser version of which seems now to feature in German rethinking of their Foreigners' Law. Italy, as we have seen, has a much shorter history of immigration, and its newly established system of formal rights is perhaps closer to the British than the German pattern. However, it is distinctive in two respects: the reliance to date on recurrent regularisation procedures, and the powerful influence of informal practices, apparent in relation to employment, social support and systems of control.

The sequential logic underlying these different trajectories is easy to trace, though the differences themselves invite questions as to the underpinning philosophy with respect to non-citizens, and each national system conveys a different set of messages. While the German regime does embody a fairly robust system of rights, the message to the non-citizen is one of only cautious acceptance. The conditions and requirements surrounding the accumulation of rights not only act as obstacles on the path to security but also signal that acceptance is only cautiously granted, particularly in relation to statuses of protection. In Britain, the fact that many early migrants arrived with citizenship status has served to establish, in principle at least, the possibility of full membership. The erosion of Commonwealth citizenship rights, of course, conveyed the opposite message, but the regime which has emerged does suggest a certain unease about the possibility of long-term partial status. In Italy the reverse is true, and an ambiguity permeates the whole system through the informal exercise of discretion, the provision of supports which fall short of full entitlement and the continuing reliance on 'irregular' work.

I hesitate to claim that these differences embody explicit intent in the thinking of legislators and the shaping of rights, but would be more inclined to view them as the outcome of embedded traditions. As we have seen, these traditions are amenable to change, through either expansion or contraction, but to take this speculation any further would require a detailed examination of the policy process. In the present work I have focused instead on national regimes for rights in their active operation, structuring my analysis around the concept of civic stratification. Such analysis draws attention to the construction of (nationally variable) systems for the classification of migrants and hence to the fact that rights are rarely self-evident or absolute. They are tied into often complex systems of differentiation which serve as both a statement of rights and a basis for limiting the claims of some groups. The area of rights and controls with respect to migration is thus shown to be one of compromise, made inevitable by the management of contradiction. The nature of such compromise and its costs is at least as deserving a focus for attention as deliberation about the future fate of the nation state.

Notes

Introduction

1 Despite its international flexibility, capital does in fact have a national home (see W. Hutton in the *Guardian*, 12 July 1995).
2 See Robertson's (1990) phases of globalisation, and Giddens (1990:16) 'globalising scope of modern institutions'.
3 Used here in Foucault's (1991) sense of the governing of a population and its territory.
4 Most of these interviews were conducted in English. However, roughly half of the Italian interviews required the use of an interpreter.

1 A cluster of contradictions: the politics of migration in the European Union

1 A proposed Directive from the European Commission would conditionally extend free movement to TCNs resident from five years or more in one of the member states (European Commission, 2001b).
2 See Report from the Ministers responsible for Immigration, SN 4038/91 (WG1 930), reproduced in House of Lords, 1992.
3 Modestly estimated at about 1 million by the European Commission in 1994 (European Commission, 1994b).
4 See House of Lords, 1989, Evidence:3; 1992, Evidence:41; 1994, Evidence:77.
5 The position of Ireland is not yet known.
6 E.g. 'ethnic' Germans returning from the ex-Soviet bloc were actively encouraged until 1989, though since then their continuing arrival has become increasingly contentious.
7 Directive 96/71 (OJ 1997 L 18/1).
8 'Free movement' is generally used as short hand for the right to work and reside. Non-EEA citizens have a literal right of free movement, i.e. to cross borders within the EU without a visa, but must report to the authorities within three days and have no right to seek employment or to settle.
9 Germany requested a 62-year-old Italian who had become dependent to leave, though there could be a human rights case against this on the basis of respect for private life (*Migration News Sheet*, November 2000).
10 On carrier liability see House of Lords, 1994, Evidence:39; on visa policy see House of Lords, 1989, Evidence:162; on the Dublin Convention see Bolten, 1992.
11 We should note there is not a common definition of a refugee operating throughout the EU, raising doubts about what constitutes a safe country for the return of asylum seekers.
12 The Council of Europe has changed its position on this issue and moved from discouraging dual citizenship to encouraging it as a means of better integration of

migrant populations (Bartsch, 1992). Germany has softened its law in this area (see Chapter 2), but retains the ideal of a sole nationality.
13 See for example the expulsion of resident serial offenders from Germany (*Migration News Sheet*, July 1998; November 1998).
14 Charles Wardle MP (House of Lords, 1992, Evidence:38) argues it is not unreasonable to require this step as a condition of free movement.
15 The rate for Germany, for example, is 0.5% and for Sweden 5.6%. Germany permits dual nationality in only a limited set of circumstances and has operated restrictive procedures for naturalisation (Baubock and Cinar, 1994), now somewhat liberalised.
16 See Owers (1994), *Guardian*, 7 April and 9 May 1995. Absurdly, this intensification has not been consistent. For example, it has been said of Britain 'we let in three quarters of a million people every year on a temporary basis and we have not the slightest idea how many leave' House of Lords, 1992, Evidence:68. Expulsion policy is now to be intensified (*Migration News Sheet*, December 2001).
17 See for discussion memo to the House of Lords from the Equal Opportunities Study Group, University of Southampton, House of Lords, 1992.

2 Rights and controls in the management of migration: the case of Germany

1 Does not apply to ethnic Germans or to those whose prior citizenship cannot be renounced.
2 That is, legally resident for eight or more years.
3 Conditions of linguistic competence and self-maintenance remain.
4 The number of asylum seekers passed 100,000 for the first time in 1980 (Joppke, 1999:87).
5 Paragraph 16 of the Basic Law, now amended to 16a, provides the highest form of protection.
6 For details see www.bmi.bund.de/dokumente/Artikel/ix_62109.htm (accessed 19 March 2002).
7 EEA refers to the European Economic Area, with slightly broader membership than the European Union. We should note the restrictions even here. Non-workers must demonstrate a capacity for self-maintenance, while work seekers will be allowed only a limited time on benefit to find work.
8 The first test is whether a German worker is available, then an EEA worker, and so on through a hierarchy of preference. The checks on available workers are very rigorous and take so long that any potential employer of a low-skilled worker would be unlikely to wait.
9 Turkish spouses in employment are slightly privileged in relation to other non-EEA workers through the protections offered by the Association agreement between Turkey and the EU. This grants them certain employment rights which have been deemed to imply a right of residence.
10 We should note that all income tests are not about what a family is prepared to live on, but a measure of income against specified minimum standards.
11 The exception is when an unemployed applicant moves from contributory benefit to means tested benefit. They can meet the income with test contributory benefit but if they have not found work by the time this expires they would move to limited status.
12 The actual differences between these two statuses are not clearly spelt out and may change over time. But, for example, unlimited permission is lost after an absence from Germany of more than six months, whereas the right of abode is not.
13 For an example of this law in practice, see the case of Erkan Taylay (Mehmet), reported in *Migration News Sheet*, January 1999.
14 There are different types of package according to culture and religion.

15 For a note on these different statuses see Federal Commissioner for Foreigners' Affairs, 1997.
16 Under the Geneva Convention recognised refugees must be granted rights equivalent to a national (ZDWF, 1996).
17 For a period Berlin denied support completely, but after campaigns against this practice, as of February 2001, they have adopted the practice of other Länder.

3 The ambiguous terrain of rights: Italy's emergent immigration regime

1 As any welfare recipient will testify.
2 As with family rights, which can be qualified according to the economic well-being of the receiving country.
3 See for example the debate about 'workfare' in relation to benefit rights.
4 Now incorporated into the Amsterdam Treaty.
5 Applications for asylum have fluctuated dramatically over the last decade. Putting aside the exceptional years of 1991 (24,490 requests – Nascimbene and Galiano, 1997) and 1997 (20,000 requests – *Migration News Sheet*, July 2000), we find 6939 requests for 1998 (*Migration News Sheet*, June 1999) as against 1323 for 1993 and 1834 for 1994 (Nascimbene and Galiano, 1997) – a rise partly due to the impact of the Dublin Convention.
6 Although this status was introduced in the 1998 law, its implementation has been rather slow. New amendments would increase the residence qualification for this status to six years.
7 Doubled from five in 1992.
8 As of December 2001.
9 12,000, 118,349, 234,841 and 248,501 (Sciortino, 1999:238) with 312,410 having registered their intention to apply in 1998 (Caritas di Roma, 1999:131). In fact there were 254,000 applicants and the final outcome is pending at the time of writing. There has been much dispute about the treatment of those who cannot prove presence in Italy before the required date. Note that figures across time do not reflect the total numbers regularised as the same person can feature in more than one procedure.
10 Interview with Head of Foreigners' Office of the Department of Labour, Rome, 12 October 1999.
11 By July 2000 this quota was used up and a further 30,000 permits were under consideration, mainly for firms in the north (*Migration News Sheet*, August 2000).
12 From 16 per cent of all non-EU permits in 1994 to 25 per cent in 1998 (Caritas di Roma, 1996, 1999).
13 If the spouse has work on entering the income can be included, but not putative income.
14 48 per cent of new permits in the north and 31 per cent in the south (Caritas di Roma, 1999).
15 Anecdotal reports repeatedly cite long delays, disorganisation, inconsistency, etc.
16 Attempts at fabrication are not uncommon.
17 But include in this people who had applied in the *sanatoria* and were awaiting a decision.
18 It is open to debate how far legislation was prompted by a recognition of basic rights and how far by an awareness of potential health hazards posed by a large clandestine population.
19 Proposals for screening the migrants for disease were contested and defeated in Rome during the spring of 2001, being seen as part of a drive to discredit migrants.
20 Usually granted for specified groups by administrative decree.
21 Particularly the case in centres which have a dual purpose of detention and provision.

Notes

22 The Albanians who arrived in 1997 were an exception in this respect, but those who had an offer of a job were later allowed to remain.
23 Such rulings have applied in the past to ex-Yugoslavs (law 390, 24 September 1992); Somalis (decree of Ministry of Foreign Affairs, 9 September 1992); Albanians (Decree law 60, 20 March 1997 turned into law 128, 19 May 1997) and now under the immigration law 40, 6 March 1998.
24 See note 5 above.
25 Informed respondents felt that the failure to identify resources for this provision was one reason behind the bill's failed passage.
26 Agreed at the Tampere European Council meeting, October 1999 (Council of the European Union, 1998).
27 Save the most basic of universal human rights.

4 The shifting contours of rights: Britain's asylum and immigration regime

1 *Jus soli* rather than *jus sanguinis*.
2 This was the critical law with respect to the right of abode, but there were further changes under the 1981 British Nationality Act, which changed the rules for acquisition of citizenship and abolished citizenship of the UK and Commonwealth.
3 74,500 clearances for temporary purposes and 690 for settlement in 1998 (Home Office, 1999a:table 2.1).
4 Notably the European Convention on Human Rights and the Geneva Convention.
5 The enforcement section declined an interview, but asked to check the final work with a view to 'accuracy'.
6 The habitual residence test, introduced in 1994, was aimed at preventing an assumed abuse of this possibility and now requires proof of an intention to settle from the work seeker.
7 Excluding the elderly, but including the non-EEA spouses of EEA workers. Members of the latter group are unique in British Immigration law in holding a residence permit, though commentators note what seems like obstructive delay in the issuing of this permit.
8 Cases can now be heard in a British court, but note that the court cannot strike down legislation.
9 Public funds are defined as income support, means-tested job seekers allowance (JSA), housing benefit, family credit, council tax benefit, housing under parts II and III of the 1985 Housing Act, child benefit and a range of disability-related benefits (see Joint Council for the Welfare of Immigrants, 1997:180).
10 Unless the British citizen is exercising free movement in returning from another member state.
11 See the case of Surinder Singh, C-370/90 European Court of Justice, July 1992.
12 Freedom from inhuman and degrading treatment.
13 Although a draft Directive issued by the Commission as the possible basis for a harmonised family policy in the EU proposed immediate family unification rights for those with ELR, this element of the proposal was withdrawn, and the British government has anyway announced its intention to remain outside this directive.
14 Cf. Harrison, 1999:2.
15 A recent judgement also confirmed that third party support is acceptable (CO/1880/97, 28 October 1999).
16 This translates into a right to be considered as an asylum applicant.
17 This is expanded further by temporary protection for particular crisis situations.
18 Speech to the European Conference on Asylum, Lisbon, 16 June 2000.
19 See *Migration News Sheet*, March 2002.
20 *Migration News Sheet*, February 2001.
21 See Social Security Advisory Committee, 1996:xiii.

22 *R v. Westminster and Others* (1997) 1 CCLR 69.
23 1997 1 CCLR 85.
24 Quoted in Seddon, 1999:13.
25 Those with children are the responsibility of NASS until removal, but generally families with vulnerable children can be offered local authority care under the Children Act (1989).
26 Letter from IND to Refugee Arrivals Project, 17 April 2000.
27 *R v. Brent LBC* ex parte D.
28 See Court of Appeal, case nos C/1999/0747, C/1999/7342, C/199/7696.
29 European Court of Human Rights, case no. 146/1996/767/964.
30 Abdulaziz (1985) 7 EHHR 471.

5 Stratified rights and the management of migration: national distinctiveness in Europe

1 Dent, 1998 reviews these issues with respect to social and economic rights.
2 While this Convention is incorporated into Community law it derives from the Council of Europe and has thirty-four parties.
3 See for example the Commission Memorandum accompanying the Draft Directive on Family Unification (European Commission, 1999), the UN DESA report 2000, Germany's new green card policy, Italy's immigration quotas and Britain's acknowledgement of the need for legal channels of entry.
4 The European Convention on Social and Medical Assistance, for example, protects against non-renewal of a residence permit for dependence on public funds after a residence period of five years (see Plender, 1999:269).
5 See ECJ case C-171/95.
6 The restriction does not include refugees recognised under the Geneva Convention.
7 This is the key condition, in addition to proof of arrival in Italy before a specified date and adequate housing.
8 Earlier for domestic workers.
9 A recent UN report argued that demand was very much higher than that anticipated by the quotas.
10 To be raised to 18 for children arriving with parents but reduced to 12 for those arriving separately.
11 However, in the latter case proof of maintenance is temporarily suspended if there is a child involved, but must be met before a transition to unlimited residence for the spouse.
12 Three years' legal residence in cohabitation with the principal for a spouse, and completion of a vocational training course for a child.
13 See ECJ case C-351/95.
14 The status can discretionally be granted through the partner.
15 Those who have children would qualify under the 1989 Children Act.
16 For example, the draft Directive proposes 18 as the upper limit for family unification for children, and Germany's latest proposal raises the maximum age to 18 only for children accompanying their parents on entry. For those arriving later the upper age limit would be lowered to 12. The draft Directive also requires immediate access to the labour market for family members, which the new German law would grant, but in some cases only for jobs for which no German, EU or resident TCN can be found.
17 See Joint Council for the Welfare of Immigrants response to the House of Commons debate, 'A complacent defence of the status quo', 6 March 2000.
18 Depending on how strictly the term 'authorised to reside' is interpreted.
19 The issue is to be revisited in another Directive.
20 Protection from inhuman and degrading treatment.

164 *Notes*

21 See T.I. v. UK, 43844/98.
22 There has been some indication that this may change, with the Secretary of State, David Blunkett, endorsing the German definition (*Guardian*, 5 September 2001), though Germany now seems set to change its position.
23 See for example the CIR-ONLUS information leaflet on the Italian Council of Ministers Directive of 6 June 1998 (Consiglio Italiano per Refugiati, via Velabro 5a, 00186 Roma).
24 Letter from IND to Refugee Arrivals Project, 27 April 2000.
25 A legitimate qualification of family rights under the ECHR (see European Commission, 1999).
26 See ECtHR case D v. UK (146/1996/767/964).
27 A concession permits the regularistion of those with fourteen years' presence. See IND information leaflet on Regularisation of Stay for Immigration Offenders, January 2000.
28 See note 24 above.

6 Gender, race and the embodiment of rights

1 In fact this tendency has continued, and there have been a number of instances of abuse of foreign labour in private care homes.
2 In the UK in 1998 19,430 women were given leave to enter as wives or fiancées as compared with 12,750 men (Home Office, 1999a); in Germany in 2000 there were 38,756 entries for foreign wives as compared to 19,433 for foreign husbands (communication from Beauftragte der Bundesregierung für Ausländerfragen); and in Italy in 1999 new permits for family reasons included 39,457 women and 14,540 men (Caritas di Roma, 2000).
3 From 8603 in 1996 to 18,863 in 2000 (communication from Beauftragte der Bundesregierung für Ausländerfragen). Note that family unification in the context of free movement in Europe is excluded from these figures.
4 Canada has moved further than most countries in incorporating a gender-sensitive practice in the granting of asylum and in 1993 the Canadian Immigration and Refugee Board issued groundbreaking guidelines on gender-related persecution.
5 The case of Lazo-Majano, in which a domestic worker was repeatedly sexually assaulted by her employer, who was a member of the Salvadoran military. The case was heard in Canada.
6 Gilani v. Secretary of State 12, in the UK, and Fatin v. INS in the US.
7 Islam v. Secretary of State for the Home Department and Regina v. Immigration Appeal tribunal and Another ex parte Shah.
8 Figures in this section are taken from Beauftragte der Bundesregierung für Ausländerfragen, 2000:table 10.
9 Many of the latter group came under arrangements for temporary protection, however, and were granted full employment rights on the basis of a time-limited stay. Some of the 'traumatised' have now been granted unlimited residence under the 'hard cases' ruling.
10 With totals of respectively 7350, 5430, 3940, 3630. However, Somalia, Nigeria, Turkey, South Africa and Sri Lanka also feature with numbers respectively of 2950, 2950, 2360, 2260, 2100 (Home Office, 1999a: table 6.1).
11 With respectively 8335, 5980, 5895, 5870, 5155, 4450 and 4040 applicants (*Guardian*, 21 May 2001).

7 Managing contradiction: civic stratification and migrants' rights

1 Conventions apply only to those countries which have signed, but also specify a minimum number of parties before they can come into effect.

2 For a comprehensive list see Plender, 1999.
3 See for example International Covenant on Economic, Social and Cultural Rights, ILO Convention concerning Migration for Employment.
4 See for example ILO Convention concerning Migration for Employment, Article 6.
5 As in the British requirement to 'satisfy an Immigration Officer' in order to gain entry.
6 Exceptions will usually be made in cases of proven domestic violence.
7 After a stay of four years; see ECJ case C-171/95.
8 See for example the Association Agreement with Poland (Plender, 1999:551).
9 See European Court of Human Rights case D v. UK, application number 30240/96.
10 ECHR Article 8 (2).
11 Usually limited to the immediate nuclear family (as in Germany), but possibly including dependent parents (as in Italy).
12 See *Migration News Sheet*, November 1999.
13 The House of Lords has ruled Germany an unsafe country for some asylum seekers (see *Refugees Daily*, 20 December 2000), notwithstanding the ruling by the ECtHR that Germany's protections against removal were adequate. See case T.I. v. UK, application number 43844/98.
14 Principally the Geneva Convention and the ECHR, but see also the European Convention for the Prevention of Torture and Inhuman and Degrading Treatment.
15 For British examples see 1996 AII ER 385, and 1997 1 CCLR 85.
16 For example, vouchers allow little flexibility in purchasing plans when only designated shops may be used and only limited change is given.
17 See European Court of Human Rights case D v. UK, application number 30240/96.
18 As in the case of a child who holds citizenship in Germany, or the involvement of a child present for seven or more years in Britain.
19 The 2002 Aliens law will abolish the use of *duldung* (or tolerated status) but the practice is likely to continue through the use of *bescheinigung* (certificate).
20 Whereby applications from before a given date are automatically granted some form of legal status.
21 Receiving respectively 78,564 and 62,971 applications in 2000 (*Migration News Sheet*, January 2001).
22 For an example of forced prostitution see *Guardian*, 30 May 2000.
23 See the House of Lords Ruling (25 March 1999) offering refugee status to two Pakistani women fleeing domestic violence (discussed in *Migration News Sheet*, April 1999); also, Germany is now set to incorporate gender persecution into the grounds for recognition under the GC.
24 With the amendment to the 1998 Immigration Law.
25 See Jack Straw's speech to the European Conference on Asylum, Lisbon, 16 June 2000.
26 See, for example, court rulings on support for asylum seekers in Britain cited in note 17 above.
27 Illustrating this point, an Italian immigration lawyer cited an exchange with a judge in which he had raised the ECHR in relation to a deportation. The judge's response had been 'Let us speak of law and not politics'.

Bibliography

Ad Hoc Group on Immigration (1991) *Report from the Ministers Responsible for Immigration to the European Council*, SN 4038/91 (WGI 930), Brussels.
Alexander, J. C. (1988) *Action and its Environments*, New York: Columbia University Press.
Allbeson, J. (1996) *Failing the Test*, London: National Association of Citizens Advice Bureaux.
Allen, S. and Macey, M. (1994) 'Some issues of race, ethnicity and nationalism in the "New Europe"', in R. Crompton and P. Brown (eds) *A New Europe? Economic Restructuring and Social Exclusion*, London: UCL Press, 108–35.
Anderson, B. (2000) *Doing the Dirty Work*, London: Zed Books.
Anthias, F. and Yuval-Davis, N. (1992) *Racialised Boundaries*, London: Routledge.
Audit Commission (2000) *Another Country*, Audit Commission Publications: Abingdon.
Balibar, E. (1991) 'Racism and politics in Europe today', *New Left Review*, 186: 5–19.
Barbalet, J.M. (1988) *Citizenship*, Milton Keynes: Open University Press.
Bartsch, H.J. (1992) 'Council of Europe – legal co-operation in 1992', *Yearbook of European Law*, 12: 675–83.
Baubock, R. (1991) *Immigration and the Boundaries of Citizenship*, Warwick: Centre for Research in Ethnic Relations.
Baubock, R. and Cinar, D. (1994) 'Briefing paper: naturalisation policies in Western Europe', in M. Baldwin-Edwards and M. A. Schain (eds) *The Politics of Immigration in Western Europe*, Ilford: Frank Cass, 192–6.
Beauftragte der Bundesregierung für Ausländerfragen (2000) 'Daten und fakten zur Ausländersituation', Bonn: BBA.
Bechhofer, F. (1996) 'Comment on Lockwood', *British Journal of Sociology*, 47: 551–5.
Beck, U. (2000) *What is Globalisation?*, Cambridge: Polity Press.
Bhabha, J. (1996) 'Embodied rights', *Public Culture*, 9: 3–32.
Bhabha, J. and Shutter, S. (1994) *Women's Movement*, Stoke-on-Trent: Trentham Books.
Blake, N. (1999) 'The mechanics of the Human Rights Act 1998', in *The Human Rights Act and Immigration and Asylum Law*, Conference sponsored by Justice and Sweet and Maxwell. London, 3 December 1999.
Blake, N. and Fransman, L. (1999) *Immigration, Nationality and Asylum under the Human Rights Act*, London: Butterworth.
Blaschke, J. (1993) 'Gates of immigration into the Fed Rep of Germany', *International Migration*, 31: 361–88.
Bobbio, N. (1995) *The Age of Rights*, Cambridge: Polity Press.

Bolderson, H. and Roberts, S. (1995) 'New restrictions on benefits for migrants', *Benefits*, January: 11–15.
Bolten, J. J. (1992) 'From Schengen to Dublin: the new frontiers of refugee law', in H. Meijers (ed.) *Schengen*, Leiden: Stichling NJCM-Borekerij, 8–36.
Bosniak, L. S. (1991) 'Human rights, state sovereignty and the protection of undocumented migrants', *International Migration Review*, 25: 737–70.
Bottomore, T. (1992) 'Citizenship and social class forty years on', in T. H. Marshall and T. Bottomore (eds) *Citizenship and Social Class*, London: Pluto Press, 55–93.
Brah, A. (1993) 'Difference, diversity, differentiation: processes of racialisation and gender', in J. Wrench and J. Solomos (eds) *Racism and Migration in Western Europe*, Oxford: Berg, 195–214.
Brah, A. (1994) 'Time, place and others: discourses of race, nation and ethnicity', *Sociology*, 28: 805–13.
Brubaker, W. R. (ed.) (1989) *Immigration and the Politics of Citizenship in Europe and America*, Lanham MD: University Press of America.
Brubaker, W. R. (1992) *Citizenship and Nationhood in France and Germany*, Cambridge MA: Harvard University Press.
Bunyan, T. (1997) *Key Texts on Justice and Home Affairs in the EU*, London: Statewatch.
Bunyan, T. and Webber, F. (1995) *Intergovernmental Co-operation on Immigration and Asylum*, CCME Briefing Paper 19, Brussels: Churches Commission for Migrants in Europe.
Calvita, K. (1994) 'Italy and the new immigration', in W. A. Cornelius, P. L. Martin, and J. F. Hollifield (eds), *Controlling Immigration*, Stanford CA: Stanford University Press, 303–26.
Carens, J. H. (1988) 'Immigration and the welfare state', in A. Gutman (ed.) *Democracy and the Welfare State*, Princeton NJ: Princeton University Press, 207–30.
Carens, J. (1989) 'Membership and morality: admission to citizenship in liberal democratic states', in W. R. Brubaker (ed.) *Immigration and the Politics of Citizenship in Europe and America*, Lanham MD: University Press of America, 31–49.
Caritas di Roma (1996) *Immigrazione: dossier statistico*, Rome: Anterem.
Caritas di Roma (1999) *Immigrazione: dossier statistico*, Rome: Anterem.
Caritas di Roma (2000) *Immigrazione: Dossier Statistico*, Rome: Anterem.
Castel, J. R. (1992) 'Rape, sexual assault and the meaning of persecution', *International Journal of Refugee Law*, 4: 39–56.
Castles, S. and Kosack, G. (1985) *Immigrant Workers and Class Structure in Western Europe*, Oxford: Oxford University Press.
Castles, S. and Miller, M. J. (1998) *The Age of Migration*, London: Macmillan.
Cator, J. and Niessen, J. (1994) *The Use of International Conventions to Protect the Rights of Migrant and Ethnic Minorities*, papers presented at the seminar, Strasbourg, 8 and 9 September 1993, under the auspices of the Secretary General of the Council of Europe.
Chell, V. (1997) 'Gender selective migration', in R. King and R. Black (eds) *Southern Europe and the new Immigrations*, Brighton: Sussex Academic Press, 75–92.
Collinson, S. (1993) *Europe and International Migration*, London: Royal Institute of International Affairs.
Cook, R. J. (1993) 'Women's international human rights law: the way forward', *Human Rights Quarterly*, 15: 230–61.
Council of the European Union (1994a) 'Council Resolution on admission of TCNs for employment', in *Official Journal of the European Communities*, No C 274/3.

Council of the European Union (1994b) *Proposal for a Joint Action on Harmonising Means of Combating Illegal Migration and Illegal Employment and Improving the Relevant Means of Control*, Council Document 12336/94.

Council of the European Union (1998) *Action Plan for Establishing an Area of Freedom, Security and Justice*, 12028/1/98, Brussels: DGH.

Crawley, H. (1997) *Women as Asylum Seekers*, London: Immigration Law Practitioners' Association.

Cross, M. (1991) 'Editorial', *New Community*, 18: 1–7.

Cruz, A. (1994) *Carriers' Liability in the Member States of the European Union*, CCME Briefing Paper 17, Brussels: Churches Commission for Migrants in Europe.

Cruz, A. (1995) *Shifting Responsibility*, Stoke-on-Trent: Trentham Books.

De Vincentiis, D. (1998) *La Nuova Disciplina dell'Immigrazione*, Naples: Edizioni Giuridiche Simone.

Dent, J. A. (1998) *Research Paper on the Social and Economic Rights of Non-nationals in Europe*, London: ECRE.

Department of Employment (1982) *Employment Gazette* (March), London: HMSO.

Deutsches Ausländerrecht (Foreigners' Law) (1997) Munich: Beck-Texte.

Dummett, A. and Nicol, A. (1990) *Subjects, Citizens, Aliens and Others*, London: Weidenfeld and Nicolson.

European Commission (1993) *The EC Member States and Immigration in 1993*, Brussels: European Commission.

European Commission (1994a) *European Social Policy: the Way Forward for the Union*, white paper, COM (94) 333.

European Commission (1994b) *On Immigration and Asylum Policies*, Communication from the Commission to the Council and the European Parliament, COM (94) 23 final.

European Commission (1995) *Report on the Operation of the Treaty on European Union*, SEC (95) 731 final.

European Commission (1999) *Proposal for a Council Directive on the Right to Family Unification*, COM (1999) 638 final; amended proposal COM(2000)624 final.

European Commission (2000) *Communication on a Community Immigration Policy*, COM (2000) 757 final.

European Commission (2001a) *Proposal for a Directive on Minimum Standards for the Reception of Asylum Seekers*, COM (2001) 181.

European Commission (2001b) *Proposal for a Council Directive Concerning the Status of Third Country Nationals Who Are Long Term Residents*, COM (2001) 127.

European Commission (2001c) *Proposal for a Council Directive on the Conditions of Entry and Residence of Third Country Nationals for the Purposes of Paid Employment and Self-Employed Economic Activities*, COM (2001) 386 final.

European Council on Refugees and Exiles (ECRE) (2000) *Non-state Agents of Persecution and the Inability of the State to Protect – the German Interpretation*, London: ECRE.

European Parliament (2000) *Asylum in the EU Member States*, LIBE 108 EN, Brussels: DG Rese.

European Parliament (2001) *Report on the Proposal for a Council Framework Decision on Combating Trafficking in Human Beings*, A5-0183/2001, Brussels: EP.

Faist, T. (1994) 'How to define a foreigner', *West European Politics*, 17: 50–71.

Federal Commissioner for Foreigners' Affairs (1997) *Facts and Figures on the Situation of Foreigners in the Federal Republic of Germany*, Bonn: FCFA.

Federal Employment Service (1995) *Work Permit for Foreign Employees*, Nurnberg: FES.

Federal Ministry of Labour and Social Affairs (2000) *The Federal Republic of Germany's IT Specialists Temporary Relief Program*, Berlin: FMLSA.
Fernhout, R. (1993) 'Europe 1993 and its refugees', *Ethnic and Racial Studies*, 16: 492–505.
Foucault, M. (1991) 'Governmentality', in G. Burchell, P. Gordon and P. Miller (eds), *The Foucault Effect*, Hemel Hempstead: Harvester Wheatsheaf.
Frankfurter Rundschau (1998) 'Hungrig im Dickicht der Stadte', 20 May.
Fraser, N. (1995) 'From redistribution to recognition', *New Left Review*, 212: 69–93.
Freeman, G. P. (1986) 'Migration and the political economy of the welfare state', *Annals of the American Academy of Political and Social Science*, 485 (May): 51–63.
Freeman, G. P. (1994) 'Can liberal states control unwanted migration?', *Annals of the American Academy of Political and Social Science*, 534 (July): 17–30.
Freeman, G. P. (1995) 'Modes of immigration politics in liberal democratic states', *International Migration Review*, 29: 881–902.
Friese, M. (1995) 'East European women as domestics in western Europe', *Journal of Area Studies*, 6: 194–202.
Garden Court Chambers (1999) *The Human Rights Act and Immigration and Asylum Law*, Conference sponsored by Justice and Sweet and Maxwell. London, 3 December.
Gellner, E. (1983) *Nations and Nationalism*, Oxford: Blackwell.
Giddens, A. (1990) *The Consequences of Modernity*, Cambridge: Polity Press.
Giddens, A. (1995) 'Government's last gasp?', *Observer*, 7 July: 25.
Glidewell Panel (1996) *The Asylum and Immigration Bill*, London: Justice.
Golinowska, S. (1995) 'Problems of economic migration in Central and Eastern Europe: the case of Poland', paper presented at the conference on the 'Integration of Central and Western Europe', University of Essex, 15–18 June.
Greatbatch, J. (1989) 'The gender difference: feminist critiques of refugee discourse', *International Journal of Refugee Law*, 1: 518–27.
Groenendijk, K. (1995) *Regulating Ethnic Immigration: the Case of the Aussiedler*, paper presented at a workshop on 'Migration: Processes and Interventions', September 1995, Amsterdam.
Groenendijk, K. and Hampsink, R. (1995) *Temporary Employment of Migrants in Europe*, Nijmegen: Katholieke Universiteit.
Guardian (1995) 'Crackdown on employers may boost race bias', 7 April.
Guardian (1995) 'New purge on illegal immigrants', 9 May.
Guardian (1995) 'Clash of cultures as British brickies rebuild Berlin', 2 October.
Guardian (1996) 'Britain's hit by "tourist benefit" cut', 14 February.
Guardian (1996) 'Building on the crack', 21 March.
Guardian (1996) 'French police check on "cheap" British labour', 3 December.
Guardian (2000) 'Misery of immigrants', 11 February.
Guardian (2000) 'Prostitutes imported into slavery', 30 May.
Guardian (2000) 'The truth about forced marriage', 3 June.
Guardian (2000) 'Power shifts to the judges', 11 September.
Guardian (2000) 'Ministers agree voucher review', 28 September.
Guardian (2001) 'Welcome to Britain', 21 May.
Guardian (2001) 'The invisibles', 23 May.
Guardian (2001) 'Deportation raids "will harm race relations"', 11 July.
Guardian (2001) 'The asylum quagmire', 5 September.
Guardian (2001) 'Green card work permits for useful immigrants', 3 October.
Guardian (2001) 'Court's line wrong on asylum detentions', 3 October.

Guardian (2001) 'Asylum seekers can be detained', 20 October.
Guardian (2001) 'Reform of asylum system underway', 29 October.
Guardian (2001) 'Hopes for a better reception for refugees', 30 October.
Guardian (2001) 'Migrants ruling angers Blunkett', 6 December.
Guardian (2002) 'German gays begin to tie the legal knot', 2 April.
Guild, E. (1992) *Protecting Migrants' Rights: Application of EC Agreements with Third Countries*, CCME Briefing Paper 10, Brussels: Churches Commission for Migrants in Europe.
Guild, E. (1994) *The Legal Framework Regulating Citizenship in the European Union*, paper presented at the conference on 'Citizenship, Nationality and Migration in Europe', University College London, 21–22 September.
Guiraudon, V. (1998) 'Citizenship rights for non-citizens: France, Germany and the Netherlands', in C. Joppke (ed.) *Challenge to the Nation State*, Oxford: Oxford University Press, 272–318.
Hall, S. (1991) 'The local and the global: globalisation and ethnicity', in A. King (ed.), *Culture, Globalisation and the World System*, London: Macmillan, 19–40.
Hammar, T. (1990) *Democracy and the Nation State*, Aldershot: Avebury.
Handoll, J. (1994) *Free Movement of Persons in the EU*, Colorado Springs: John Wiley.
Harrison, S. (1999) 'The impact of article 3 ECHR', in *The Human Rights Act and Immigration and Asylum Law*, Conference sponsored by Justice and Sweet and Maxwell, London, 3 December 1999.
Heinhold, H. (2000) *Legal Handbook for Refugees*, Karlsruhe: von Loeper.
Hix, S. (1995) *The 1996 Intergovernmental Conference and the Future of the Third Pillar*, CCME Briefing Paper 20, Brussels: Churches Commission for Migrants in Europe.
Hix, S. and Niessen, J. (1996) *Reconsidering European Migration Policies: the 1996 Intergovernmental Conference*, Brussels: Churches Commission for Migrants in Europe.
Home Office (1998) *Fairer, Faster and Firmer*, CM 4018, London: HMSO.
Home Office (1999a) *Control of Immigration Statistics UK 1998*, CM 4431, London: Government Statistical Service.
Home Office (1999b) *Asylum Statistics UK 1998*, London: Government Statistical Service.
Home Office (2002) *Secure Borders, Save Haven*, CM 5387, London: HMSO.
Hoogenboom, T. (1992) 'Integration into society and free movement of non-EC nationals', *European Journal of International Law*, 3: 36–52.
House of Lords (1992) *Community Policy on Migration*, HL Paper 35, London: HMSO.
House of Lords (1994) *Visas and Control of External Borders of the Member States*, HL Paper 78, London: HMSO.
House of Lords (1989) *1992: Border Control of People*, HL Paper 90, London: HMSO.
Hune, S. (1991) 'Migrant women in the context of the International Convention on the protection of the rights of all migrant workers and members of their families', *International Migration Review*, xxv: 800–17.
Hutton, W. (1995) 'Myth that sets the world to right', *Guardian*, 12 June.
Immigration Law Practitioners' Association (2001a) *ILPA European Update*, June, London: ILPA.
Immigration Law Practitioners' Association (2001b) *ILPA European Update*, September, London: ILPA.
Independent on Sunday (2000) 'Refugee doctors face £1000 fee', 12 November.
Independent on Sunday (2001) 'Focus: the asylum crisis', 25 February.
Independent on Sunday (2001) 'Run by pimps from Africa to Italy – via the UK', 11 March.

Indra, D. (1987) 'Gender: a key dimension of the refugee experience', *Refuge*, 6: 3–4.
Information and Studies on Multiethnicity (ISMU) (1996), *The First Report on Migrations*, Milan: Quaderni ISMU.
International Journal of Refugee Law (IJRL) (1999) *Cases and Comments*, 11, 3: 498–527.
Joint Council for the Welfare of Immigrants (1987) *Out of Sight*, London: JCWI.
Joint Council for the Welfare of Immigrants (1993) *The Right to Family Life for Immigrants in Europe*, London: JCWI.
Joint Council for the Welfare of Immigrants (1997) *Immigration, Nationality and Refugee Law Handbook*, London: JCWI.
Joppke, C. (1999) *Immigration and the Nation State*, Oxford: Oxford University Press.
Juss, S. (1997) *Discretion and Deviation in the Administration of Immigration Control*, London: Sweet and Maxwell.
Kelly, N. (1994) 'Guidelines for women's asylum claims', *International Journal of Refugee Law*, 6: 517–34.
Kofman, E., Phizacklea, A., Parvati, R. and Sales, R. (2000) *Gender and International Migration in Europe*, London: Routledge.
Kussbach, E. (1992) 'European challenge: East–West migration', *International Migration Review*, xxvi: 646–67.
Kymlicka, W. (1989) *Liberalism, Commuity and Culture*, Oxford: Clarendon Press.
Kymlicka, W. (1995) *Multicultural Citizenship*, Oxford: Clarendon Press.
Layton-Henry, Z. (1992) *The Politics of Immigration*, London: Blackwell.
Leidholt, D. (1996) 'Sexual trafficking of women in Europe', in R. Amy Elman (ed.) *Sexual Politics and the European Union*, Providence: Bergahn Books, 83–96.
Lister, R. (1997) *Citizenship: Feminist Persepectives*, London: Macmillan.
Lockwood, D. (1996) 'Civic integration and class formation', *British Journal of Sociology*, 47: 531–50.
Marshall, T. H. (1950) *Citizenship and Social Class*, Cambridge: Cambridge University Press.
Martiniello, M. (1994) 'Citizens of the European Union', in R. Baubock (ed.) *From Aliens to Citizens*, Aldershot: Avebury, 29–47.
Meyer, J., Boli, J., Thomas, G. M. and Ramirez, F. O. (1997) 'World society and the nation state', *American Journal of Sociology*, 103: 144–81.
Migration News (1999) California: http://migration.ucdavis.edu.
Migration News Sheet (various) Brussels: Churches Commission for Migrants in Europe.
Miles, R. (1990) 'Whatever happened to the sociology of migration?', *Work Employment and Society*, 4: 281–98.
Miles, R. (1993) 'The articulation of racism and nationalism', in J. Wrench and J. Solomos (eds), *Racism and Migration in Western Europe*, Oxford: Berg, 35–52.
Miles, R. (1994) 'Explaining racism in contemporary Europe', in A. Rattansi and S. Westwood (eds) *Racism, Modernity and Identity*, Cambridge: Polity Press, 189–221.
Mingione, E and Quassoli, F. (1998), 'The insertion of immigrants in the underground economy in Italy', in R. King, G. Lazaridis and C. Tsardanis (eds), *Eldorado or Fortress: Migration in Southern Europe*, London: Macmillan, 29–56.
Morokvasic, M. (1991) 'Fortress Europe and migrants women', *Feminist Review*, 39: 69–84.
Morris, L. D. (1994) *Dangerous Classes*, London: Routledge.
Morris, L. D. (1997a) 'A cluster of contradictions: the politics of migration in the EU', *Sociology*, 31: 241–59.

Morris, L. D. (1997b) 'Globalisation, migration and the nation state: the path to a post-national Europe?', *British Journal of Sociology*, 48: 192–209.
Morris, L. D. (1998) 'Governing at a distance: rights and controls in British immigration', *International Migration Review*, 32: 949–73.
Morris, L. D. (2000) 'Rights and controls in the management of migration: the case of Germany', *Sociological Review*, 48: 224–40.
Morris, L. D. (2001) 'The ambiguous terrain of rights: Italy's emergent immigration regime', *International Journal of Urban and Regional Research*, 25: 497–516.
Munz, R. (2001) 'Germany's immigration reform', in *Policy Recommendations for EU Migration Policies*, Brussels: King Baudouin Foundation.
Murray, A. (1998) 'Debt bondage and trafficking', in K. Kempadoo and J. Doezema (eds) *Global Sex Workers*, London: Routledge, 51–65.
Nascimbene, B. and Galiano, G. P. (1997) 'Italy', in J.-Y. Carlier, D. Vanheule, K. Hullmann and C. P. Galiano (eds) *Who is a Refugee? A Comparative Case Law Study*, The Hague: Kluwer Law International, 457–69.
National Association of Citizens Advice Bureaux (1996) *A Right to Family Life*, London: NACAB.
National Association of Citizens Advice Bureaux (2000) *A Person Before the Law*, London: NACAB.
Niessen, J. (1992) 'The Member States against the Commission', *Migrantenrecht*, 1: 7–12.
Observer (1999) 'Sex slavery spreads across UK', 14 March.
Observer (2000) 'Sex gangs sell prostitutes over the Internet', 16 July.
Observer (2000) 'Skilled migrants to be let into UK', 3 September.
Observer (2000) 'Nowhere left to run to', 31 December.
Observer (2000) 'Refugees pour back to London', 31 December.
Observer (2001) 'Teenage slaves bought to order', 14 January.
Observer (2001) 'Barbed wire and cameras for asylum seekers', 4 November.
O'Keefe, D. (1992) 'The Schengen Convention: a suitable model for European integration?', *Yearbook of European Law*, 12: 184–219.
O'Leary, S. (1995) 'The social dimension of Community citizenship', in A. Rosas and E. Antola (eds) *A Citizens' Europe*, London: Sage, 156–81.
Owers, A. (1994) 'The age of internal controls?', in S. Spencer (ed.), *Strangers and Citizens*, London: Rivers Oram Press, 264–81.
Parry, G. (1991) 'Conclusion: paths to citizenship', in U. Vogel and M. Moran (eds) *The Frontiers of Citizenship*, Basingstoke: Macmillan, 166–201.
Pateman, C. (1988) *The Disorder of Women*, Cambridge: Polity Press.
Pastore, M. (1998) 'L'Italia e gli accordi di Schengen', *Critica Marxista*, 6: 69–80.
Peers, S. (1996) 'Towards equality', *Common Market Law Review*, 33: 7–50.
Peers, S. (2000) *EU Justice and Home Affairs Law*, Harlow: Longman.
Phillips, A. (1992) 'Universalist pretensions in political thought', in M. Barrett and A. Phillips (eds) *Destabilising Theory*, Cambridge: Polity Press, 10–30.
Phizaclea, A. (1996) 'Migration and globalisation: a feminist perspective', paper presented at 'New Migration in Europe' ERCOMER conference, April.
Plender, R. (1999) *Basic Documents on International Migration Law*, The Hague: Kluwer Law International.
Pugliese, E. (1993) 'Restructuring of the labour market and the role of Third World migrations in Europe', *Environment and Planning D: Society and Space*, 11: 513–22.
Rattansi, A. (1994) '"Western" racisms, ethnicities and identities in a "postmodern" frame', in A. Rattansi and S. Westwood (eds) *Racism, Modernity and Identity*, Cambridge: Polity Press, 15–18.

Rattansi, A. and Westwood, S. (eds) (1994) *Racism, Modernity and Identity*, Cambridge: Polity Press.
Rex, J. (1986) *Race and Ethnicity*, Milton Keynes: Open University Press.
Reyneri, E. (1998a) *Addressing the Employment of Immigrants in an Irregular Situation*, Symposium on 'International Migration and Development', UN Task Force on Basic Social Services for All, 29 June–3 July.
Reyneri, E. (1998b) 'The role of the underground economy in irregular migration to Italy, *Journal of Ethnic and Migration Studies*, 24: 303–21.
Reyneri, E (1998c) 'The mass legalisation of migrants in Italy', *South European Politics and Society*, 3: 83–104.
Reyneri, E (1999) *Immigration and the Underground Economy in New Receiving South European Countries*, paper presented at 'European Socio-Economic Research Conference', Brussels, April.
Richardson, D. (1998) 'Sexuality and citizenship', *Sociology*, 32: 83–100.
Robertson, R. (1990) 'Mapping the global condition', in M. Featherstone (ed.) *Global Culture*, London: Sage, 15–30.
Robertson, R. (1992) *Globalisation*, London: Sage.
Rose, N. and Miller, P. (1992) *British Journal of Sociology*, 43: 173–205.
Salt, J., Singleton, A. and Hoggarth, J. (1994) *Europe's International Migrants*, London: HMSO.
Sassen, S. (1998) *Globalisation and its Discontents*, New York: The New Press.
Scarman, Lord (1981) *The Brixton Disorders*, Cmnd 8427, London: HMSO.
Schuck, P. H. (1989) 'Membership in the liberal polity', in W. R. Brubaker (ed.) *Immigration and the Politics of Citizenship in Europe and America*, Lanham MD: University Press of America, 51–65.
Sciortino, G (1991) 'Immigration into Europe and public policy: do stops really work?', *New Community*, 18: 89–99.
Sciortino, G. (1999) 'Planning in the dark: the evolution of Italian immigration control', in G. Brochman and T. Hammar (eds), *Mechanisms of Immigration Control*, Oxford: Berg, 233–60.
Seddon, D. (1999) 'Support arrangements: the possibilities of challenge', in Garden Court Chambers, *The Human Rights Act and Immigration and Asylum Law*, conference sponsored by Justice and Sweet and Maxwell, London, 3 December 1999.
Sivanandan, A. (1991) 'Editorial', *Race and Class*, 32: v.
Smith, A. (1995) *Nations and Nationalism in a Global Era*, Cambridge: Polity Press.
Smith, D. M. and Blanc, M. (1995) 'Some comparative aspects of ethnicity and citizenship in the European Union', in M. Martiniello (ed.) *Migration, Citizenship and Ethno-national Identities in the European Union*, Aldershot: Avebury, 70–92.
Social Security Advisory Committee (1996) *Benefits for Asylum Seekers*, HC81 session 1995/6, London: HMSO.
Solomos, J. (1995) 'The politics of citizenship and nationality in a European perspective', in M. Martiniello (ed.) *Migration, Citizenship and Ethno-national Identities in the European Union*, Aldershot: Avebury, 40–52.
SOPEMI (1998) *Trends in International Migration*, Paris: OECD.
Soysal, Y. (1994) *Limits of Citizenship*, Chicago IL: University of Chicago Press.
Staples, H. (1999) *The Legal Status of Third Country Nationals Resident in the EU*, The Hague: Kluwer Law International.
Statewatch (1997) 'Amsterdam Treaty', 13 (May–June): 13–17.
Statewatch (2000a) 'Deaths and demonstrations spotlight detention centres', 10 (Jan–Feb): 19–21.

Statewatch (2000b) 'Judge questions constitutionality of immigration law', 10 (Nov–Dec): 5.
Statewatch (2001a) 'Immigration bill restrictive and repressive', 11 (Aug–Oct): 3.
Statewatch (2001b) 'Campaign enters second stage', 11 (Nov–Dec): 2–3.
Statewatch (2001c) 'Amended immigration law proposed', 11 (Nov–Dec): 3–4.
Steiner, H. J. and Alston, P. (1996) *International Human Rights in Context*, Oxford: Clarendon Press.
Tanton, P. (2000) 'Mail order marriage and global imperialism', PhD thesis, University of Essex.
Taylor, C. (1994) *Multiculturalism*, Princeton NJ: Princeton University Press.
Therborn, G. (1995) *European Modernity and Beyond*, London: Sage.
Thomas, D. Q. and Beasley, M. E. (1993) 'Domestic violence as a human rights issue', *Human Rights Quarterly*, 15: 36–62.
Tosi, A. (1996) *Housing Rights, Insecurity of Tenure, and Poverty in Italy*, Brussels: FEANTSA.
Tosi, A., Kazepov, Y. and Ranci, C. (1998) *Italy 1997 Report*, Brussels, FEANTSA.
Tosi, A. (1995) *Italy 1994 Report*, Brussels, FEANTSA.
Tosi, A. and Ranci, C. (1999) *Support in Housing in Italy*, Brussels, FEANTSA.
Trucco, L. (1999) 'Italy', in Faculty of Law, University College Dublin (ed.) *Refugee Law Comparative Study*, Dublin: Department of Justice, Education and Law Reform.
Truong, T.-D. and del Rosario, V. O. (1995) 'Captive outsiders: the sex traffick and mail-order brides in the European Union', in J. Wiersma (ed.) *Insiders and Outsiders*, Kampen: Kok Pharos Publishing House, 36–91.
Turner, B. (1988) *Status*, Milton Keynes: Open University Press.
Turner, B. (1990) 'The two faces of sociology: global or national?', *Theory Culture and Society*, 7: 343–58.
Turner, B. (1993) 'Outline of a theory of human rights', *Sociology*, 27: 485–512.
UNHCR (2000) *Refugees Daily*, 20 December.
United Nations Department of Economic and Social Affairs (DESA) (2000) *Replacement Migration: Is It a Solution to Declining and Ageing Populations?*, http://www.un.org/esa/population/publications/migration/migration.htm (accessed 8 April 2002).
Wallace, C., Chmuliar, O. and Sidorenko, E. (1995) 'The Eastern frontier of Western Europe: mobility in the buffer zone', *SWS Rundschau*, 1: 41–69.
Waters, M. (1996) 'Human rights and the universalisation of interests', *Sociology* 30: 593–600.
Webber, F. (1999) 'Mechanics: the Immigration and Asylum Act', in Garden Court Chambers *The Human Rights Act and Immigration and Asylum Law*, Conference sponsored by Justice and Sweet and Maxwell, London, 3 December 1999.
Wilpert, C (1999) '"New" Migration and Informal Work in Germany', paper drawn from the TSER research project *Migrant Insertion in the Informal Economy*, Berlin: Technische Universität.
ZDWF (Zentrale Dokumentationsstelle der Freien Wohlfahrtspflege für Flüchtlinge) (1996) *Guidelines for Persons Recognized as Entitled to Asylum*, Bonn: UNHCR/SCO.
Zolberg, A. (1989) 'The next waves: migration theory for a changing world', *International Migration Review*, xxiii: 403–30.

Index

Amsterdam Treaty 11, 12, 13, 16, 17, 145
asylum: British asylum regime 83, 84, 89–98, 112–15, 138, 151, 153; domestic violence as a basis for 132–3; erosion of the right to 16–17, 18, 31, 81, 104, 150, 151, 155–6; gender basis of 131–3; German asylum regime 29, 31, 41–50, 106, 112, 114, 115, 116, 119, 133, 150–1, 153; harmonisation of 113–14, 116, 156; Italian asylum regime 74–8, 107, 113, 115, 116, 120, 151, 153; rape as a basis for 131–2; *see also* Dublin Convention, Geneva Convention, refugees
Asylum and Immigration Act (1996) 26, 83
asylum seekers: civic stratification 150–2, 154–5; demonisation of 3, 25; detention of 96–8, 116; deterrence of 151, 156; dispersal of 41–2, 92, 93, 96, 114–15, 151, 152; family unification 43, 49, 85–6, 109, 110, 111; housing, access to 42, 46, 47, 92, 114; racial harassment of 42, 92; removal of 94, 98, 138; voucher system 91, 92, 93, 96, 116, 151; welfare, access to 41, 42, 46, 47, 91, 92, 93, 114; work, access to 41, 43, 44, 46, 49, 75, 76, 83, 84, 106, 107, 108, 112, 120; *see also* asylum
Austria: family unification 149–50

benefit tourism 14, 26
Britain: Asylum and Immigration Act (1996) 26, 83; asylum regime 81, 83, 84, 89–98, 112–15, 138, 151, 153; benefit tourism 14, 26; British Nationality Act (1983) 137, 141; carriers' sanctions 89–90; civic stratification 80, 85, 101, 107, 119–20, 138–9, 148; clandestine migrants 82, 98–9, 117, 138–9, 152; Commonwealth citizens, rights of 80, 119, 137, 141, 154, 157, 158; detention of asylum seekers 96–8, 116; employers' sanctions 18, 83, 107, 148; entry clearance conditions 86, 87; exceptional leave to remain 85, 86, 101, 113; family unification 81, 84, 85, 86, 87, 88, 110, 111, 119, 137–8, 149, 150; habitual residence tests 14, 26; Human Rights Act (2000) 80, 84, 87, 88, 90, 96, 97, 100, 101, 114, 116, 117, 118, 156; Immigration Act (1971) 80, 137; Immigration and Asylum Act (1999) 91, 95, 96, 99; immigration regime 14, 26, 80–8, 98–102, 107, 110, 117–20, 137–9, 147; National Assistance Act (1948) 90, 93, 94, 95; National Asylum Support System 91–3, 94; naturalisation rules 120, 155; race and civic stratification 137–9; racial discrimination 85, 86; removal of asylum seekers 94, 98, 138; self-reliance requirements 110, 147; sex trade 127; skilled labour shortages 82, 84, 106; voucher system 91, 92, 93, 96, 116, 151; welfare, access to 87–8, 90, 110; work permits 25, 81–2, 84, 125
British Nationality Act (1983) 137, 141

citizenship 4, 30, 50, 51, 122, 143–4;

176 *Index*

and gender 123–4; rights of 3, 4, 6, 122–3, 153
civic stratification 7, 19–22, 27, 122, 123, 144–9, 153, 156–7; asylum seekers 150–2, 154–5; Britain 80, 84, 85, 101, 107, 119–20, 138–9, 148; European Union 6, 7, 148–9; gender 123–6, 129–31, 153–4; Germany 29, 32, 36–7, 38, 40, 43, 44, 46, 49–52, 109, 119, 158; Italy 50–2, 63, 65, 71, 78–9, 107, 120–1; race 133–9, 141–2, 153, 154; third country nationals 14–15, 20–1, 23, 28–32, 50–2, 62, 63, 65, 78–9, 84, 85, 100–2, 104–11, 119–21, 135–40, 145–9, 154; women 123–6, 129–31, 153–4
Convention for Suppression of the Traffic in Persons and of the Exploitation of the Prostitution of Others 127–8
Convention on Migrant Workers and Their Families 15, 54

Denmark: Amsterdam Treaty opt-out 11, 13
domestic workers 21–2, 117, 124–6, 154
Dublin Convention 113, 116, 17, 18, 74, 75, 90, 150, 155

European Convention on Human Rights 6, 16, 103, 108, 112, 113, 114, 116, 117, 118, 121, 145, 149, 150, 152, 156
European Convention on the Legal Status of Migrant Workers 15
European Economic Area nationals: family unification 34, 85, 108, 109, 149; freedom of movement 10, 12, 16, 24–5, 32, 80, 81, 85, 103, 108, 145, 146; freedom to work 20, 25, 32, 81, 103, 105, 107, 145, 146
European Union: Amsterdam Treaty 11, 12, 13, 16, 17, 145; asylum policy, harmonisation of 113–14, 116, 156; Dublin Convention 17, 18, 74, 75, 90, 113, 116, 150, 155; European Citizenship 16, 20, 22, 26, 145; family unification 22, 23, 108, 111–12, 149–50; free movement of labour 8, 10, 11, 12, 13, 14, 16, 20, 24–5, 32, 80, 81, 85, 103, 108, 145, 146; immigration, harmonisation of 10, 104, 121; labour regulations, avoidance of 18, 25; Maastricht Treaty 10, 11, 16; Posted Workers Directive 14; racism and immigration controls 23–5; readmission agreements 17, 18; refugees, legal status of 20, 21; Rome, Treaty of 11; Schengen accord 54; Single European Act 11, 12, 22; single market 7, 10, 11, 12, 22, 31, 145; skilled labour shortage 5, 25, 26, 30, 33, 38–9, 82, 84, 105, 106; Treaty on European Union 145; *see also* European Convention on Human Rights

family life: right to 129–31, 149–50
family unification 4, 5, 20–1, 22, 23, 81, 84, 85, 86, 87, 88, 108, 111–12; asylum seekers 43, 49, 85–6, 109, 110, 111; Britain 81, 84, 85, 86, 87, 88, 110, 111, 119, 137–8, 149, 150; Germany 31, 34–6, 43, 49, 109, 110, 111, 129–30, 149; harmonisation of 149–50; Italy 60–1, 110–11; refugees 109, 110, 111
Foreigners' Law 32–3, 34, 36, 37, 39; asylum provisions 41–7; *bewilligung* 39; family unification 35–6; *Gestattung* 41, 48; refugee status 43–7; self-reliance requirements 34, 35, 36, 37; time-limited residence statuses 34–6; tolerated presence (*duldung*) 44, 45, 47–50, 106, 116, 152; unlimited residence, progression to 36–8
France: British sub-contractors, prosecution of 13–14

gender: civic stratification 123–6, 129–31, 153–4
Geneva Convention 112, 113, 150, 155; protocol on asylum 89
Germany: asylum regime 18, 29, 31, 41–50, 106, 112, 114, 116, 119, 133, 150–1, 153; *bewilligung* 39; Bosnian refugees, management of 44–5, 117, 135, 136; citizenship statuses 28, 30, 31, 135; civic stratification 29, 32, 36–7, 38, 40, 43, 44, 46, 49–52, 109, 119, 158; clandestine migrants 40, 117, 118, 152; family unification 31, 34–6, 43,

Index 177

49, 109, 110, 111, 129–30, 149; Foreigners' Law 32–9, 41–50; *Gestattung* 41, 48; green card 25, 34, 38, 106; guestworkers 8, 28, 29, 31, 38, 50, 119, 124, 154, 155, 157; humanitarian leave (*befugnis*) 43, 44, 45, 46, 48–9, 50, 106, 112; immigration regime 18, 26, 30–40, 50–1, 106, 109, 116–17, 119, 135–7; Kurds, civic status of 135, 136, 141; Nationality Law 28, 29, 32, 34, 38, 50; naturalisation rules 30, 31, 120, 155; race and civic stratification 135–7, 141; racial harassment of asylum seekers 42; readmission of labour 18; reception centres 41–2; refugee statuses 43–7; residence permits 34–8, 43, 44, 45, 46, 48–9, 50, 109; self-reliance requirements 34, 35, 36, 37, 38, 109, 147; skilled labour shortage 30, 33, 38–9, 82, 106; time-limited residence statuses 34–6; tolerated presence (*duldung*) 44, 45, 47–50, 106, 116, 152; Turkish resident workers, civic status of 31, 106, 109, 135, 136, 141; women migrants, discrimination against 37, 109; work permits 35, 36; *see also* Foreigners' Law
globalisation 1, 2, 3, 10, 143
green card 25, 34, 38, 106
guestworkers 8, 17–18, 28, 29, 31, 38, 50, 119, 124, 154, 155, 157

Human Rights Act (2000) 80, 84, 87, 88, 90, 96, 97, 100, 101, 114, 116, 117, 118, 156

immigration: Britain 14, 26, 80–8, 98–102, 107, 110, 117–20, 137–9, 147; civic stratification 29, 32, 36–7, 38, 40, 43, 44, 46, 49–52; Germany 18, 26, 30–40, 50–1, 106, 109, 116–17, 119, 135–7; Italy 53–63, 78–9, 107–8, 110–11, 120–1, 139–40, 147; international controls 23; racial discrimination in immigration laws 23–5, 85, 86
Immigration Act (1971) 80, 137
Immigration and Asylum Act (1999) 91, 95, 96, 99
International Convention on the Protection of the Rights of all Migrant Workers and Their Families 15, 21
Ireland: Amsterdam Treaty opt-ins 11
Italy: asylum regime 74–8, 107, 113, 115, 116, 120, 151, 153; civic stratification 63, 65, 71, 78, 107, 120–1; clandestine migrants 17, 55–60, 64–5, 71, 73, 152; emergency provisions for foreigners present without permission 67, 68–71; employment quotas 58, 59, 63, 125–6; expulsion of migrants 71, 72, 73, 74; family unification 60–1, 110–11; immigration regime 53–63, 78–9, 107–8, 110–11, 120–1, 139–40, 147; labour market, policing of 64, 65, 72; low-skilled labour, demand for 17, 55, 107; Martelli law 61, 65; migrants, policing of 64, 68, 70, 71, 72, 73; naturalisation rules 55, 120; race and civic stratification 139, 140, 141; readmission of labour 18; reception centres 65–7, 70, 115; refugees, access to work 107; refugees, family unification 111; regularisations (*sanatoria*) 54, 55, 56, 57, 58, 59, 107, 118, 139, 152, 157, 158; residence permits 55, 56, 59, 60, 61; self-reliance requirements 55, 59, 63, 148; temporary holding centres 73, 74, 75, 77; temporary protection refugees 74, 75, 76; voluntary organisations and the provision of social services 67–8, 69, 70; welfare, access to 55, 65, 67–9, 111

Maastricht Treaty 10, 11, 16
Marshall, T. H. 4, 30, 50, 51, 144
Martelli law 61, 65
migrants: civic stratification 14–15, 20–1, 23, 28–32, 50–2, 62, 63, 65, 71, 78–9, 84, 85, 100–2, 104–11, 119–21, 135–40, 145–9, 154; clandestine 4, 11, 17–18, 21, 40, 55–60, 64–5, 71, 73, 82, 98–9, 116, 117, 118, 127, 138–9, 152–3; family life, right to 87, 88, 89; international protection of 15–16, 21; *see also* third country nationals

nation state: citizenship 3; cultural homogeneity of 3; domestic

178 *Index*

interpretation of international obligations 156–7; sovereignty, erosion of 2, 3; welfare provision 13–15
National Assistance Act (1948) 90; exclusions from 93, 94, 95
National Asylum Support System 91–3, 94
Nationality Law 28, 29, 32, 34, 38, 50

Oakington detention centre 96

post-national society 3, 5, 143

race: and civic stratification 133–9, 141–2, 153, 154
racism 3, 5, 11, 22; asylum seekers, racial harassment of 42, 92; indirect racism 11; racial discrimination in immigration laws 23–5, 85, 86
reception centres 41–2, 65–7, 70, 115
refugees: Bosnian refugees, management of 44–5, 117, 135, 136; family unification 109, 110, 111; legal status of 20, 21; work, access to 49, 75, 106, 107; *see also* asylum seekers
Rome, Treaty of 11

Schengen accord 54
sex trade 21–2, 126–9, 153
Single European Act 11, 12, 22
single market 7, 10, 11, 12, 22, 31, 145

third country nationals: civic stratification 14–15, 20–1, 23, 28–32, 50–2, 62, 63, 65, 78–9, 84, 85, 100–2, 104–11, 119–21, 135–40, 145–9, 154; family unification 22, 23, 60–1, 109, 111; freedom of movement 12, 13, 20, 22–3, 24, 103, 108, 145; housing, access to 56–7, 61–2; integration of 22; legal status of within the European Union 11, 12, 13, 14, 15, 18; residence rights 81, 100–1; social support of 67–8, 69, 70; welfare, access to 65, 87–8, 90, 110, 111; work, access to 20–1, 38, 55, 56, 57, 58, 59, 63, 78, 81–2, 105–8, 136, 153; *see also* migrants
Turkey: Association and Co-operation Agreements 19, 31, 106, 109; family unification 109, 135; workers resident in Germany, civic status of 31, 106, 109, 135, 136, 141

United Nations: International Convention on the Protection of the Rights of all Migrant Workers and Their Families 15, 21

welfare: asylum seekers' access to 41, 42, 46, 47, 91, 92, 93, 114; free movement of labour, effect of 13–15; migrants' access to 65, 87–8, 90, 110, 111; residence, relationship to 109; self-reliance, relationship to residence permits 34, 35, 36, 37, 38; third country nationals' access to 65, 87–8, 90, 110, 111
women: asylum 131–3; civic stratification 123–4, 153–4; discrimination against 109; domestic violence as a basis for asylum 132–3; domestic workers 154; domestic workers, abuse of 21; labour migration 124–6, 141–2; legal status of migrants 21–2; rape as a basis for asylum 131–2; sex trade 21–2, 126–9, 153